John Smith

Galic Antiquities

Consisting of a history of the Druids, particularly of those of Caledonia; a dissertation on the authenticity of the poems of Ossian; and a collection of ancient poems, translated from the Galic of Ullin, Ossian, Orran, &c.

John Smith

Galic Antiquities
Consisting of a history of the Druids, particularly of those of Caledonia; a dissertation on the authenticity of the poems of Ossian; and a collection of ancient poems, translated from the Galic of Ullin, Ossian, Orran, &c.

ISBN/EAN: 9783337324346

Printed in Europe, USA, Canada, Australia, Japan

Cover: Foto ©ninafisch / pixelio.de

More available books at **www.hansebooks.com**

A COLLECTION

OF

ANCIENT POEMS,

TRANSLATED FROM THE

GALIC.

D A R G O:

A P O E M [*].

The ARGUMENT.

COMHAL, failing to Innisfail, lands on a defart ifle through night. Here he meets with Dargo, who was fuppofed to have been loft on their return from a former expedition. To comfort Dargo, who had got fome intimation of the death of his fpoufe Crimora, Ullin introduces the epifode of Colda and Minvela. Arriving at Innisfail in the morning, they engage Armor, a chief of Lochlin, who falls in battle.—Crimoina, who had followed Armor in difguife, is difcovered at night mourning over his grave, and carried to the hall of Innisfail, where Ullin, to divert her grief, relates the ftory of Morglan and Minona. The next day, Comhal propofes to fend her home; but, on her choofing to live in Morven, fhe is brought there, and becomes the fecond wife of Dargo.
Some time after this, Connan, at a hunting party, fuggefting fome doubts of Crimoina's attachment to them, as they were at variance with her people, propofes to make trial of her love by ftaining Dargo with the blood of a wild boar which they had killed, and carrying him home as dead. Crimoina was fo affected with the fuppofed death of her hufband, that, after having fung his elegy to the harp, fhe fuddenly expired befide him.

PART I.

SEE! Dargo refts beneath his lonely tree, and liftens to the breeze in its ruftling leaf. The ghoft of Crimoina rifes on the blue lake below: the deer fee it, and ftalk, without fear, on the

[*] This poem, which goes under the name of *Dan an Deirg*, has been in fuch eftimation as to pafs into a proverb; *Gach dan gu dan an Deirg*.

Perhaps it owes much of the regard paid it, to that tender and plaintive, tho' fimple, air to which it is ftill fung. There are few who have any at all of Offian's poems,

the upland rock. No hunter, when the sign is seen, disturbs their peace; for the soul of Dargo is sad and the swift-bounding companion of his chace howls beside him.—I also feel thy grief at my heart, O Dargo; my tears tremble as dew on the grafs, when I remember thy woful tale.

COMHAL sat on that rock, where now the deer graze on his tomb. The mark of his bed are three gray stones and a leaflefs oak; they are mantled over with the mofs of years. His warriors rested around the chief. Leaning forward on their shields, they listened to the voice of the song. Their faces are sidelong turned; and their eyes, at times, are shut. (The bard praised the deeds of the king, when his blasting sword and the spear of Innisfail † rolled before them, like a wreath of foam, the battle.

THE song ceased; but its sound was still in our ear, as the voice

poems, but can repeat, at least, some part of Dargo.

As the narration of this poem, however, is put for the most part in the mouth of Ullin, and as the transactions of it suit his time better than Offian's, who, if then born, must have been very young, we may suppose *Dan an Deirg* to have been the composition of Ullin. Of this hoary and venerable bard, Offian always speaks with reverence, and ascribes to him many episodes in his larger poems.

† As the names of Lochlin, Erin, and Innisfail, often occur in this and some of the other poems that follow, it may be proper to remember, that by *Lochlin* is meant Norway, or Scandinavia in general; by *Erin*, Ireland; and by *Innisfail*, a part of the same country inhabited by the Falans. Sometimes *Innisfail* seems to denote some of the Hebrides; and *Inniflore* stands always for the Orkneys, or at least the greatest part of them.----It may be also proper to observe the footing on which the kings of Morven or Caledonia were with these neighbouring countries. With the inhabitants of *Innisfail* and *Inniflore*, they generally lived on good terms; and seem to have been their superiors. With the legal sovereigns of *Erin* and their people they were nearly allied; and frequently assisted them against the usurpations of the Firbolg, and the incursions of the Scandinavians. With their southern neighbours, beyond the friths of Forth and Clyde, the kings of Morven seem to have had very little friendly intercourse.

voice of the gale when its courſe is paſt. Our eyes were turned to the ſea. On the diſtant wave aroſe a cloud.) We knew the ſkiff of Innisfail. On its maſts we ſaw the Cran-tara* hung. "Spread," ſaid Comhal, " the white wings of my ſails. On the waves we fly to help our friends."

NIGHT met us, with its ſhades, on the deep. Waves lifted before us their white breaſts, and in our ſails was the roar of winds.

" THE night of ſtorms is dark; but a deſart iſle is nigh. It ſpreads its arms like my bow when bent, and its boſom, like the breaſt of my love, is calm. There let us wait the light; it is the place where mariners dream of dangers that are over."

OUR courſe is to the bay of Botha. The bird of night howled above us from its grey rock. A mournful voice welcomed its ſullen note from a cave. " It is the ghoſt of Dargo †," ſaid Comhal; " Dargo, whom we loſt returning from Lochlin's wars."

WAVES lifted their white heads among the clouds. Blue mountains roſe between us and the ſhore. Dargo climbed the maſt to look for Morven; but Morven he ſaw no more. The thong broke in his hand; and the waves, with all their foam, leapt over his red wandering hair. The fury of the blaſt drove our ſails, and we loſt ſight of the chief. We raiſed the ſong of grief in his praiſe,

* The Cran-tara means in general a ſignal of diſtreſs. It was properly a piece of wood half-burnt, and dipt in blood, which was conveyed with all poſſible expedition from one hamlet to another in caſes of imminent danger. The *Cran-tara* ſignifies the " beam of gathering;" and the fire and blood might intimate either the danger apprehended from the invaders, or a threatening to ſuch as did not immediately repair to the chieftain's ſtandard.---The cuſtom ſeems to have been common to other northern nations. See Ol. Mag. p. 146.

† *Dargo*, " red-haired;" *Comhal*, "mild brow."

praife, and bade the ghofts of his fathers convey him to the place of their reft.

But they heard us not, faid Comhal; his ghoft ftill haunts thefe dreary rocks. His courfe is not on funny hills; on green moffy vales in Morven. Ye ghofts of woody Lochlin, who then purfued us in the ftorm; vain is your attempt, if you think to detain Dargo. Your numbers may be many, but you fhall not prevail. Trenmor † fhall come from Morven's clouds, and fcatter, with his blaft, your dim forms. Your curling mifts, like the beard of the thiftle of Ardven, fhall fly before the ruler of the ftorm.—And thou, Dargo, fhalt ride with him, on the fkirt of his robe, and rejoice with the air-borne fons of thy people.—Raife, Ullin, the fong, and praife his deeds: he will know thy voice, and rejoice in the found of his fame. And if any of the ghofts of Lochlin are near, let them hear of the coming of Trenmor.

Peace to thy foul, faid Ullin, as he reared his voice; peace to thy foul, dweller of the caves of the rock; why fo long in the land of ftrangers? Art thou forced to fight the battle of clouds with Lochlin's ghofts, alone; or do the thoufand thongs of air confine thee? Often, O Dargo, didft thou contend with a whole hoft; and, ftill, thy ghoft maintains the unequal combat. But Trenmor fhall foon come, and lift the broad fhield and airy blade in thine aid. He will purfue the troubled ghofts of Lochlin before him, like the withered leaf of Malmor's oak, when it is caught in the folds of the whirlwind.—Peace to thy foul, till then,

† *Trenmor,* " tall and mighty;" the great-grandfather of Fingal.

then, O Dargo: and calm be thy reſt, thou dweller of the rock, in the land of ſtrangers.

And doſt thou bid me remain on this rock, bard of Comhal; will the warriors of Morven forſake their friend in the hour of danger? cried Dargo, as he deſcended from the ſteep of his cliff.

Galchos knew the voice of Dargo, and made the glad reply he was wont when called to the chace; the chace of the dun-bounding ſons of the deſart. Quick, as an arrow in air, he ſprings over waves. His feet are ſcarce bathed in the deep. He leaps to the breaſt of Dargo.—The dim-twinkling ſtars looked, through the parted clouds, on their meeting of joy. It was like the embrace of friends, when they meet in the land of ſtrangers, after the ſlow years of abſence.

How, ſaid Comhal, is Dargo alive! How didſt thou eſcape ocean's floods, when they rolled their billows over thy head, and hid thee in their foam?

The waves, ſaid Dargo, drove me to this rock, after toiling a whole night in the ſtream. Seven times, ſince, has the moon waſted its light and grown again: but ſeven years are not ſo long on the brown heath of Morven. All the day I ſat on that rock, humming the ſongs of our bards; while I liſtened to the hoarſe ſound of the waves, or the hoarſer ſcreams of the fowls that rode on their top. And, in the night, I converſed with the ghoſts and the owl; or ſtole on the ſea-fowl that ſlept on the beachy rock.— Long, Comhal, was the time; for ſlow are the ſteps of the ſun, and ſcarce-moving is the moon that ſhines on this lonely place.— But why theſe ſilent tears, what mean theſe pitying looks? They are not for my tale of wo; they are for Crimora's death. I know

S   ſhe

she is not: for I saw her ghost, sailing on the low-skirted mist, that hung on the beams of the moon; when they glittered, through the thin shower, on the smooth face of the deep. I saw my love, but her face was pale. The briny drops were trickling down her yellow locks, as if from ocean's bosom she had rose. The dark course of the tears was on her cheek, like the marks of streams of old, when their floods overflowed the vale. I knew the form of Crimora. I guessed the fate of my love. I raised my voice, and invited her to my lonely rock. But the virgin-ghosts of Morven raised the faint song around the maid. It was like the dying fall of the breeze in the evening of autumn; when shadows slowly grow in Cona's vale, and soft sounds travel, through secret streams, in the gale of reeds. The listening waves, bending forward, stood still, and the screaming sea-fowl were quiet, while the tender air continued.

"Come," they said, "Crimora*, to Morven; come to the hills of woods; where Sulmalda, the beauteous love of Trenmor, bends the airy bow, and pursues the half-viewless deer of the clouds. Come, Crimora, and forget thy grief in the land of our joy."

She followed; but left me a pitying look, and I thought I heard her sigh. It was like the distant wave on the lonely shore, when the mariner hears its moan from the mouth of his cave, and fears the coming storm. Still I listened; but the soft music ceased: the fair vision vanished. It vanished like the hunter's dream of love, when the sound of the horn, on the heath, awakes him. I cried; but they heard me not. They left me to mourn on my solitary rock; like the dove which his mate hath forsaken.—Since that

time,

* *Crimora*, " large, or generous heart." *Sul-malda*, " mild-looking eye."

time, my tears have always begun with the dawn of the morning, and defcended with the fhades of the night.—O when fhall I fee thee again, Crimora! Tell me, Comhal, how died my love.

Thy love heard of thy fate, and three funs beheld her white hand fupport her bending head. The fourth faw her fteps on the winding fhore, looking for the cold corfe of Dargo. The daughters of Morven beheld her from their mountains. They defcended, in filence, along their blue ftreams. Their fighs lift their wandering hair, their foft hands wipe away the dimming tear.—They came, in filence, to comfort Crimora; but in her bed of ooze, they found the maid. They found her cold as a wreath of fnow; fair as a fwan on the fhore of Lano.—The gray ftone and green turf on Morven's fhore, now compofe Crimora's dwelling.—The daughters of Morven mourned her fate, and the bards praifed her beauty.—So may we, Dargo, live in renown; fo may our fame be found, when we moulder in the narrow houfe!

—But fee that light of Innisfail; fee the Crantara fly? Danger is nigh the king. Spread the fail, and ply the oar; fwift fly the bark over the fea. Let our fpeed be to yonder fhore, that we may fcatter the foes of Innisfail.

The breeze of Morven comes to our aid. It fills the wide womb of our fails with its breath. Our mariners rife on their oars, and lafh the foaming waves on their gray-bending head. Each hero looks forward to the fhore! each foul is already in the field.—But the eye of Dargo is bent downwards, as he fits in the filence of his grief. His head refts on his arm, over the dark edge of his father's fhield. Comhal obferves the mournful chief; he obferves his tears, dim-wandering, through the boffy plain of his

S 2   fhield;

shield; and he turns his eye on Ullin, that he may gladden his soul with the song.

"COLDA † lived in the days of Trenmor. He purfued the deer round Etha's bay. The woody banks echoed to his cry, and the branchy fons of the mountain fell. Minvela faw him from the other fide. She would crofs the bay in her bounding fkiff. A blaſt from the land of the ſtrangers came. It turned the boat on the ſtormy deep. Minvela rofe on its back. Colda heard her cries. —' I die,' fhe faid, ' Colda! my Colda, help me!'

"NIGHT drew its mantle over the wave. Fainter her voice founded in his ear; fainter it echoed from the fhelving banks. Like the diſtant found of evening ſtreams, it died at length away, and funk in night.—With morning he found her on the founding beach. Her blood was mixt with the oozy foam.—He raifed her gray ſtone on the fhore, nigh a fpreading oak and murmuring brook. The hunter knows the place, and often refts in the fhade when the beams of the fun fcorch the plain with the noon-day heat.

† The epifode of Colda is often repeated by itfelf, but the circumſtances of the poem leave no room to doubt of its proper place being here. As it is beautiful, and not long, I take the liberty of inferting it for the fake of the Galic reader.

Ri linn Threinmhoir nan fgia'
Ruaig Caoilte am fia' mu Eite;
Thuit leis daimh chabrach nan cnoc,
'Scho-fhreagair gach flochd da eighe.
Chunnaic Min-bheul a gaol,
'S le curach faoin chaidh na dhail.
Sheid ofna choimheach gun bhaigh,
'S chuir i druim an aird air a barca.
Chualas le Caoilte a ghaodh
" A Ghaoil, a Ghaoil, dean mo cho'nadh."

Ach thuirling dall-bhrat na h oidhche
'S dh'fhailnich a caoi-chora'.
Mar fhuaim fruthain ann cein,
Rainig a h eigh ga chluafan,
'S air madain ann on'adh na tragha
Fhuaras gun chail an og-bhean.
Thog e'n 'a cois tragha a leachd
Aig fruthan broin nan glas-ghengin;
'S iul don t Sealgair an t aite,
Smor a bhaigh ris ann teas na greine.
'S bu chian do Chaoilte ri bron
Feadh an lo, ann coillteach Eite,
'S fad na h oidhche chluinnte a leon;
Chuireadh e air eoin an uifge deifinn.
Ach bhuail Treunmor beum-fgeithe,
'S da ionfuidh, le buaidh, leum Caoilte;
Uigh air uigh phill a ghean,
Chual e chliu, 's lean e'n t feilge.

heat.—Colda long was fad. All day, through Etha's woody banks, he ftrayed alone. All night the liftening fea-fowl, with his moan on the fhore, were fad.—But the foe came, and the fhield of Trenmor was ftruck. Colda lifted the fpear, and they were vanquifhed. His joy, by degrees, returned; like the fun, when the ftorm on the heath is paft. He purfued again the brown deer of Etha, and heard his fame in the fong of the bards."

I REMEMBER, faid Dargo, the chief. Like the faint traces of a dream that is long fince paft, his memory travels acrofs my foul. Often he led my infant fteps to the ftone on the banks of Etha. The tear, as he leaned on its gray mofs, would fall from his grief-red eye: he would wipe it away with his fnowy locks. When I would afk him why he wept?—" Yes," he would reply, " it is here Minvela fleeps." And when I would bid him cut me a bow; " It is," he would fay, " the tomb of my love indeed. O let it be thy haunt, when thou fhalt hereafter purfue the chace, and reft at noon till the warm beam is over!"—And often I did fit, O Colda, over her tomb and thine, while I gave thy fame to the mournful fong. O that my renown, like thine, might furvive, when I myfelf am high, on thefe clouds, with Crimora!

AND thy fame fhall remain, faid Comhal.—But fee thefe fhields, rolling like moons in mift. Their bofles glitter to the firft gray beams of the morning. The people of Lochlin are there; and the walls of Innisfail tremble before them. The king looks out at his window; and, through the dimnefs of his tears, beholds a gray cloud. Two drops fall on the ftone on which he leans; he perceives that our fails are the gray cloud. The tear of joy ftarts into his eye, " Comhal, he cries, is near!"

LOCH-

LOCHLIN too hath feen us, and bends his gathered hoft to meet us. Armor leads them on, tall above the reft, as the red ftag that heads the herd of Morven. Againft me he lifts that hand, from which I loofed the thongs on the fhore of Erin. Let each, my friends, gird on his fword, and bound afhore on his fpear. Let each remember the deeds of his former days, and the battles of Morven's heroes.—Dargo, fpread thy broad fhield: Carril, wave thy fword of light: Connal, fhake thy fpear, that often ftrewed the plain with dead: And, Ullin, raife thou the fong, to fpirit us on to battle *.

WE met the foe. But they ftood, firm, as the oak of Malmor, that does not bend before the fury of the ftorm. Innisfail faw, and rufhed from their walls to help us. Lochlin was then blafted before us, and its dry branches ftrewed in the courfe of the tempeft. Armor met the chief of Innisfail; but the fpear of the king fixed his thick fhield to his breaft. Lochlin, Morven, and Innisfail wept for the early fall of the chief; and his bard began the mournful fong in his praife.

" Tall wert thou, Armor, as the oak on the plain: fwift as the eagle's wing was thy fpeed; ftrong, as the blaft of Loda, thy arm; and deadly, as Lego's mift †, thy blade! Early art thou gone to the airy hall: why, thou mighty, art thou fallen in youth? Who

fhall

---

* To fing the *Brofnacha-catha*, or " the incitement to war," was part of the office of the bards.

† The lake of Lego in Ireland, and the lake of Lano in Scandinavia, have the fame noxious quality afcribed to their vapours by the ancient bards. In this fimile, fome repeat the one, and fome the other. Lano, in the mouth of a Scandinavian bard, might be more proper; but Lego feems to fuit better with the verfe, and makes the found fmoother.

Bha t airde mar dharaig 'sa ghleann.
Do lua's mar iolair nam bean gun ghcilt;
Do fpionna mar ofna' Lodda na fheirg,
'S do Lnn, mar cheo *Lège*, gun leigheas.

† The

shall tell thy aged father, that he has now no son; or who shall tell Crimoina that her love is dead?—I see thy father, bending beneath the load of years. His hand trembles on the pointless spear; and his head, with its few gray hairs, shakes like the aspen leaf. Every distant cloud deceives his dim eye, as he looks, in vain, for thy bounding ship. Joy, like a sun-beam on the blasted heath, travels over his face of age, as he cries to the children at their play, 'I behold it coming.' They turn their eye on the blue wave, and tell him they see but the sailing mist. He shakes, with a sigh, his gray head, and the cloud of his face is mournful.—I see Crimoina smiling in her morning dream. She thinks thou dost arrive in all thy stately beauty. Her lips, in half-formed words, hail thee in her dream, and her joyful arms are spread to clasp thee.—But, alas! Crimoina, thou only dreamest. Thy love is fallen. Never more shall he tread the shore of his native land. In the dust of Innisfail his beauty sleeps! Thou shalt awake from thy slumber to know it, Crimoina; but when shall Armor awake from his long sleep? When shall the heavy slumber of the tenant of the tomb be ended? When shall the sound of the horn awake him to the chace? When shall the noise of the shield awake him to the battle?—Children of the chace, Armor is asleep, wait not for his rising; for the voice of the morning shall never reach his dwelling: sons of the spear, the battle must be fought without him; for he is asleep, and no warning boss shall awake him.—Tall wert thou †, Armor, as the

oak

---

† The ancient bards frequently conclude their episodes with a repetition of the first stanza. Instead of this, however, many repeat here the following verses:

Beannachd air anam an laoich
Bu gharg fraoch ri dol 's gach greis,
Ard Ri' Lo'icann, ceann an t slusigh,
'S iomad ruaig a chuire' leis.

" Peace to the soul of the hero whose wrath

oak on the plain. Swift as the eagle's wing was thy fpeed: ftrong, as the blaft of Loda *, thy arm; and deadly, as Lego's mift, thy blade."

THE bard ceafed. The tomb of Armor was reared; and his people, with flow unequal fteps, departed. Their nodding mafts are heavy on the deep. Their fongs are heard, at times; but their found is mournful. They are like the figh of mountain-winds in the waving grafs of the tomb, when the night is dark and the vales are filent.

PART II.

THE tales of the years that are paft, are beams of light to the foul of the bard. They are like fun-beams that travel over the heath of Morven; joy is in their courfe, though darknefs dwells around.—Joy is in their courfe, but it is foon paft; and the path of darknefs, like the fhadow of mift, purfues them. It will foon overtake them on the mountains, and the footfteps of the glad beams will ceafe to be feen. Thus the tale of Dargo travels over my foul, a beam of light, though the gathering of clouds is nigh it. —Shine on, O beam, as thou didft in the ftrife of Armor, when the ftrength

wrath in the ftrife of war was deadly. Peace to the people's chief, and to Lochlin's king; often did the vanquifhed fly before him."

* The Loda, or Lodda, of Offian, is fuppofed to have been the fame with the Odin or Woden of the Scandinavians.

This hero was more ancient than Homer; as his fon Skiold was, according to the Danifh chronologies, a thoufand years older than Pompey. His many conquefts and warlike exploits feem to have procured him divine honours from his countrymen, after his death.

strength of the bard was great, and his foul swelled, like Fingal's sail, in the storm of danger.

WE * turned in, that night, to the gray tower of Innisfail, and rejoiced in the song and the shell. The burst of grief, at times, reaches our ears. " Ullin and Sulma, examine whence it comes."

WE find Crimoina stretched on the grave of Armor.—When the battle had ceased, and her lover had fallen, she too had sunk in her secret place. All day, beneath the shade of a young oak she lay. At night, she made her bed on the grave of her love.—We gently tore her from her place, as our tears descended in silence. The grief of the virgin was great, and our words were uttered only in sighs.

WE brought her to the halls of Innisfail; and sorrow came, like a cloud, on every face. Ullin, at length, took the harp, and bade it give its tenderest air. Slow, solemn, and soft, his fingers steal along the trembling strings. The sound melts the soul. It calms the tumult of wo in the breast.

† " WHO bends, he said, from his airy cloud! who pours the piteous

---

* Upon the authority of the tale, a sentence or two are here thrown in to conduct the narration, as the verse is deficient.

† The smooth and elegiac strain of this episode, when set off with all the charms of music, could not fail to affect every person possessed of any sensibility of heart. For the sake of those who may understand the original, it is here subjoined.

Co so tuirling on cheo!
Sa dortadh a leoin air a ghaoith?
O's domhain a chreuchd tha na chliabh;

'Sis doilleir am fiadh ud ra thaobh!
Sud taiblhse Mhorghlain na mais'
Triath Sli'-ghlais nan ioma' sruth;
Thainig e gu Morbheinn le ghaol
Inghean Shora bu chaoine cruth.
Thog eisin t'ar n aonach gun bhaigh.
Min'onn dh'fhag e na tigh.
Thuirling dall-cheo le oidhche na nial.
Dh'eigh na fruthaibh ;- shian na taibhse.
Thug an og-bhean siul ris an t sliabh,
S chunnacas le'a fiadh ro'n cheo:
Tharruing i'n t freang le rogha beachd:
Fhuaras an gath ann uchd an oig!
Thiolaic sinn 'san tulaich an laoch,
Le gath is cuibhre na chaol-tigh.
B'aill le Min'onn luidh sa' shoid;

Ach

piteous figh on the wind! The dark wound is ftill in his breaft, and the half-viewlefs deer is befide him? Who is it but the ghoft of the faireft Morglan, king of the ftreamy Sliglas?—He came with the foe of Morven, and purfued the deer of our land. His love was with him; the fair-haired, white-handed, daughter of Sora. Morglan had gone to the hill: Minona ftaid in the booth. The thick mift defcends. Night comes on, with all its clouds. The torrent roars in its fall. Ghofts fhriek along its hollow-founding courfe. Minona looks for her love. She half-efpies a deer, flow-moving in the mountain mift. Her hand of fnow is on the bow. She draws the ftring. The arrow flies. Oh! that it had erred farther from the mark. The deer is borne by her Morglan. The arrow is found in his youthful breaft!

"WE reared the hero's tomb on the hill, and placed the arrow and the horn of the deer in his darkly filent houfe. There, too, his bounding dog was laid, to purfue the airy deer.—Minona would fleep with her love. But we fent her home to her land; where fhe, long, was fad. But her grief wafted away with the ftream of years; and fhe now rejoices with Sora's maids, though, at times, her fighs are heard.—Who bends from his airy cloud? who pours his figh on the wind? The dark wound is ftill in his breaft, and the half-viewlefs deer is befide him."

DAY came to Innisfail, with its gray-dark light. Take, Ullin, thy fhip, faid Comhal, and bring Crimoina to her land; that, in the midft of her friends, fhe may again rejoice, like the moon

when

Ach phill i, le bron, da tir.
Bu trom a tuirf, 's bu chian:
Ach fiuth bhliadhnaidh chaith air falbh e.

Tha i 'nois fubhach le oigh'ean Shora,
Mur cluinntear a bron air uairibh.—
Co fo tuirling, &c.

when it lifts its head through clouds and smiles on the valley of silence.

BLESSED, said Crimoina, be the chief of Morven, the friend of the feeble in the day of their danger!—But what should Crimoina do in her land; where every rock and hill, every tree and murmuring brook, would awake her slumbering sorrow? The youths whom I scorned, when they would behold me, would laugh, and say, Where is now thy Armor? You may say it, but I will not hear you; I live in a land that is distant. I end my short day with the maids of Morven. Their hearts, like that of their king, will feel for the unhappy.

WE brought Crimoina with us to our land. We gave her fair hand to Dargo. But still, at times, she was sad; the secret streams, as they passed, heard on their banks her sigh.—Crimoina, thy day, indeed, was short. The strings of the harp are wet, while the bard repeats thy tale.

ONE day as we pursued the deer on Morven's darkly heath, the ships of Lochlin appeared on our seas, with all their white sails, and nodding masts. We thought it might be to demand Crimoina. " I will not fight," said Connas of the little soul, " till I first know if that stranger loves our race. Let us pursue the boar, and dye the robe of Dargo with his blood. Then let us carry the body of her husband home, and see how she will mourn for his loss."

WE heard, in an evil hour, the advice of Connas. We pursued the foaming boar. We brought him low in the echoing woods. Two held him in all his foam, while Connas pierced him through with the spear.

DARGO lay down, and we sprinkled him over with the blood.

T 2   We

We bore him on our spears to Crimoina; and sung, as we went along, the song of death. Connas ran before us with the skin of the boar. I slew him, he said, with my steel; but first his deadly tusk had pierced thy Dargo. For the spear of the chief was broke, and the loose rock had failed below him.

CRIMOINA heard the tale of the tomb. She saw her Dargo brought home, as dead. Silent and pale she stood, as the pillar of ice that hangs, in the season of cold, from the brow of Mora's rock. At length she took her harp, and touched it, soft, in praise of her love. Dargo would rise, but we forbade till the song should cease; for it was sweet as the voice of the wounded swan, when she sings away her soul in death, and feels in her breast the fatal dart of the hunter *. Her companions flock, mournful, around; they

---

* This simile is differently expressed; being sometimes derived from the *swan*, (Mar bhinn-ghuth *ealaidh* 'n guin bais), and sometimes from the *minstrel*, which is expressed by a word of nearly the same sound, (mar bhinn-ghuth *filuidh*, &c.) with a slight variation in the rest of the stanza.---Which of the words was originally used by Ullin, is uncertain; but the first is here retained as the most beautiful, though perhaps the most exceptionable, reading. The singing of the swan has been always considered as a dream of the Greek and Latin poets: and though the Celtic may need no defence, as his expression is so dubious and so differently repeated; yet, in support of them, I must observe, that it is universally affirmed in the west of Scotland, as an undoubted fact, that the wild swans which frequent these parts in winter, and which are spe-

cifically different from the tame, emit some very melodious notes on certain occasions; particularly when two flocks of them meet, when they are wounded, and when about to take their flight, being birds of passage in these countries. Their note has, in the Galic, a particular name, which would not readily be the case if the thing had not a foundation in nature: and there is likewise a tune or song called *Luineag na h Ealui*, " the swan's ditty," the words and air of which are in imitation of this bird's singing. A part of this *Luineag* is here subjoined.

Gui' eug- i, Gui'eug-o
Sgeula mo dhunach
Gui'eug-i
Rinn mo leire'
Gui'eug-o
Mo chasan dubh
Gui'eug-i
'Smi sein gle' gheal
Gui'eug-o.

they affuage her pain with their fong, and bid the ghofts of fwans convey her foul to the airy lake of the clouds. Its place is above the mountains of Morven.

"BEND," fhe faid, "from your clouds, ye fathers of Dargo; bend, and carry him to the place of your reft. And ye maids of Trenmor's airy land, prepare the bright robe of mift for my love. O Dargo, why have I loved, why was I beloved fo much! Our fouls were one; our hearts grew together, and how can I furvive when they are now divided?—We were two flowers that grew in the cleft of the rock; and our dewy heads, amidft fun-beams, fmiled. The flowers were two; but their root was one. The virgins of Cona faw them, and turned away their foot; ' They are lonely,' they faid, ' but lovely.' The deer, in his courfe, leaped over them; and the roe forbore to crop them. But the wild boar, relentlefs, came. He tore up the one with his deadly tufk. The other bends over it his drooping head; and the beauty of both, like the dry herb before the fun, is decayed.

"My fun on Morven now is fet, and the darknefs of death dwells around me. My fun fhone, how bright! in the morning; its beams it fhed around me, in all its fmiling beauty. But ere evening it is fet, to rife no more; and leaves me in one cold, eternal, night. Alas, my Dargo! Why art thou fo foon fet? Why is thy late-fmiling face o'ercaft with fo thick a cloud? Why is thy warm heart fo foon grown cold, and thy tongue of mufic grown fo mute!— Thy hand, which fo lately fhook the fpear in the battle's front, there lies cold and ftiff: and thy foot, this morning the foremoft in the fatal chace, there lies, dead as the earth it trod. From afar, o'er feas, and hills, and dales, have I followed till this day, my love!

thy

thy steps.—In vain did my father look for my return; in vain did my mother mourn my absence. Their eye was often on the sea; the rocks often heard their cry. But I have been deaf, O my parents, to your voice; for my thoughts were fixed on Dargo.—O that death would repeat on me his stroke! O that the wild boar had also torn Crimoina's breast! Then should I mourn on Morven no more, but joyfully go with my love on his cloud!—Last night, I slept on the heath by thy side; is there not room, this night, in thy shroud? Yes, beside thee I will lay me down: with thee, this night too, I will sleep, my love, my Dargo *!"

WE heard the faultering of her voice: we heard the faint note dying in her hand. We raised Dargo from his place. But it was too late. Crimoina was no more. The harp dropped from her hand. Her soul she breathed out in the song. She fell beside her Dargo.

HE raised her tomb, with Crimora, on the shore; and hath prepared the gray stones for his own in the same place.

SINCE then, twice ten summers have gladdened the plains; and twice ten winters have covered with snow the woods. In all that time, the man of grief hath lived in his cave, alone; and listens only to the song that is sad. Often I sing to him in the calm of noon, when Crimoina bends down from her flakey mist.

* A stanza or two more, which are sometimes added to this lament of Crimoina, are omitted; as there is here, especially in the original, a kind of pause, which seems to have been intended for the conclusion.

'S rinneadh leaba dhuinn an raoir,
Air an raon ud chnoc nan fealg;
'S ni'n deantar leab' air leth a nochd dhuinn,
S' ni'u fgarar mo chorp o'm Dhearg.——

GAUL:

G A U L[*]:

A P O E M.

THE ARGUMENT.

OSSIAN, having retired, through night, to the ruins of Fingal's palace, to lament the his reverse of fortune, lights upon a piece of an old shield, which he recognizes to be that of Gaul, the son of Morni.——This circumstance introduces the history of an expedition of Fingal to Ifrona, whither Gaul had followed him, but did not arrive there till Fingal had departed. Gaul, after a brave resistance, is at length overpowered by numbers, and left upon the shore dangerously wounded. Here his spouse Evirchoma (whose anxiety had led her to come with her child to meet him) finds him, and attempts to carry him home. But the wind proving contrary, and Gaul dying of his wounds, she is so overcome with toil and grief, that she is obliged to desist, and stop in the shelter of a small isle, where Ossian, who had gone in quest of her and Gaul, finds both expiring. He carries them to Strumon; the desolate appearance of which is described, with the lamentation of Fingal over Gaul, who had been one of his chief heroes.——This poem is addressed to Malvina, the daughter of Toscar.

AWFUL is the silence of night. It spreads its mantle over the vale. The hunter sleeps on the heath. His gray dog stretches his neck over his knee. In his dreams he pursues the sons of the mountain, and with joy he half-awakes.

SLEEP

[*] Gaul the son of Morni was a distinguished character in the wars of Fingal, and consequently in the poems of Ossian. This piece, which celebrates his memory, is in the original called *Tiomna 'Ghuill*. It is still pretty well known; but the most common editions of it are a good deal adulterated by the interpolations of the *Ur-sgeuls*, or "later tales." It begins in this manner:

Nach tiamhaidh tofd fo na h oidhche,
Si tiofgadh a dui'neoil air gleanntaidh!
Dh'aom fuain air iuran na feilge
Air an raon, fa chu ra ghlun.
Clanna nan fliabh tha e 'ruaga'
Na aifling, 'fa fhuain ga thre'gfin.

SLEEP on, and take thy reſt, light-bounding ſon of the chace; Oſſian will not diſturb thee. Sleep on, ye ſons of toil; the ſtars are but running their mid-way courſe, and Oſſian alone is awake on the hills. I love to wander alone, when all is dark and quiet. The gloom of night accords with the ſadneſs of my ſoul; nor can the morning ſun, with all his beams, bring day to me.

SPARE thy beams then, O ſun! like the king of Morven, thou art too laviſh of thy bounty. Doſt thou not know thy light, like his, may one day fail. Spare thy lamps which thou kindleſt, by thouſands, in thy blue hall above; when thou thyſelf retireſt to thy repoſe, below the duſky gates of the weſt. Why ſhould thy lights fail, and leave thee in thy mournful halls, alone, as his friends have done to Oſſian? Why, mighty beam, ſhouldſt thou waſte them on Morven; when the heroes have ceaſed to behold them; when there is no eye to admire their green-ſparkling beauty?

MORVEN, how have thy lights failed! Like the beam of the oak in thy palaces, they have decayed, and their place is the dwelling of darkneſs. Thy palaces themſelves, like thoſe who rejoiced within them, are fallen on the heath, and the thick ſhadow of death ſurrounds them. Temora is fallen; Tura is an heap; and Selma is ſilent. The ſound of their ſhells is long ſince paſt. The ſong of their bards and the voice of their harps are over. A green mound of earth, a moſs-clad ſtone lifting through it here and there its gray head, is all that preſerves their memory. The mariner beholds, no more, their tall heads riſing through clouds, as he bounds on the deep; nor the traveller as he comes from the deſart.

I GROPE for Selma. I ſtumble on a ruin. Without any form

is

is the heap. The heath and the rank grafs grow about its ftones; and the lonely thiftle fhakes here, in the midnight breeze, its head. I feel it heavy with the drops of night.—The owl flutters around my gray hairs: fhe awakes the roe from his bed of mofs. He bounds lightly, without fear; for he fees it is but the aged Offian. —Roe of mofly Selma, thy death is not in the thought of the bard. Thou haft ftarted from the bed where often flept Fingal and Ofcar, and doft thou think Offian will ftain it with his fpear? No; roe of the bed of Fingal and Ofcar, thy death is not in the thought of the bard.—I only ftretch my hand to the place where hung my father's fhield; where it hung, on high, from the roof of Selma. But the blue bending fhell of heaven, O Selma! is now thy only covering. I feek the broad fhield among the ruins: my fpear ftrikes againft one of its broken boffes.—It is the bofs in which dwelt the voice of war! Its found is ftill pleafant to my ear: it awakes the memory of the days that are paft; as when the breath of winds kindles the decaying flame on the heath of hinds. —I feel the heaving of my foul. It grows like the fwelling of a flood; but the burden of age preffes it back: retire, ye thoughts of war!—Ye dark-brown years that are paft, retire. Retire with your clanging fhields, and let the foul of the aged reft. Why fhould war dwell, any more, in my thoughts, when I have forgot to lift the fpear? Yes, the fpear of Temora is now a ftaff; never more fhall it ftrike the founding fhield.—But it does ftrike againft a fhield: let me feel its fhape.—It is like the wafting moon, half-confumed with the ruft of years.—It was thy blue fhield, O Gaul!—the fhield of the companion of my Ofcar!— But why this melting of my foul?—Son of my love! thou haft

U received

received thy fame. I will retire and give the name of Gaul to the song.—Harp of Selma, where art thou? And where art thou, Malvina? Thou wilt hear with joy of the companion * of thy Oscar.

THE night was stormy and dark: ghosts shrieked on the heath: torrents roared from the rock of the hill: thunders rolled, like breaking rocks, through clouds; and lightnings travelled on their dark-red wings through the sky.—On that night, our heroes gathered in Selma's halls; the halls that are now an heap! the oak blazed in the midst. Their faces shone in its light, joyful between their dark locks; and the shell went round, with its sparkling joy †. The bards sung, and the soft hand of virgins trembled on the string of the harp.

THE night flew on the wings of gladness. We thought the stars had scarce measured half their way, when gray morning arose, from the troubled clouds of her repose in the east. The shield of Fingal

---

* The disparity of age between Gaul and Oscar was considerable. Yet the similarity of their characters might naturally attach them to each other. The original word, however, which is rendered *companion*, is obsolete, and may only import that they went *hand in hand* to battle. I insert so much of the passage as may enable those who understand the langage to judge of the meaning of the expression.
Sa choppain eigheach nam blar!
Is far-aoibhin leam fathasd t fhuaim;
Tha e dusga' nan laidh chualdh feach:
'Sa dh'aindeoin aois, tha manam a 'leimnich.
———Ach nam smuainte nam blar,
'S mo shleagh air fas na luirg;
An sgla' choppach tuille cha bhuail i;
Ach ciod fo'n fhuaim a dhuisg i?

Bloidh fgeith air a caithe le haois!
Mar ghealach ear-dhu' a cruth.
Sgia Ghuill si a t'ann
Sgia cho'lain mo dheagh Oscair!

† There are several opinions with regard to the liquor used in these *feasts of shells*. The most probable is, that it was made of a juice extracted from the birch-tree, and fermented. This would be more palatable than that which it is said they made of a certain kind of heath, and more suited to their exigencies than any spoils of wine which they might, at times, carry away from the Roman province. Or they might possibly have malt-liquors from other parts of the island before they themselves paid any attention to agriculture.

gal was ftruck. This bofs ‡ had then another found. The heroes heard its voice, like thunder on the diftant heath; and they rufhed with joy from all their ftreams. Gaul heard it; but the water of Strumon rolled its flood, and who could crofs its mighty tide?

WE failed to Ifrona: we fought; and recovered the fpoil of our land. Why didft thou not wait at thy moffy ftream till we returned, thou lifter of the blue fhield! Why, fon of Morni, was thy foul fo impatient for the battle?—But thou wouldft not lofe thy fhare in any field of fame. Gaul prepared his fhip, light rider of the foamy wave, and fpread his fails to the firft ray that ftreaked the clouds of the eaft. He followed to Ifrona the path of the king.

BUT who is that on the fea-beat rock, fad as the gray mift of the morning? Her dark hair floats, carelefs, on the ftream of winds; her white hand is around it, like the foam of floods. Two dewy drops ftart into her eyes as they are fixed on the fhip of Gaul; and on her breaft hangs, in the midft of his fmiles, her child. She hums in his ear a fong. Sighing, fhe ftops fhort. She has forgot what it was. Thy thoughts, Evirchoma, are not of the fong: they fail, along with thy love, on the deep. The leffened fhip is half in view. A low-failing cloud now fpreads its fkirt between, and hides it like a dark rock in the paffing mift. " Safe be thy courfe, rider of the foamy deep; when, my love, fhall I again behold thee!"

---

‡ The bofs of Fingal's fhield, found juft now in the ruins of his palace. The *Beim-fgeithe,* or " ftriking the fhield," was the ufual mode of giving the alarm or challenge to battle among the Caledonians.

Evirchoma * returns to Strumon's halls; but her steps are slow, and her face is sad. She is like a lonely ghost in a calm, when he walks in the mist of the pool, and the wind of hills is silent. Often she looks back, in the midst of her sighs, and turns her tearful eye towards Ocean. " Safe be thy course, rider of the foamy deep; when shall I again behold thee!"

Night with all her murky darkness met the son of Morni in the midst of his course. The dim moon hid herself in the caves of clouds, and no star looked out from the windows of the sky. His bark in silence rides the deep: and, in our course, we miss the chief, as homeward we bound to Morven.

Ifrona hides itself in the morning mist. The step of Gaul is careless on its shore: he wonders he does not hear the roar of battle. He strikes his shield, that his friends may know of his coming. " Does Fingal," he says, " sleep; and the battle unfought? Heroes of Morven, are you here?"

O that we had! Then had this spear defended thee from the foe; or low had its owner fallen. No harmless staff, the prop of tottering years, was then Temora's spear. It was the lightning that overturns the lofty trees in its red-winged course, when the mountains tremble before it. Ossian was then no blasted tree that stands alone on the heath, shaking before every breeze, and half-bent over the stream by wintry storms. No; I stood like the pine of Cona, with all my green branches about me, smiling at the storm of heaven, and tossing themselves with joy in the roar of winds.

---

* *Aoibhir-chaomha,* " mild and stately," the wife of Gaul, and daughter of *Casdu-conglas.* Mention is made of her in the 3d book of Temora, and some other of Ossian's poems.

† " Fil-

winds. O that I had been nigh the chief of Strumon, when blew the storm of Ifrona!

WHERE, then, ye ghosts of Morven, were you? Were you asleep in your airy caves, the dark-gray chambers of the clouds, or sporting with the withered leaf, the play of whistling boys, when you did not warn your sons of the danger of Gaul?—But you did warn us, friendly spirits of our fathers! Twice you drove back our sails to Ifrona's shore, as you sent your terrible roar along the deep. But we did not understand the sign. We thought you had been the ghosts of foes, that meant to oppose our return.—The king drove his blade through the gray folds of their robe, as over his head they passed. " Pursue," he said, " the thistles beard in other lands; or sport, where you can, with the sons of the feeble."

MOURNFUL they flew upon their blast. Their sound was like mountain-sighs on dark streams, when cranes foretel the storm. Some thought they half-heard from them the name of Gaul.

* * * * * * * * * *

" AM I alone in the midst of thousands? Is there no sword to shine, with mine, in the darkness of battle?—The breeze blows towards Morven. Thither is the course of white-headed billows. Shall Gaul lift his sails? His friends are not with him. What shall Fingal say, who bade his sons to mark the path of Gaul in battle †? What shall the bards say if they see a cloud on the fame of the son of Morni? Morni! my father! wouldst thou not blush if thy son retired? Yes, with thy white hairs, thou wouldst hide thy face in the presence of the heroes of other times, and sigh in the wind above the vale of

Stru-

† " Fillan and Oscar, of the dark-brown hair! fair Ryno, with the pointed steel! advance with valour to the fight, and behold the son of Morni. Let your swords be like his in the strife, and behold the deeds of his hands." Fingal, B. 4.

Strumon. The ghosts of the feeble would behold thee and say, 'There the father of him who once fled in Ifrona.' No; thy son will not fly, O Morni! his soul is a beam of fire; it catches in its red flame the groves. If wide they spread their wings, as wide it spreads its rage.—Morni, come in thy mountain cloud, and behold thy son. Thy soul was a crowded stream that swelled and foamed, when rocks in the narrow path opposed its course; the same shall be the soul of Gaul.—Evirchoma! Ogal!—But lovely beams mix not with the tempest of heaven: they wait till the storm is over. The thoughts of Gaul must now be of battle. All other thoughts away.—O that thou wert with me, Ossian, as in the strife of Lathmon!—But my soul is a spirit of the storm. Dark-eddying it rushes, alone, through the troubled deep. It heaves a thousand billows over trembling isles; then careless rides upon the car of winds."

THE shield of Morni is struck again in Ifrona *. No half-consumed, earth-crusted board was this orb then! Ifrona rocked with its sound, and its thousands gathered around Gaul. But the sword of Morni is in the terrible hand of the chief; and, like the green branches of the forest, their ranks are hewn before him. Their

blue

* The conduct of Gaul on this occasion may be censured as rash, in drawing upon himself a whole host when he was alone. But as he had before struck his shield, in hopes his friends had been near him, it is probable that he could not well decline an engagement to which himself had founded the alarm.—It may further be observed, that the behaviour of Gaul on this occasion corresponds very much with his character in the poem of *Lathmon*, and indeed with the manners of the times, which made it disgraceful for a hero to retire on any pretext whatever. The conduct of Oscar in the *War of Caros* affords a remarkable instance of this. The great resemblance betwixt Celtic manners and the laws of chivalry in later times, makes it probable, that the first had suggested most of those ideas on which the latter were founded.

† In

blue arms are ſtrewed upon the heath, and the birds of death are hovering round.

Thou haſt ſeen, Malvina, a mighty wave recoiling, white, from the broad ſide of a whale, when her path is in the foamy deep. Thou haſt ſeen, on the top of that wave, a flock of hungry ſea-fowl gathered about the whale which they dare not approach; tho' they ſee her float, half-dead, on ocean's ſtream, with her white belly turned above like ſails: ſo ſtood the ſons of Ifrona, afraid; and kept at bay by the ſword of Gaul.

But the ſtrength of the chief of Strumon begins to fail. He leans to the ſide of a tree. His blood marks, with wandering ſtreams, his blue ſhield, and a hundred arrows with their heads of ſteel have torn his ſide. Still, however, he holds his ſword, a meteor of death, in his hand, and the foes are afraid.

But ſons of Ifrona! what means that ſtone which you try to lift? Is it to mark to future times your fame †? Ah! no; the thoughts of your ſoul are hard as ſteel. Scarce can ſeven hurl the rock from the hill: it rolls its courſe againſt the thigh of Gaul.— The chief ſinks upon his knee; but over his broad, brazen ſhield, he ſtill looks terrible. His foes are afraid to come nigh. They leave him to pine away in death, like an eagle that lies upon a rock, when the bolt of heaven hath broke its wings.

O that we had known in Selma that ſuch, whirlwind of battle! was thy fate. Then had we not liſtened to the ſongs of virgins, nor to the voice of harps and bards. The ſpear of Fingal had not ſlept ſo quiet by the wall; nor the ſon of Luno reſted in

his

---

† In ancient times, pillars of ſtone were frequently erected in the field of battle to commemorate the victory.

his sheath. Then had we not wondered, that night, to see the king half-rising from the feast, and looking to his shield. " I thought," he said, " the light spear of a ghost had touched its boss; but it was only the passing breeze."

GHOST of Morni ! why didst thou not strike it louder again; or pour thy knowledge on the dream of our rest ? Why didst thou not come to Ossian, and say, " Awake, be thy path again on the wave of the deep."—But thou hadst been flying in haste to Ifrona, to mourn over the fall of thy son.

MORNING arose on Strumon. Evirchoma awoke from her troubled dreams. She heard the sound of the chace on Morven, and wondered no voice of Gaul was there. She listens; but the rock does not echo to his cry. The groves of Strumon hear only the sighs of the fair.

EVENING comes; but no dark ship is seen, light-bounding over the deep. The soul of Evirchoma is mournful.

" WHAT detains my hero in the isle of Ifrona ? Why, my love, art thou not returned with Morven's chiefs ? Thou hast perhaps missed them on the deep. But yet thou mightest have ere now returned. How long shall thy Evirchoma bend from the rock of waves? How long shall the tear wander, like a stream in mist, upon her cheek ?—Is the child of our love forgot ? If not, where are the wonted smiles of his father ? The tears of Ogal * descend with mine; and his sighs to mine reply. O that his father heard him,

as,

---

* *Ogal*, " young Gaul." In those times men did not receive their proper names till they had distinguished themselves by some renowned action, or discovered some peculiar characteristic in their person or behaviour. This, like all the other customs of the ancient Caledonians, had a happy tendency to inspire their youth with the love of virtue and bravery; the only avenue to that immortality of fame of which they were always so ambitious.

as, lifping, he half-repeats his name; then quick would be the fteps of his return to relieve him. But ah me! I remember my dream through night; and I fear the day of thy return, O Gaul, is over.

"The fons of Morven, methought, purfued the chafe; but abfent was the chief of Strumon. At a diftance I faw him reclined on his fpear; on one foot only leaned the chief. The other feemed a column of gray mift. It varied its form to every breeze. I approached my love; but a blaft from the defart came. He vanifhed.—But dreams are the children of fear. Chief of Strumon, I fhall again behold thee. Thou wilt lift thy fair head before me, like the beam of the eaft, when he looks on Cromla's † haunted heath, where fhook all night, amidft the terror of ghofts, the weary traveller. The fpirits of the dark retire on their deep-ruftling blaft; and he, glad, takes his ftaff, and purfues the reft of his journey.

"Yes, my love, I fhall behold thee. Is not that thy fhip that climbs the diftant wave: its fails are like the foam of the rock; like a tree that waves its top in fnow? Is it thy fhip; or is it a cloud of mift that deceives, through the darkening fhades, my tearful eye?—Still it appears like the fhip of my love.—Yes, dark-bounder on the rolling deep, it is thou.—Dufky night, hide not from my view his fails. Thou beginneft to hide them under thy raven wings: but I will bound, in this fkiff, on the darkly-rolling deep; and meet in the folds of night my love."

X SHE

† *Crom-ft lia*', "bending hill," or "the hill of bending." It was probably a Druidical place of worfhip, which might affix to it the ideas of awe and terror here afcribed to it.

* This

She went †; but no ship meets her on the deep. It was but a cloud low-sailing on its wave; the bark of some mariner's ghost, pursuing the sport of his former days.

The skiff of Evirchoma flies before the wind. Ifrona's bay receives it through night, where lonely waves roll themselves beneath the gloom of hanging woods. The thin moon glides from cloud to cloud. Its course, through trees, is on the edge of the hill. The stars, at times, glance through their parted mist, and hide themselves again under their vapoury veil. With the faint light, Evirchoma beholds the beauty of her child. " Thou art lovely in the dreams of thy rest."—Over him she bends a while in sighs; and then leaves him in the womb of her skiff. " Rest in peace, my child; I seek thy father along this winding beach."

Thrice she leaves him, and thrice she quick returns. She is like the dove that leaves in the cleft of Ulla's rock her young, when she wanders, over the plain, in search of food. She sees the dark berry on the heath below her; but the thought of the hawk comes across her soul, and she oft returns to behold her young, before she tastes it.—Thus the soul of Evirchoma is divided, like a wave which the rock and the wind toss, by turns, between them.—" But what voice is that from the breast of the breeze? it comes from the tree of the lonely shore."

" Sad," it says, " I pine here alone; what avails that my arm was so strong in battle? Why does not Fingal, why does not Ossian,

know,

† This expedition of Evirchoma will not appear unnatural or extravagant, if we consider, that, in those days, the women frequently bore a part in the most arduous undertakings both by sea and land. Besides, she might not probably intend to go far from the shore at her first setting out, as she thought she had seen the ship of Gaul at no great distance.

* What

know, that I am thus low on the shore of night? Ye lights above, that at times behold me, tell it in Selma, by your red signs, when the heroes come forth from the feast to behold your beauty. Ye ghosts that glide on nightly beams, if through Morven be your eddying course, tell, as you pass, the tale in the ear of the king. Tell him, that here I pour out my soul; that cold in Ifrona is my dwelling; that two days have brought me no food, and that my drink is the briny wave.—But tell not this in Strumon; let not your knowledge come to the dreams of Evirchoma. Be the rustling of your blasts far from her halls: shake not roughly your wings, as, even at a distance, you pass. My love might hear it; and some dark-boding thought might travel, as mist, across her soul. Be therefore your course, ye spirits of night, far off; and let the dreams of my love be pleasant.—The morning, Evirchoma, is yet distant. Sleep on, with thy lovely child in thy arms, and pleasant be thy dreams in the murmur of Strumon! Pleasant, in the valley of roes, be thy dreams, O Evirchoma! let no thought of Gaul disturb thee. His pains are forgot, when the dreams of his love are pleasant."

" AND dost thou think thy love could sleep, and her Gaul in pain? Dost thou think the dreams of Evirchoma could be pleasant, while thou wert absent? No; my heart is not unfeeling as that rock; nor did I receive my birth in Ifrona's land *.—But how

X 2 shall

* What this Ifrona was, is uncertain; but it seems to have been remarkable for the cruelty of its inhabitants. In the following lines of a fragment concerning the death of Clonar, who had been slain there, many properties of the *Celtic hell* are ascribed to it; from which, and the similarity of the names, it is probable it might have been considered as a type of it.

I sin alluidh na Freoine,
Le d' thiugh-cheo buan, 's led' ua' bheiflan;
A thir nam pian! gun mhiadh gun bhaigh;
Dol a d' dhail be fud mo dheisinn.

" Ifrona,

shall I relieve thee, Gaul; or where shall Evirchoma find food in the land of foes?—I remember the tale of Casdu-conglas.

"WHEN I was young, in my father's arms, his course was one night on the deep with Crisollis, beam of love. The storm drove us on a rock. Three gray trees dwelt lonely there, and shook in the troubled air their leaf-less heads. At their mossy root a few red berries crept. These Casdu-conglas pulled. He pulled them, but he tasted not. Thou needest them, he said, Crisollis; and, to-morrow, the deer of his own mountain will supply Casdu-conglas.—The morning came; the evening returned: but the rock is still their dwelling.—My father wove a bark of the branches of the gray trees*; but his soul is feeble for want of food. 'Crisollis,' he said, 'I sleep. When the calm shall come, be thou gone with thy child to Idronlo; the hour of my waking is distant.'—Never shall the hills of I-dronlo behold me,' she replied, 'without my love. O why didst thou not tell me thy soul had failed! both might have been sustained by the mountain-berries. But the breasts of Crisollis will sup-

"Ifrona, horrible isle! covered with thick and ever-during mist: thou noisome abode of wild and venomous beasts: thou land of pain, where fame and friendship are strangers.—I tremble to go near thee."

As the name of *Glen-Freoin* is still retained by a valley in the neighbourhood of Clyde, it is probable the scene of this poem was somewhere on that coast, the inhabitants of which were generally at variance with the people of Morven. The situation of many places shew, that anciently, *I*, or *Inis*, did not always signify an island, but sometimes a promontory, or any place nearly inclosed by the sea: as *Deiginish, Craiginish,* &c.

* The *Curachs* (or *vimenei alvei* of Solinus) which were the first boats of the Caledonians, were made of wicker, and covered again with hides. The name, for some time, seems to have continued, after the construction of their vessels was much improved, as the ancient poems give sometimes the name of *Curach* to vessels of a considerable size. That which brought St Columba and his companions to Iona, was called *Curach*, though near 40 feet long, if we may credit tradition.

supply her love. I feel them full within, and thou, my love, muſt drink. For my ſake thou muſt live, and not fall here aſleep.'— He roſe: his ſtrength returned: the wind retired: they reached I-dronlo. Often did my father lead me to Criſollis' tomb, as he told the lovely tale. ' Evirchoma,' he ſaid, ' let thy love to thy ſpouſe be ſuch, when the days of thy youth ſhall come.' And it is ſuch, O Gaul; theſe breaſts will ſupply, this night, thy ſoul. To-morrow we ſhall be ſafe on the ſhore of Strumon.

" LOVELIEST of thy race," ſaid Gaul, " retire thou to Strumon's ſhore; let no beam of light find thee in Ifrona. Retire in thy ſkiff with Ogal: why ſhould he fall like a tender flower, which the warrior, unfeeling, lops off with the end of his ſpear; himſelf of no ſon the father. He lops it off, with all its drops of dew; as, careleſs, he walks along, humming the ſong of the cruel. Retire, and leave me in Ifrona; for my ſtrength, like the ſtream of ſummer, is failed: I wither like the green herb before the blaſt of winter. No friendly beam of the ſun, no returning ſpring ſhall revive me.—Bid the warriors of Morven bring me to their land: but no, the light of my fame is clouded. Let them only raiſe my tomb beneath this tall tree. The ſtranger will ſee it as he looks around him from his watery courſe. Sighing, he will ſhake his head, and ſay, There is all that remains of the mighty!"

" AND here too ſhall be all that remains of the fair; for I will ſleep in the ſame tomb with my love. Our narrow bed ſhall be the ſame in death; our ghoſts in the folds of the ſame gray cloud ſhall be joined. The virgins of Morven will mark, through moon-beams, our ſteps, and ſay, ' Behold, they are lovely.' Yes, traveller of the

watery

watery way, drop the double tear; for here, with her beloved Gaul, is the flumbering Evirchoma.

"But ah! what voice is that in the breeze? The cries of Ogal pour, helplefs, in my ear. They awake my fleeping foul. Yes; my foul rolls reftlefs within, and tofles from fide to fide in its uneafy bed. And why heaves thus the foul of Gaul; why burfts that figh from the warrior's breaft? Feel thus the hearts of fathers for their fons; have they, at times, the foul of a mother? Yes, for I feel the ftirrings of thine: let me bear thee to the fkiff where our child was left. Come, the burden of my love will be light: Evirchoma will be ftrong when her Gaul is in danger.—Give me that fpear, it will fupport on the fhore my fteps."

She bore him to her fkiff. She ftruggled all night with the wave. The parting ftars beheld the decay of her ftrength: the morning light beheld it fail, as the mift that melts in the beam of heat *.

I slept, that night, on the hunter's heath. Morni, with all his gray, parted locks, rofe in my dreams. Above me he leaned on his trembling ftaff. His face of age was fad; it was marked with the courfe of the tear. The ftream wandered, here and there, on his cheek. The deep furrows, which time had worn, were full. Thrice looked the red eye of the aged over the deep; and thrice arofe his figh. " Is this," he faintly faid, " a time for the friend of Gaul to fleep?"—A blaft comes, ruftling, along the bended trees. Its noife awakes the cock of the heath. At the root of his dark-brown

---

* In the moft common editions of *Tiamna 'Ghuill* a long dialogue is foifted in here, which is rejected as fpurious, or belonging to fome other Gaul whofe wife was called *Aina*. It begins with

A Righbhin is binne ceol
Gluais gu malda, 's na gabh bron, &c.

brown bufh, he lifts his head from beneath his wing ; and, trembling, raifes the mournful, plaintive voice.—I ftarted at the cry from my dream. I faw Morni rolled away, a gray cloud, in the fold of the blaft. I purfued the path which he marked on the fea. I found on the blue face of the wave, fheltered by a defert ifle, the fkiff. On the dark fide of it leaned the head of Gaul. Under his elbow refted the fhield of battle. Over its edge half-looked the wound, and poured the red-ftream around its bofs. I lifted the helmet from his face. His yellow locks, folded in fweat, were wandering on his brow. At the burft of my grief he tried to raife his eye ; but it was heavy. Death came, like night on the eye of the fun, and covered it with all its darknefs.—Never more, O Gaul, fhalt thou behold the father of thy Ofcar.

BESIDE the fon of Morni is the decayed beauty of Evirchoma. Her child fmiles, carelefs, in her arms ; and plays with the head of the fpear. Her words were few : her voice was feeble. I gave her my hand to raife her up. She laid it on the head of Ogal, as, fighing, fhe pierc'd with her look my melting foul.—No more fhall Evirchoma rife ! Sweet helplefs child, thou needeft no longer cling to the breaft of thy mother. Oflian fhall be thy father : but Evirallin is not; and who fhall fupply the place of Evirchoma ! —But I feel the meltings of my foul return.—Why fhould Oflian remember all the griefs that are paft ? Their memory is mournfully-pleafant; but his tears would fail.

WE came to Strumon's mofly ftreams. Silence dwelt around their banks. No column of fmoke, blue-curling, rifes from the hall. No voice of fongs is there ; no foft trembling found of the harp. The breeze rufhes, whiftling, through its open porch; and

lifts

lifts the dry, ruftling leaf, upon its eddying wing. The perching eagle fits already on its lofty top, and marks it out as the place of her repofe. " Here," fhe feems to fay, " I may fafely build my neft; for who can climb its height, to make my brown fons afraid?"— The dun little fon of the roe beholds her, as, wandering below, he looks up to what he thinks a gray rock.—He beholds her, and is afraid. He hides himfelf under a broad fhield, near the gate of the houfe.—Stretched acrofs the threfhold, fwift Cof-ula lies. He hears a ruftling near. He thinks it may be the tread of Gaul. In his joy he ftarts up, and fhakes from his dim eye the tear. But when he fees it is only the fon of the roe, he turns his mournful face away. He lies again on his cold ftone, and the fong of his grief is difmal.

But who can tell the fadnefs of Morven's heroes? They come in filence, each from his own winding vale; flowly moving, like the dark fhadow of mift on the brown rufhy plain, when the wind is fcarce awake on the hill. They fee the bulwark of the battle low; and their burfting tears, like the ooze of rocks, defcend. Fingal leaned to a blafted pine, that was overturned at the head of Gaul. His gray locks, as he bends, half-hide his tears; but in his white beard they meet the whiftling wind.

" And art thou fallen," at length he faid; " art thou fallen, firft of my heroes! when my ftrength has failed? Shall I hear thy voice no more in my halls, nor the found of thy fhield in my battles? Shall thy fword no more lighten the dark path of my danger; nor thy fpear fcatter whole hofts of my enemies? Shall thy dark fhip ride no more the ftorm, while thy joyful rowers pour before them the fong on the watery mountains? Shall the children of Morven

no

no more awake my foul from its thought, as they cry, ' Behold the fhip of Gaul!' Shall the harps of virgins, and the voice of bards, no more be heard when thou art coming?—I fee not the red-ftreaming of thy banners on the heath; the tread of thy foot is not there; nor the found of thy unmiffing arrow. The bounding of thy dogs is not on the hill; they mournfully howl in the door of thy empty houfe. The deer grazes on the plain before them: but they weep on; they do not heed him; for they fee not Gaul returning.—Alas! fons of the chafe, the day of his return is paft. His glad voice fhall call you no more, in the morning, to purfue the fteps of roes through rocky mountains. Here, forgetful of the chafe, he refts; nor can even the found of Morven's fhield, O Gaul, awake thee!

" STRENGTH of the warrior, what art thou! To-day, thou rolleft the battle, a cloud of duft, before thee; and the dead ftrew thy path, as the withered leaves mark the courfe of a ghoft of night. —To-morrow, the fhort dream of thy valour is over; the terror of thoufands is vanifhed. The beetle, on his dufky wing, hums the fong of triumph over the mighty; and, unmolefted, offends him.—

" WHY, fon of the feeble, didft thou wifh for the ftrength of the chief of Strumon, when thou didft behold him brightening in the courfe of his fteel, as brightens a pillar of ice in the midft of fun-beams? Didft thou not know that the ftrength of the warrior foon fails, as melts in the beam that ice which thou haft been viewing? Its date is fhort; like the bright cloud that glitters to the ray of the evening. The hunter fees it from his rock, as he hies him home, and admires the rain-bow form of its beauty.

beauty. But a few moments, on their eagle-pinion, pafs; the fun fhuts his eye of light; the blaft whirls that way his ruftling courfe, and a dark mift is all that remains of the gay form.—It is all, O Gaul! that now remains of thee.—But thy memory, chief of Fingal's heroes, fhall remain. No cloud of mift that fhall pafs away, on its own gray wings is thy fame.

"RAISE †, ye bards, his tomb; with that of the fun-beam of his love, Evirchoma. This gray ftone fhall mark to the traveller the place of his repofe; and that tall oak fhall fhade it from the noon-day heat. The paffing breeze fhall bid its boughs be early green, and long preferve their beauty. Its leaves fhall fhoot out their head, through the fhower of the fpring, while other trees are ftill bare, and the heath around them blafted. The birds of fummer, from their diftant land, fhall firft perch on Strumon's oak; from afar they fhall behold its green beauty. The ghoft of Gaul will hear, in his cloud, their fong; and the virgins of the race to come will praife Evirchoma. The memory of you two, while thefe monuments remain, fhall travel through future years together.—Then, when thou, O ftone, fhalt crumble into duft; and thou, O tree, moul-

† This paragraph lofes much of the artlefs fimplicity of the original, as it could not be rendered with perfpicuity without paraphrafing fome of its images. The original paffage is here annexed, that fuch as choofe to do it may have it in their power to compare it with the tranflation.

Cairibh, a chlanna nan teud,
Leaba Ghuill, 's a dheo-greine la' ris;
Far an comh'raichear a leab' ann cein.
Ged' raibh geugan ard ga sgaile'
Fui' sgei' na daraig is guirme bla',
Is luaithe fas, 's is buaine dreach;
A thruchdas a duilleach air anail na frois,

'S an raon man cuairt di seargte.
A duilleach, o iomal na tire,
Chitear le coin an t famhruidh;
Is luidhidh gach eun mar a thig
Air barra' geige na Strumoin.
Cluinnidh Goll an ceilair na cheo,
'S oighean a' seinn air Aoibhir-chaomha.
'S gus an caochail gach ni dhiu so
Cha sgarar ar cuimhne o' cheile.
—Gus an crion gu luaithre a chlach,
'S ao searg as le h aois a gheug so,
Gus an sguir na sruthain a ruith
'S an dea' mathair-uisge nan sleibhte;
Gus an caillear ann dilinn aois
Gach filidh 's dan is aobhar sgeil,
Cho'n fheoruich an t Aineal " Co mac Morna;.
No c'ait an co'nuidh' Ri' na Strumoin?"

moulder with age away; when thou, mighty ſtream, ſhalt ceaſe to run, and the mountain-ſpring ſhall, no more, ſupply thy courſe; when your ſongs, O bards, in the dark flood of Time ſhall be loſt; and the memory of yourſelves, with thoſe you ſung, in its vaſt current be ſwept away and forgot:—Then, perhaps, may ceaſe to be heard the fame of Gaul; and the ſtranger may aſk, " Who was Morni's ſon, and who was Strumon's chief?"

DUTHONA:

A POEM*.

The ARGUMENT.

FINGAL, purfuing Dorla who had carried off the fpoils of Selma in his abfence, lands in the night in Duthona, the ifland of his friend Conar. His landing is obferved and oppofed by Dorla, who had alfo called here and fubdued Conar. Fingal thinking he had been oppofed by his friends, was fatisfied with making them retreat a little, till day-light fhould fhew them their miftake. But learning how matters ftood from Conar, who is accidentally difcovered in a cave where he had been confined by Dorla, fpies are fent to watch the motions of the enemy. —Next morning Fingal and the remains of Conar's people engage with Dorla, who falls in battle.—Minla the daughter of Conar, who had been found concealed in the habit of a young bard, is unexpectedly reftored to her father, who gives her in marriage to one of Fingal's heroes.

WHY doft thou roar fo loud, O fea, on Morven's rocky coaft; and why, O wind of the fouth, doft thou pour thy ftrength againft the fhore of my echoing hills? Is it to detain my fails from the land of the foe, and ftop my growing fame?—But, ocean, thy billows roar in vain; and thou, wind of the fouth, mayeft blow; but you cannot detain the fails of Fingal, from the land of the diftant Dorla. The roar of your ftrength fhall foon decay;

---

* *Du'-thonna,* "the ifle of dark waves." This poem, from one of the incidents mentioned in it, is often called *Dan Oi'-mara,* or "The fong of the maid on the fhore." The verfification in feveral places is broken, and only fupplied from the traditionary tale which accompanies the poem. A few lines in the beginning are omitted, and the tranflation begins with the following ftanza:

Is girbh leam heucai h do thonn,
A mhuir cheann-ghlas, ri bonn mo fhleibh:
Is ofnaiche att'ar, citi', a deas,
Chon e mo leas gu du' fheid fibh, &c.

decay; and the blue face of my feas shall be calm behind, when you retire to reft in the green groves of the defart.—Yes, thy ftrength, O wind, shall fail; but the fame of Fingal shall remain: my renown shall be heard in the land that is diftant.

THE king fpoke, and his heroes gathered around. The bushy hair of Dumolach fings in the wind. Leth bends over his shield of brafs; it is marked with many a fcar. Morlo toffes in air his glittering fpear; and the joy of battle is in the eye of Gormallon.

WE rush through ocean's furgy foam. Whales, trembling, fly before us on the deep. Ifles fee us, and fly out of our way; they hide themfelves behind the path of our ship. Duthona lifts its head like a rock of ooze, which the diftant wave feems, at times, to intercept. " It is the land of Conar," faid Fingal; " the land of the friend of my people!"

NIGHT defcends on the fable deep. The mariner cries, It is dark. He wanders from his courfe: he looks in vain for the guiding ftar.—He half-fees it, through the torn fkirt of a showery cloud: with joy he bids his companions behold it. They look up; but the window of the cloud is shut, and the light is again concealed.—The fteps of the night, on the deep, are dark. Let our courfe be to the shore till morning arife with her yellow locks in the eaft; till dark waves clothe themfelves in light, and mountains lift their green heads in day.

OUR courfe is to Duthona's bay.—But fee that dim ghoft on the rock! He is tall as the gray pine to which he leans. His shield is a broad cloud. Behind it rolls in darknefs the rifing moon. That column of dark-blue mift, ftudded above with a red ftar, is his fpear; and that meteor that gleams on the heath, his fword. Winds, in their eddies, lift at times, like smoke, his hair. These flames, in two caves below it, are his eyes.—Often had Fingal seen the sign of battle; but who could believe it in the land of Conar, his friend?

THE king ascends the rock. The blade of Luno waves a meteor of light in his hand, and Carril walks behind him. The spirit beholds the warrior approach: on the wings of his blast he flies. Fingal pursues him with his voice: the hills of Duthona hear the sound. They shake with all their gray rocks and groves. From their dreams of danger, the people start along the heath, and kindle the alarm of the flame.

ARISE, my warriors, said the returning king, with a sigh; arise, let each gird on his mail, and spread his broad shield before him. We must fight; but not with the wonted joy of our strength when the roar of the battle rose. Our friends meet us through night; and Fingal will not tell his name *. Our foes might hear it, and say, " The warriors of Morven were once afraid." No; let each gird on his mail, and spread the shield: but let the spear err of its mark, and the arrow fly to the wind. With morning light we shall be seen of our friends, and our joy shall be great in Duthona.

WE

---

* In those days of heroism it was reckoned cowardice to tell one's name to an enemy, lest it should be considered as claiming kindred with him and declining the combat. The same extravagant notions of honour seem to have prevailed among some other nations of antiquity. In the Argonautic expedition, Jason, after having been hospitably entertained by Cyzicus king of the Deliones, was driven back on his coast, through night, and he and his people taken for Pelasgians, with whom they were then at war. Rather than dispense with this punctilio of honour, Jason fought till day-light shewed his friends their mistake, after a great many of them, with their king, had been killed. Vid. Ancient Univ. Hist. *of Fab. and Heroic Times*, § 6.

We met, in our rattling steel, the darkly-moving host. Their arrows fell, like a shower of hail, on our shields; but we fought not the fall of our friends. They gathered about us, like the sea about a rock. The king saw that his people must fight or fall. He came from his hill in the awful stride of his strength, like a ghost that hath clothed himself in storms. The moon raised her head above the hill, and beamed on the shining blade of Luno. It glittered in the hand of the king, like a pillar of ice in the fall of Lora, when the sun is bright in the midst of his journey. Duthona saw its blaze, but could not bear its light. They retired, like darkness when it sees the steps of the morning, and sunk in a wood that rose behind.

Slow-moving like Lubar, when he repeats in Dura's plain his course, we came to a hollow stream that ran before us on the heath. Its bed is between two banks of ferns, amidst many an aged birch. There we talked of the storms of battle and the actions of former heroes. Carril sung of the times of old: Ossian praised the deeds of Conar; nor did his harp forget the mild beauty of Minla.

The voice of the song ceased. The breeze whistled along the gurgling stream. It bore to our ear the sound of grief. It was soft as the voice of ghosts in the bosom of groves, when they travel over the tombs of the dead.

Go, Ossian, said the king, and search the banks of the stream; some one of our friends lies there, on his dark shield, overturned like a tree in the strife of night. Bring him to Fingal, that he may apply the herbs of the mountain; lest any cloud should darken our joy in the land of Duthona.

I WENT, and liftened to the fong of wo; my tears flowed, in filence, over the ftream.

"FORLORN and dark is my dwelling in the ftorm of night[*]. No friendly voice is heard, fave the cry of the owl from the cleft of her rock. No bard is nigh in my lonely cave, to deceive the tedious night.—But night and day are the fame to me; no beam of the fun travels here in my darkly dwelling. I fee not his yellow hair in the eaft; nor, in the weft, the red beam of his parting. I fee not the moon, failing through pale clouds, in her brightnefs; nor trembling, through trees, on the blue face of the ftream. No warm beam from either vifits the cave of Conar. O that I had fallen in the ftrife of Dorla; that the tomb had received my Minla! Then had the fame of Duthona paffed away, like autumn's filent beam, when it moves over the brown fields between the fhadows of mift. The children under Duthrona's oak feel it warm, and blefs the beam. It is over; they bend their bows, and forget it.—Forget me alfo, children of my people, if Dorla does not meet you, like the blafting wind of the froft, when the rofe-buds of the wood are tender. O that I had met death before you; when I ftrode with Fingal before the ftrength of Swaran! Then my tomb might rife before the king, and my fame be fung by the voice of Offian. The bards of the diftant years, fitting around the winter-flame, would fay, when the feaft was over, 'Liften to the fong of Conar.'— But now my fame fhall not be heard; my tomb fhall not be known. The ftranger ftumbles on a gray ftone in Duthona. Its head is covered with the rank, whiftling grafs. He turns it away

with

---

[*] This fong of Conar has in the original an air of melancholy extremely fuitable to the occafion of it.

Is doracha 'fan doirinn mo cho'nuidh!
Gun ghuth am choir ach ian t'amhaidh;
Threig am Bard :—tha'n oidhche mall;
O's oidhche gach la dhamhfa, &c.

with the end of his spear. He perceives the mouldering tomb. 'Who sleeps,' he asks, 'in this narrow house?' The children of the vale reply, 'We know not; the song doth not record his name."

—But it shall record thy name, O Conar! thou shalt not be forgotten by the voice of Cona. Come, leave thy cave, and lift again the spear of battle. The foe shall wither, like the frosted fern, before thee; and thy fame shall flourish, as the green oak of Duthona, when it lifts its tall head above the mist of the vale, and spreads its glittering leaf to the shower of the sun.

" Friendly is thy voice, son of night; for ghosts affright not me. No; their voice is pleasant to forsaken Conar. O let thy converse be oft in my cave! our words shall be of the narrow house, and of the airy dwellings of heroes. Of other worlds we shall speak: but of my friends, of my fame, we shall be silent.—My fame is departed like the melting of mists on Mora, when the sun is high, and the clouds retire to the desart. My friends, too, are distant: between their peaceful shields they sleep, and no dream of me disturbs them. And let them sleep; spirit of the friendly soul, my dwelling shall soon be with thee in the peaceful abode of thy rest. Together we shall visit the children of grief in their nightly cave, and make them forget their pain in their dreams*. We will wander with their souls through fields of fame; and bid the mighty shake in their presence. Their thong shall be a robe: their cave the noble Selma. The wind in their ear shall be the music of harps, and the whistling grass the song of virgins. Till then be thy

---

* The bard, it would appear from this passage, was of opinion, that dreams were sometimes occasioned by the agency of departed spirits, who had the power of impressing the mind with sensations of either the pleasing or painful kind.

thy vifits to Conar frequent; for thy voice to me is pleafant, air-borne fon of the night."

I CUT the thongs from the hand of the chief, and brought him to the king. Their faces brightened with joy between their gray locks, when they met; for they remembered their early days: The days, when firft they drew the ftring in the moffy vale of ftreams; when the ftag was but the thiftle's beard, and the deer the wandering down of the defart. Their years afterwards grew together; and roes, before their fwift fteps, bounded on Gormal.

BUT who, faid Fingal, hath confined the friend of Morven to his cave? Strong muft be his arm; and unerring his fteel in the ftrife of battle.

"DORLA heard that my arm had failed; and he came to my halls by night, when my friends were abfent. I fought; but his numbers prevailed. Dorla is ftill in Duthona: Minla is forrowful in his prefence; and my people, through their fecret vales, are fcattered."

FINGAL heard the words of Conar; and the gathering of his mild brows, like clouds that cover the ftorm, is terrible. He fhakes the afpen fpear in his hand, and looks on the fword of Luno. "This is no time," he fays, "for reft; when he who fpoiled Morven is fo nigh. His people too are many; for they met us in the midft of night, when we thought they had been the hoft of Conar.—Offian, be thy fteps, with Gormallon, along the fhore. Dumolach and Leth! to Conar's halls; and if Minla be there, fpread before her your dark-broad fhields, and defend her. Morlo, be thou on the heath, that our foes may not fpread the fail to the wind, before the fun fhall light us to battle. And where art thou, Carril of the fong?

song? Be nigh the chief of Duthona with thy harp. Its sound is a beam of light that rises in the midst of storms. The tempest, when it shines, retires; and the darkness flies to the desart."

CARRIL came with his harp. Its sound was soft, as the gliding of ghosts on the bank of Lora; when they hide themselves in the white mist of noon, and their sound is on the gale of the stream. —Move in silence, stream of night, that we may listen to the song of the bard.

" OVER Lara of streams there bends an oak. Below it, one lone thistle lifts, between two mossy stones, its head. It sheds, in the passing stream, its drops of dew. Two ghosts are seen there at noon, when the sun is on the plain, and silence reigns in Morven. One is thy ghost, aged Ural? Thy hair wanders, a whiter mist, over two clouds that form thy darkened eyes.—And who is that in the cloud of snow before thee? Who but that fair huntress of the roe, thy daughter?

" THE youths of Lara were at the chase: they were spreading the feast in the booth of the desart. Colgar saw them; and came to Lara in secret, like the torrent that rushes, sudden, from the hill, when no shower is seen by the sunny vale.——' Daughter of Ural, thou must go with Colgar. The thongs must confine thy father. He might strike the shield. The youths might hear its sound in the desart.'

" COLGAR, I love thee not. Leave me here with my father. None is with him. His eyes are dark, and his gray hairs are lonely.

" COLGAR would not hear. The daughter of Ural must go with him; but her steps on the heath are mournful. She moves, sad,

like

like the mift of fhowers, when the fun is dim in his cloud, and the valley of ftreams is filent. A roe bounds on the heath; he fteals below them towards a fmall ftream. His brown fides, at times' appear thro' the green rank ferns.—' Colgar, give me that bow; I have learnt to pierce the deer.'—He gave the bow. She drew the ftring. Colgar fell.—She returned to Lara, and the foul of her father was glad. The evening of his life was like the departure of the fun on the mountain of fpring; like the leaf of autumn, when it drops in the filent vale. The days of Morála on the hills were many; in death fhe refted, in peace, with her father.——Over Lara of ftreams there bends an oak. Below it are two beds. One, Ural, is thine; and thine, daughter of the bow, is the other befide it *."

I went with Gormallon to the fhore. Below its rocks we found a youth. His arm, iffuing from the light mail, refted on a broken harp, and the ftaff of a fpear is befide him. The moon, rifing like a half fhield, looked through the beard of the rock on his bended head. In the midft of his grief it waved from fide to fide, like a pine in the figh of winds.

Who is this, faid Gormallon, that dwells lonely in the midft of night? Art thou of the hoft of Dorla; or from the halls of Conar?

I am, (replied the youth, trembling as the leaf in the blaft, as the grafs in the ftream of winds,) I am of the bards who lived in Conar's halls. Dorla heard my fong, and fpared me. Hereafter I

may

---

* The bards always adapted the fub- of Conar, was what gave rife to this, the ject of their fongs to the fituation of their happy end of which would give the old hearers. The refemblance between the man fome gleam of comfort. cafe of Ural's daughter and the daughter

* Gormay remember that he carried the arms from Selma, and spread the battle on the fields of Duthona.

"REMEMBER him thou mayest *; but what canst thou say in his praise? He stole the arms from Selma; and came upon Conar, when his friends were absent. His arm is feeble in danger, but strong when none is to oppose. He is a cloud that rises only in a calm; a dark mist, that never lifts his head from the fen, till the winds of the vale have retired.---But the storm from Morven shall overtake this cloud; Fingal shall scatter his beauty."

"I REMEMBER the king," said the youth, "since he was in the halls of Duthona. The voice of Ossian I remember, and the stately warriors of Morven. But Morven is far from Duthona."---The sigh stopt his words, and the bursting of his grief was heard, like the breaking of ice on Lego, or the mountain winds in the cave of Ardven.

"FEEBLE † is thy soul," said Gormallon; "thou art not of the halls of Conar, nor of the race of his bards. They sung of the deeds of battle. Their souls swelled with the joy of danger, as swell the white sails of Fingal under the blast of Morven. Thou art of the friends of Dorla.—Go, then, thou feeble arm, and tell him that Morven pursues him. Never more shall he see the deerless hills of his heathy desart."

GORMALLON, reproach not the youth, said I. The soul of the brave, at times, may fail; but it returns again, like the sun when the storm is over. He smiles from the height of his course, and the clouds are scattered. The green-headed pine waves no longer

* Gormallon speaks.
† The most of this paragraph, and part of that before and after it, are selected from the traditionary tale of the poem. The dialogue is there carried on to a greater length, but appears too frivolous to be translated.

longer its fpiry top; the blue face of the fea is calm; and the glittering vales, in the midft of fun-beams, rejoice.

I TOOK the youth by the hand. I brought him to Carril of fongs, till the ftrife of battle fhould be over; for the light now fhone on the arms of Dorla. His people, fpeechlefs and pale, behold the ftrength of Morven and the fword of Conar. They ftand in their place like the benighted hunter on Cromla, when the terror of ghofts furrounds him. The cold fweat bedims his eye: his trembling knees forbid his flight; and down he finks in the midft of his journey.

DORLA beheld the white eyes of his people, and the big tear hangs forward in his own. The fpear of Morven glittered in his hand as he fpoke.

" WHY ftand we in pale filence here, like thefe gray trees around us? The warriors of Morven are few; and our numbers may prevail. They may have their fame, but have not we alfo fought with heroes? Or, fhould any think of flight, where is the way to our fhips, but through the midft of the foe?—Let us then rufh on in our wrath, that our arms may be ftrong, and the joy of our friends be great when we return to the ftreams of Caruth."

* * * * * * * * * *

CONAR ftruck the fhield of Duthona. His fcattered people heard it. They lift their heads from their fecret place, like the ftreams of the heath of Cona, which in the day of drought hide themfelves under the ftones of the brook; but when the warm fhowers defcend, they come forth from their retreat; and, roaring, rufh from every hill.

WE met: we fought; and Dorla fell by the fpear of Conar. The king

king faw the foe brought low. He came in his mildnefs, and fpoke to the people of fallen Dorla.

"FINGAL delights not in the fall of his foes, altho' they make him unfheathe the fword. Return to your land; and come not again to Morven, nor to the fea-beat fhore of Duthona. Short is the wintery day of the people that lift the fword againft Fingal. A pillar of fmoke that comes acrofs the tempeft is the life of thofe who fight with the warriors of Morven. Return; and carry the fallen Dorla to his land, that the white hand of his fpoufe may rear his tomb, and her tearful eye behold his ghoft, in the vapour of mift, on Caruth.—Why didft thou rife fo early from thy reft; fpoufe of the fallen Dorla? What doft thou there, leaning on thy gray rock, with thy locks wandering in the drops of dew. Why travels thy eye on the diftant wave; thefe are not the fails of thy love? Thou feeft but the foam that breaks round the fporting whale on the bubbling deep.—Murmuring Caruth hears the fighs of the fair, and its banks learn the name of Dorla. Her two children lean to their mother's knee. They fee the round tear hang on her cheek. They lift their little hand to feize the bright pearl. 'Why,' they fay, 'does our mother weep; and where flept, laft night, our father?' ——So perhaps, Offian, is thy Everallin now anxious for thee. She leads thy little Ofcar to Morven's brow, that fhe may view the diftant fea. He toffes his bulrufh fpear before him, and looks ftern over the little fhield of woven reeds. Think of them, my fon, and fpare the warrior, who, like the unhappy Dorla, leaves behind him a weeping fpoufe.—Alas, Dorla, why art thou fo early fallen!"

Evirallin! Ofcar! ye beams of joy which are now no more! How can Offian touch the harp or fing of war, when your lovely
forms

forms shoot, like falling stars, across his soul? O that I were a companion of your blue course, light-travellers of the mountains on high! When shall our ghosts meet in clouds, and glide in the evening gale, when its dusky wave scarce bends the top of pines on Cona? When shall we lift our unshorn heads in other lands, like stars of night in the heathy desart? O that it were soon! that my bed were made in the down of clouds! What the bed of heath is to the weary hunter of Lona, that is the tomb to the heavy bard. I will sleep. Gray stone, wilt thou and the song preserve then my name? No; the season of thy age, O stone, will come, and thou wilt sink down with me to the place where the weary repose on their lowly bed of earth. The stranger will lean on his spear, and ask for thy place; but the sons of little men will not know it. Light of the song, canst thou shew the stranger the place; canst thou tell where sleeps the gray stone of the bard? No; like me, thou art old; the mist of years hath closed upon thy light. Our memory shall pass away like the tale of Duthona, which already is dim on the soul of the bard.

THE people of Dorla ride in silence over the deep. No song rolls before them on the wave. The bards lean their heads upon their harps. Along the wet strings wander, through tears, their gray hairs. The mariner loses, in the mist of thought, his course. The rower, sighing, stops in the midst of his stroke.—Ah! children of grief, remember your steps are on the deep. The storm and the night are behind you.

WE come to the halls of Conar; but the chief is mournful. The sigh lifts the mail upon his breast. It rises like a wave when it folds the storm in its bosom. The light of his eye travels not in its wonted brightnefs through his hall; it is dim as the winter-fun, when the thunder-fhower rides, in its own dark cloud, before it.---None fays to the chief, " Why art thou fad?" For, abfent is that ftar of night; the bright, foft-looking eye of Minla.

FINGAL beheld the darknefs of the chief, and covered his own grief under the plume of his helmet. " Carril," he foftly faid, " where is thy foul of fong? Come, and with thee bring thy harp."

CARRIL comes, bending gray on his ftaff. The voice of the harp is in his hand. Behind him walks the young bard from the fhore of night: but his light mail falls to the ground. A white hand rifes to cover the fpreading blufh. Whofe hand is that fo white? whofe face, through wandering locks, blufhes fo mild?— " Minla," cried Conar, " is it thou!"---Her arms in filence fold themfelves about his neck.---The foul of the aged returned, as the fun when the ftorm is over. He gave the fair to Gormallon; and we fpread the fails, with fongs, for Morven *.

---

* This is among the few ancient Galic poems which have a happy conclufion, and on that account deferves to be preferved. The ancient bards, no doubt, employed their mufe in celebrating joyful as well as mournful events. But, as melancholy tender fcenes are moft apt to make a lafting impreffion on the memory, the latter are often remembered when the former are loft and forgotten.

D E R M I D*:

A POEM.

The ARGUMENT.

This poem opens with an addrefs to the valley of Cona, in which its prefent filence is contrafted with its former bufy fcenes. Of thefe the ftory of Dermid's killing a wild boar of an enormous fize, is fingled out. After Dermid had killed this boar, he is defired by Connan, who bore him a grudge which the poem accounts for, to meafure his length, with his bare foles, againft the direction of the briftles on his back. Dermid, it feems, thought it might be a reflection upon his valour to decline the requeft. He complied; but the confequence proved fatal.
Graina, Dermid's wife, having been alarmed by the ftory of an old man whom fhe had met, after parting with Dermid, ran to his affiftance with a fpear, and arrived juft as that which he had was broken in his encounter with the boar: but fhe herfelf being wounded by a random fhot in the courfe of the chafe, fits down near enough to be witnefs of the death of her beloved Dermid. Both are interred in the fame place, and their elegy fung by the bards.

HOW peaceful, this night, art thou, O vale of Cona! No voice of thy hounds, no found of thy harps is heard. The fons of the chafe are gone to their reft, and the bed has been made for the bards. The murmur of thy ftream, O Cona, is fcarce perceived: the breeze fhakes not the dew off thy bended grafs.

The

* Dermid, the fon of Duino, is frequently mentioned in other poems of Offian, and much celebrated in the tales of later times. Thefe, mixing their marvellous with the original poem, have rendered it in a great meafure abfurd and extravagant. But they are for the moft part of fo heterogeneous a nature as to be eafily feparated.

† Cia

The gray thistle hangs over thy bank its sleepy head; its hairs are heavy with the drops of night.—The roe sleeps, fearless, in the booth of the hunter; his voice hath ceased to disturb her. She sees his tomb, amids green ferns, before her. Light-leaps over its mound her little kid. He rubs with his horn the mofs from its gray stone; and on the soft heap, when tired of play, he lays himself down to rest.

VALE of Cona †, how art thou changed! And thou, hill of Golbun, how quiet is now thy heath! Thou coverest thy head with thy dark veil of mist; and slumberest in the noon of day. No voice of the hunter, no cry of the hound, travels along thy darkbrown side to awake thee.—I move forth when all is calm; I lean my gray head on my spear, and listen if I may hear the echo of thy rocks. But thou art silent, O Golbun, in thy bed of clouds: no voice of thine is heard; save when thou repliest to the sportive cry of the deer, when evening has half-hid the sun in the wave of the west. Then, thou dost reply; but thy words are few: thou soon composest thyself again to thy slumber.

THOU wert not thus quiet, O Cona, when the king pursued thy deer, and made thy stream shake between its woody locks; nor was thy silence such, O Golbun, when the son of Duino pursued thy boar, foaming like Lora in his winding course.

LISTEN

† Cia tiamhaidh thu nochd a *Ghlean-caathan!* Gun ghuth gaothair thu, 's gun cheol, &c. The *Gleann-caathan*, or *Cona*, of Offian has been supposed by some to be Glenco in Argyleshire; and by others, Strathconan in Murray. Both seem to be at too great a distance from the scene of this poem, if we may rely on tradition, which places it in *Sli'gaoil* near Kintyre. What appears most probable is, that Fingal often shifted his habitation for the convenience of hunting, and might give several other places the same name with that of his principal residence.
——parvam Trojam, fimulataque magnis, Pergama.

LISTEN, son of Alpin, to the tale; thou wilt pour its light on the dark stream of future years.

THE morning was calm on Cona. Mountains saw in Ocean their gilded heads. The son of the deer beheld his young branches in the stream, when the sound of Fingal's horn is heard. Starting, he asks his mother what it means. She, trembling, bids him fly to the desart.—

"THIS day," said the king, "we pursue the boar, the deadly boar of Golbun."

* * * * * * * * * * †

WE sent the sons of the chase to the hill. Their cries, as they climb, are deep and loud. Golbun with all its woods resounds.

THE sound rose on Dermid's ear, as he lay in the cave of his rest. As a mountain-stream in the midst of rain, so leapt his soul with joy at the voice of the chase. " My red spear, where art thou? and where art thou, my dark bow?"

NOT so glad was Graina in her cave, to which she had retired with her love from Connan's hate. The dark soul of Connan had loved Graina; but Graina gave her heart to Dermid. " Heed not," she said, " the cry of the hounds; the chace of heroes is not awake on the hill."

" FAIR is thy form, my love; and like the bloom of trees in spring

† Some repeat here a small fragment called *Nòs Seilge*, or " The manner of hunting." As this poem is wholly a hunting adventure, it is probable these verses ought to have a place in it, if their incorrectness did not forbid it. The most accurate of them are the following, which denote their armour to have been nearly the same as in going down to battle.

Gun ar n eide' 's gun ar n airm
Cha rachamaid a sheilg nan cnoc;
Bhiodh luireach oirn 's ceann-bheairt chorr,
'S da shleagh mhor ann dorn gach fir,
Bhiodh sgia uain' air a gheibhe' buaidh,
'S cloidhe cruaidh gu sgolta cheann,
Bogha cruadhach agus iughair
'S caogad guineach ann am bolg.

spring is thy beauty; yet this day I must leave thee, with thy child, in the cave. I must mix with heroes on Golbun."

AND wilt thou leave me, said Graina, loveliest of men; wilt thou leave me, thou light of my soul in darkness? Where is my joy but in the face of Dermid? where is my safety but in thy shield of brass? Wilt thou leave me, thou fairer than the sun when he smiles, after the shower, on th eleaf of the birch; thou milder than his evening beams, when they play on the down of the mountain? Thy son and I will be sad, if thou art absent, Dermid.

"GRAINA, dost thou not remember the moans of the crane, as we wandered early on the hill of our love *? With pity, thou didst ask the aged son of the rock, Why so sad was the voice of the crane? 'Too long,' he replied, 'he hath stood in the fen; and the ice hath bound his lazy foot.—Let the idle remember the crane, lest one day they mourn like him.'—Graina, I will not rest longer here. Fingal might say, with a sigh, 'One of my heroes is become feeble.'—No; king of Morven, the soul of Dermid is not a stream that will fail; the joyful murmur of its course shall always attend thy steps. Rest thou in thy cave, my love; with night I will return with the spoil of roes.

HE went, swift as the path of an arrow, when it whistles thro' the yielding air on its two gray wings. Graina climbs, pensive and slow, the hill, to view the chase of roes from her rock. The light of her countenance is mild, but dim; like the moon in the night of calm, when it moves in silence through the clouds, and seems

the

---

* 'S moch a ghoireas a chorr
  Air an lon ata 'n *Slia'gail.*
Slia'gaoil, " the hill of love," is still the proper name of a mountain near Kintyre, said to have been the residence of these lovers, and to have received from them its name.

† The

the darkened fhield of a ghoft, hung on high in his own airy hall*! She meets a fon of age in the woods. Bending, he weeps over a gray ftone. " Here," he faid, " fleeps the fpoufe of my love; here, I reared over her the green turf.—Many were our days on the heath. We have feen one race, like the leaf of autumn, pafs: we have feen another lift in its place its green head, and grow old. We have turned away our foot from trees, left we might crufh them in youth; and we have feen them again decay with years. We have feen ftreams changing their courfe; and nettles growing where feafted kings. All this while our joy remained; our days were glad. The winter with all its fnow was warm, and the night with all its clouds was bright. The face of Minalla was a light that never knew a wane; an undecaying beam around my fteps. But now fhe fhines in other lands; when, my love, fhall I be with thee?

" THERE too, fair maid, thou beholdeft another tomb. Under it is the cold bed of the fon of Colla. It was made by the trembling hand of his father. By the boar of the woods my fon was flain. He fell near the cave of his dwelling. His fpoufe was preparing the feaft for his return; ' I go,' I faid, ' to look for his coming.' I went; I heard his cry; I ran with the fhort fteps of age to affift him. Hanging by my robe, his fon attends. We find his father dead. The boar had broke his fpear in twain; and the fword in his cave was left. His child takes him by the hand, and bids him rife. ' Why,' he faid, ' fhouldft thou fleep without?'—Alas! he
hears

---

* The original word *(Ealachainn tai-bhfe)* fignifies properly " the armoury of a ghoft." The whole comparifon, which is exceedingly beautiful, as well as fanciful, is fubjoined.

Bha a braghad gu feimh a 'soillfe'
Mar ghealach ri oidhche fhaimhe;
Si gluafad ro na neula balbha,
Mar fgia air *ealachainn* taibhfe.

hears thee not; for the tusk of the boar hath torn him, and his sleep is heavy.—This morning sounds Fingal's horn to pursue the fatal boar. But its voice reaches not the ear of Tuthal; the morning that shall rouse my son is distant. O Tuthal, why hadst not thou thy father's spear?"

"Mournful," said Graina, "is the tale of Colla. My tears in a stream could flow on the tombs of thy spouse and son. My tears could flow; but I must fly with speed. My Dermid pursues the fatal boar; who knoweth, my love, but thou mayst need a spear? Colla, keep thou this child till I return. I fly to my love with a stronger spear."

Dermid had come to the vale of Cona, like a fair light that grows in darkness. We rejoiced in his presence, as the mariners when the star, that long concealed itself in its cloud, looks again on their dark course, and spreads its beam around. The voice of songs is on the deep; and seals lift up, through trembling waves, their heads to listen to the music.

We climb Golbun of green hills, where the branchy horns of deer are seen in mist, and where lie thick the mossy beds of roes. From echoing rocks we start the boar, the red deadly boar of Golbun. We pursue him with all our dogs; but he leaves them weltering in blood behind.

Who, said the king, shall kill the boar of Golbun; the boar that is red with the blood of heroes; that hath slain so many of our hounds? His shall be a spear, the gift of a king; a shield with all its studs; and the herbs of the secret stream, to heal the hero's wounds.

Mine,

MINE, replied Dermid, shall be the gift of the king; or I fall by the bristly foe, and lose the fame of the song.

HE spoke, and flew over the heath in the gleam of steel. His course was like the red cloud that bears the thunder on its wing when the fields of Fingal are silent and dark. Quaking heroes lift from Morven their eye, and behold in sky the fight of ghosts. It is Trenmor hurling his wrath against Lochlin's sons, when they come to pursue his airy deer.

ALREADY the roar of Dermid is on Benala. From Benala he flies to Benlora. Now the hill of Ledroma shakes under his feet; and now the hill of Elda.

THE boar flies before him, but not so fast. His path is marked with wreaths of foam. His noise is like the white tumbling of waves on the isle of storms; like the falling of rocks amidst the groves of the desart.—See! they ascend Drimruath: the spear of Dermid almost reaches the foe. It falls heavy on its sides; it marks them with red streams. It sounds like the fall of trees, with all their aged branches, on a rock. The vales along their winding banks resound.—But see! with fury red-glaring in his eye, he turns, as the stream of flames on a hill when the dark winds have changed.—As it were a bulrush or slender reed of Lego, he grinds the hard, tough spear of Dermid *.

" O THAT thou wert near me, Graina! that my love would come from her cave, and bring me the spear of battle!"

* The original of these two lines is a most remarkable *echo to the sense*. The one line is full of that harsh, grinding sound which it describes, and the other as smooth as the bulrush or reed of Lego of which it speaks. The contrast between them has also a fine effect.

Chagnadh e a shleaghan reidh ruadh'
Mar chuile na Leige, no mar luachair.

"Bring it I do, my Dermid. From my cave I saw thy diſtreſs. Thither again I return. There look for me, my love, when the ſtrife on the hill is over."

And what though he find thee too, hapleſs maid! Alas! the days of thy years are run.—An arrow in its wandering flight had met the fair in the courſe of the chaſe. In her breaſt of ſnow it is lodged; but ſhe conceals it with her robe from Dermid.—Dear haſt thou paid, O Dermid, for that weapon in thy hand; who ſhall tell thee what it coſt thee?

With all his terrible might, the chief lifts his ſpear. Like a meteor of death, red-iſſuing from Lano's cloud, a flood of light, it quick-deſcends. The head is lodged in the rough breaſt of the boar: the ſhaft flies, over trees, through air. His ſword is in the hero's hand; the old companion of his deeds in the hour of danger. Its cold point pierces the heart of the foe:—The boar, with all his blood and foam, is ſtretched on earth †.

We rejoiced to ſee Dermid ſafe; we rejoiced all, but Connan. Meaſure, ſaid that little ſoul, the boar which thou haſt ſlain. Meaſure him with thy foot bare; a larger hath not been ſeen.

The foot of Dermid ſlides ſoftly along the grain; no harm hath the hero ſuffered.

Measure, ſaid Connan, the boar againſt the grain; and thine, chief of ſpears, ſhall be the boon thou wilt aſk.

The ſoul of Dermid was a ſtranger to fear; he obeyed again the voice of Connan.—But the briſtly back of Golbun's boar, ſharp as

† It is from this event that the clan of the Campbells, who derive their pedigree from this Dermid, have aſſumed the boar's head for the creſt of their arms. In the compoſitions of the later bards they are often called *Sliochd Dhiarmid an Tuirc*, or, "The race of Dermid who flew the boar."

as his arrows and strong as his spear, pierces with a thousand wounds his feet. His blood dyes the ground; it flows in wandering rills through the grass. The herbs of the mountain are applied; but their virtue fails.—Dermid falls, like a tall pine, on the heath ‡.

Ah! how quick the colour forsakes his cheek. It was red as the fruit that bends the mountain tree *; but now it grows pale as the withered grass. A dark cloud spreads over his countenance, as thick mists that veil the face of the wintery sun, when the evening comes before its time.

" The shades of night gather on my eyes. I feel the decay of my strength. The tide that flowed in my heart hath ebbed away. Behind it I remain a cold, unmoving rock.—Thou shalt know it, Graina, and be sad; ah! the pain of death is to part with my love.—But the shades of the night are gathering over my soul. Let Dermid sleep; his eyes are heavy."

Who shall tell it to Graina?—But Graina is nigh. She leans be-

‡ The death of Dermid, in the manner it is here told, will appear somewhat odd. It is probable he had received some other wound in a more mortal part; and that some of the poem, where his death may have been better accounted for, is lost. The current tradition with regard to this passage is, that Dermid was vulnerable in no part but in the sole of his foot, and that the great art of Connan was to get him wounded there. Whether this account of the matter, though common, be very old or very satisfactory, is a point in which the translator is not concerned.

* In poems chiefly depending on tradition, there must be in different editions a considerable variation. Their comparisons frequently differ; but they are always beautiful, and have the same scope. Thus, for instance, instead of the above simile, many have here another of the same nature, taken from the strawberry:

Ged' bu deirge do ghruaidh nan t subh
Bhiodh air uilin enuic 's an sheur;
Dh' fhas i nois dui'-neulach uaine,
Mar neul fuar air neart na grein.'

—Such as may, here, miss the dialogue concerning *Cuach Fhinn*, or the medicinal cup of Fingal, will remember that it is of so different a complexion from the rest of the poem, that no apology needs be made for rejecting it as the interpolation of some later bard.

beneath the shade of a tree. She hears the moans of her love: they awake her slumbering soul. Hark! she pours her faint song on the calm breath of the breeze. See! her blood and her tears wander on her white breasts, like dark streams on the mountains of snow.

"My love is fallen! O place me in his bed of earth; at the foot of that rock, which lifts, through aged trees, its ivy head. The sheeted stream, with murmuring grief, shall throw its waters over our tomb; but O! let it not wet the dark-brown hair of my love.—The stream still murmurs by; some day its course may wash away the mound. The hunter, as whistling he goes careless by, will perceive the bow of Dermid, and say, ' This is Dermid's grave.' His spouse perhaps may be with him. Near the bow, she will observe this arrow in my breast; and say, as she wipes her eye, ' Here was Graina laid beside her love.'—Musing, they move silently along; their thoughts are of the narrow house. They look on each other, through glistening eyes. ' The fondest lovers,' they say, ' must part at last."

—" But stop, hunters of the mountain, and give the mighty his praise. No mean hunter of a little vale was he, whom you have passed, so careless, by. His fame was great among the heroes of Morven; his arm was strong in their battles. And why should I speak of his beauty; shall his comeliness remain with him in the tomb!—His breast was as the down of the mountain, or the snow on the tree of the vale, when it waves its head in the sun.—Red was the cheek, and blue the eye, of my love. Like the grass of the rock, slow-bending in the breeze, were his brows; and sweeter than the music of harps or the songs of groves, was thy voice to virgins,

virgins, O Dermid!—But the music of thy voice is ceased, and my spirits can no more be cheered. The burden of my grief is heavy: The songs of Morven's bards cannot remove it. It will not listen to all the larks that soar in the lowly vale, when the dewy plains rejoice in the morning sun of summer.—But what hath Graina to do with the sun of the morning; or what hath Dermid to do with summer? When shall the sun rise in the tomb? When shall it be summer in the grave, or morning in the narrow house? Never shall that morning shine, that shall dispel our slumber, O Dermid*!"

WE

---

* Cha de.lruich a mhaidin gu *La bhrath*
A ch'fhogras do phramh, a Shuinn!

The word *la bhrath*, in its literal and primary sense, signifies " the day of burning," which was the Druidical term for the dissolution of the world *by fire*, as *gu dilinn* was their name for the alternate revolution which they supposed it should undergo *by water*. In a metaphorical sense both words came to denote *never*, or " till the end of the world," which for many ages back has been their only acceptation. Hence, a translator is naturally led to render these and the like words by their present meaning, without adverting to their etymology or ancient signification. This is one reason why more religious ideas do not appear in the works of Ossian, which, if examined, in the original, will be found to contain many allusions to the Druidical tenets. The word under our present consideration, tho' it is now universally understood to signify *never*, was used, long after the introduction of Christianity, to denote the dissolution of the world by fire, as among the Druids from whom it was borrowed. In that famous prophecy of St Columba, to which his monastery owed so much of its repute, it has this meaning, *Seachd la' ro an bhrath*, &c. " Seven days before the dissolution of the world, a flood shall cover the other kingdoms, but Iona shall swim above it." Ossian, who uses the word frequently in his poems, probably affixed to it this idea, much oftener than that of *never* as we do at present. In the original the word is always more emphatical than can easily be expressed in a translation. An instance or two will make this obvious to such as understand both languages. One occurs in the battle of Lora, where Bosmina says to Erragon,

" 'S nim faicear a d' thalla *gu brath*
Airm agh'or mo dheagh Ri'."

" *Never* shall they behold in thy halls the victorious arms of the king."

In the first book of Temora, Fingal mourning over the fallen Oscar, says

" Gu *la brath* chon eirich Oscar!"

" *Never more* shall Oscar rise," is scarce so emphatical.

WE laid the lovely pair in their bed of earth. The spear of his strength, with his bow, is beside Dermid; and with Graina is laid the arrow that was cold in her breast. Fingal bended on his spear over their grave. A dark stream descended on his cheek. His bards saw his grief. Each assumed his harp, and gave the name of the dead to the song.—Heroes, mournful, stood around. Tears flowed from the eye of hounds, as they rested on dark-brown shields at their feet.

"PEACEFUL, O Dermid, be thy rest; calm, son of Duino, be thy repose, in thy dark and lowly dwelling!—The din of arms is over; the chase of the boar is ceased; the toil of the day is ended; and thou, heedless of the return of the morning, art retired to thy slumbering rest.—The clang of the shield, the noise of the chace shall not awake thee. No; Dermid, thy sleep is heavy!

"BUT who can give thy fame to the song, thou mighty chief! Thy strength was like the strength of streams in their foam: thy speed like the eagle of Atha, darting on the dun trembling fawn of the desart. In battle, thy path was like the rapid fall of a mountain stream*, when it pours its white torrent over the rock, and sends abroad its gray mists upon the wing of winds. The roar of its stream is loud through Mora's rocks. Mountain-trees, with all their moss and earth, are swept along, between its arms.—But when it reaches the calm sea of the vale, its strength is lost, and the noise of its course is silent. It moves not the withered leaf if the

---

* The following lines, altho' defective, being only one of the editions from which this passage is made up, are so beautiful as to deserve their room:

Bha do neart mar thuilteach uifge,
Dol a[g]us a chlaoidh do namh;

Ann eabhaig mar iolair nan speur,
No sleud eisg a' ruith air fail'.
A thriath threun a b' aille leadan
Na aon shleafgach tha 'san Fheinn,
Gu ma samhach a raibh t or-chul,
Ful' chudrom na foide re!

* In

the eddying wind doth not aid it.—On eddying winds let thy spirit be borne, son of Duino, to thy fathers; but light let the turf lie over thy beauteous form, and calm in the grave be thy slumber!

" A VESSEL rides the surgy deep*. It bounds from ridge to ridge. Its white sails are spread to the wind. It braves the fury of the storm.—' It is the son of Duino's!'—Yes, stranger, it was the son of Duino's; but now the son of Duino is no more. There, he hovers, a faint form, above; and the boar is half-viewless beside him.

" THE horn sounds on the mountain. The deer start from the moss of rocks; from the banks of their secret streams. The unerring dart of the hunter pursues them on the heath. One of them is arrested in the midst of his course. Panting he tastes the cooling fount. His knees shake, like the reedy grass in the stream of winds. He falls as he climbs the bank. His companions attempt with their head to raise him, but in vain; they are forced to forsake him and fly.—They fly, but the hunter pursues them. ' His speed is like the speed of Dermid!'—Alas! stranger, it is not he. The son of Duino sleeps in his lowly dwelling, and the hunters horn cannot awake him.

" THE foes come on with their gathered host. A mighty stream meets them in their course. Its torrent sweeps them back, and overturns their grove of spears.—' It is,' saith the son of the stranger, ' one of the warriors of Morven; it is the strength of Dermid!' —The strength of Dermid, replies his companion, hath failed.

At

* In this elegy of the bards over Dermid, the various accomplishments of that hero are remarked; and appear the more striking from their being put, for the most part, in the mouth of strangers.

At the foot of that ivy rock I saw, as I passed, his tomb. The green fern had half-hid the gray stone at his head. I pulled its rank growth away: Why shouldst thou, vile weed, I said, obscure the fame of the hero?

" A YOUTH comes, whistling, across the plain. His arms glitter to the sun as it sets. His beauty is like that sinking beam, that spreads around him its rays; and his strength is like his beauty.—The virgins are on the green hill above; their robes are like the bow of the shower; their hair like the tresses of the sun, when they float on the western wave in the season of calm. They admire the stately beauty of the warrior, as lightly he moves along.—' The youth,' they say with a sigh, ' is like Dermid.'---The memory of the son of Duino rises on their soul, as a beam that breaks on blasted Mora, through the torn edge of a dusky cloud. In sorrow they bend their heads. The tears shine through their spreading locks, like stars through the wandering hair of the moon. They fall like the tears of Ossian when they flow for Oscar of Lego.

" THE children of youth are tossing their little spears. They see the hero on the plain. ' There comes Dermid!' Their reedy spears are thrown away, and they forsake the shield of willow. Their steps of joy are quick to meet the maker of their bows. But they see it is not he, and in mid-way they stop. Slow, they return to their play; but the noise of their harmless battle is not heard, for their little souls are sad for Dermid.

" THE voice of music and the sound of the harp are heard in Fingal's hall. The benighted traveller is charmed as he approaches. A moment he leans his breast upon his staff, and, sidelong,

long, bends his liftening ear.---' It is Dermid!' he fays; and haftens to overtake the fong.---A beam of light, clear but terrible, comes acrofs his foul. He makes two unequal ftrides; in the midft of the third he ftops. ' Dermid is no more!'---He wipes with the fkirt of his robe his eye; and, fighing, flowly-walks along.---It is the voice of the bards thou doft hear, O ftranger; they are pouring the fame of Dermid on future times; clothing his name with the nightly fong. The chief himfelf, in Selma thou fhalt find no more. He fleeps with Graina in the cold and narrow houfe. On Golbun's heath thou wilt find it, at the fide of the ftream of roes.---A rock, dark-bending with its ivy mantle above, fhelters from ftorms the place. A mountain-ftream leaps over it, white, and murmuring travels on. A yew fpreads its dark-green branches nigh: the deer refts undifturbed at noon beneath its fhade. The mariner leaning to his maft, as he paffes on the darkly-rolling wave, points out the place, and tells his mates the woful tale. The tear bedims their eye. They cannot mark the fpot: they heave the deep note of grief, and fail to the land of ftrangers. There, they tell the tale to liftening crowds around the flame of night. The virgins weep, and the children of youth are mournful. All day they remember Dermid and Graina; and in the dreams of their reft they are not forgotten."

AND often you defcend to the dreams of Offian too, children of beauty. Often you poffefs his thoughts, when he fits, alone, at your tomb; and liftens if he may hear the fong of ghofts. At times, I hear your faint voice in the figh of the breeze, when I reft beneath your green tree, and hang my harp on its low-bending

C c branch,

branch.---But Offian is a tree that is withered*. Its branches are blafted and bare; no green leaf covers its boughs. From its trunk no young fhoot is feen to fpring. The breeze whiftles in its gray mofs: the blaft fhakes its head of age.---The ftorm will foon overturn it, and ftrew all its dry branches with thee, O Dermid! and with all the reft of the mighty dead, in the green winding vale of Cona.

How peaceful art thou, O vale of Cona! Thy warriors and thy hunters are all gone to reft. Let the bed be alfo made for the bard; for the fhades of night thicken around him, and his eyes are heavy.

---

* No image could better reprefent the forlorn condition of the poet than this which he has chofen. The words, too, in which he defcribes it, are full of that foft and mournful found which is expreffed in the Galic by the diphthong *ao*, and the tripthong *aoi*; founds which, fo far as I know, are peculiar to the Galic language, and highly congenial to the more foft and mournful feelings.

Tha mife mar gheig na h aonar,
Si gu mofgaio maol gun duileach,
Gun mhaothan ri taobh, no ogan,
Ach ofna bhroin a' caoi' na mullach.
'S fogus an doinion, a fgaoileas
A crionach aofd' air feadh a ghlinne.
Mu leabaidh Dhiarmaid s nan laoch lughar
Aig Caothan nan luban uaine.

FINAN

The ARGUMENT.

The children of Morven, having given Ossian a description of two ghosts which they supposed they had seen in the clouds, are informed of their names;—the manner of their death;—the grief of their father Murno;—the ceremony of his resigning his arms in old age, when his race became extinct;—with the song of the bards on that occasion;—and the episode of Turloch and his children, which had been introduced to comfort Murno and the lover of Lorma.

WHAT is it you behold in the face of night, children of the sportful days? Is it the snow that rests white on Morven's top; or the gray smoke of the halls of air? Do you behold the daughter of night pale in clouds; or is her face seen in the calm stream in Cona's vale? Hear you the mournful spirit of the mountain; or do you listen to the voice of ghosts in the gale of winds?

" Morven, O bard, is white. The moon is in the stream: the spirit of the mountain speaks; and the voice of ghosts is in the gliding gale. But in none of these is our thought. Our eye is in

---

* Often called *Dan chlanna Muirne*, " the song of the children of Murno." As the number of names in this poem may render it somewhat intricate, especially near the beginning, it may be proper to remember, that Murno was the father of Finan and Lorma; that Ardan was *his* father, Torman his bard, and Dunalva the place of his residence.

two clouds; their mist in moon-beams is white: their steps are from Alva of roes; on the wind of night flows their streamy hair. Two dark-gray dogs attend the one. His bow in his dim hand is strung.---From the white side of the other runs a coloured stream; her long robes seem stained with blood. Her face is sad, but lovely; and the tear is still on her cheek.---Keep off, O blast, a little while, till we behold the forms.---But thou rollest them together in thy dark cloud; and scatterest, like gray smoke, their limbs.---Over the rushy vale, over the hill of hinds, they wander on the wings of their rustling mist.---Bard of other times, dost thou know the forms; canst thou tell the children of Morven their names?"

THE years that are past return: the soul of Ossian is full of the song. Its voice comes like the sound of waves; it travels on the evening gale after their force on the distant shore is broke, and the stormy winds are laid.---Children of Murno, I remember your song; its sound has been long from Selma.

CHILDREN of youth, your eyes, like mine, may one day fail. You may ask the children of the years to come, what they see in the face of clouds. " We see," they will say, " two youthful ghosts; and beside them, in his dun cloud, bends their aged father. They will then ask of you the tale of the ghosts of night. Listen to it from Ossian, lest you should say, " We know not."

WHO comes trembling on the staff of age? His eyes dwell in dark, red-edged clouds: within them is the shower of tears. His gray hair is on the gale of winds, and the sigh of his voice is mournful.---Murno, why so sad? Are not the eyes of Finan flames in battle; lifts he not the shield with heroes? Are not the steps of Lorma also on the hill of roes; bends she not the bow with virgins?

gins? Why then, Murno, is thy face of age so sad; is there no sound in the harp of Torman?

"Not without cause is Murno sad; not without cause is his countenance mournful. Finan! thou liftest the shield no more in battle. Lorma! thy steps are not on the hill of roes with virgins. My children! in the tomb you are both asleep; and the soul of your father is sad. It is sad in the midst of harps, like a cloud of mist in the valley of the sun, when the hills expect the shower.

"Torman, take that moony shield: that sword which is a stream of light; that spear, tall as an oak of the vale; and that burnished helmet which shines so bright. They are the arms which Ardan wore: the arms that were worn by the father of Murno. From a chief of other lands he won them, when first Trenmor and he, in one day, lifted against foes the spear. 'Let the first of your fields,' said their fathers, 'be marked with fame. From his first name grows the renown of the hero *.'—

"They rushed to the war of Clutha, like two young eagles of heaven, when they first pursue in their rushing course one young fawn on Dora. Many were the heroes that rolled in dust before Trenmor; and Ardan won these arms from Duthorran. But thy race, O Ardan, shall no longer wield them. Only two trees, tall on the banks of Alva, were they! The mossy branches of one lone tree is bare; and the green youth of another, like the shorn flower in the sun, is withered. The son is laid on the tomb, and the father bends over the narrow house. The first blast shall lay him low; and the race no more is found.—Torman, hang in Ardan's hall the

arms

* This line is a common proverb in Galic, used to recommend an early attention to character. *'Se cliu duine a cheud iomra.'*

arms of battle. The feeble in the days to come may fee them, and admire the race that has failed. They will try to lift the arms, but cannot : ' Mighty,' they will fay, ' was the race of Alva.'

" Two bards bore to Dunalva the arms, and bade them remain to future times. One fhield was hung, a darkened moon, on high. Another, with the head of a fpear, was laid deep in its bed of earth. Nor retired the arms of heroes to their reft, without their own peaceful fong.

" Descend, faid the bards, O Ardan, thou rider of Morven's mift in the ftorm ; defcend from thy cloud, and behold thy arms! Let the dim fmile of joy, between thy tears, arife ; for thy race brought no ftain upon the fame of thy fteel, though now they fhall no longer lift it. Thy fpear, in their hand, always fhone where the battle was darkeft ; but the blood of the feeble was never a dark fpot on its blue edge. Thy fhield was a rock, which the lightning of battle often tore : in no feeble hand was it ever lifted. Murno was a ftorm that tears the oak; and a flame that confumes the grove was Finan.

" Descend, Ardan, from thy mift; guard the fhield of thy race in Dunalva †. Let no little foul touch it ; let no hand of the cruel come nigh it. Such were not the lifters of this fhield ; the bounders on this fpear ; the heroes of the race of Ardan.—Keep off, fon of the little foul ; what haft thou to do with the arms of heroes?

Retire

† It was probably from poetical fights or antique notions of this nature, that the belief fprang, which ftill prevails in the Highlands, of every family-feat or houfe of diftinction being inhabited by one or two *genii*, who are fuppofed to fuperintend the affairs of it, and to punifh fervants for their mifdemeanours. What gave ftill more weight to this opinion, were the corrections frequently beftowed on fervants in the dark ; the effects of which fometimes fhewed, that they did not proceed from fuch " unreal mockeries."

Retire to thy fecret ftream, where was never heard the noife of the fpear, the echo of the battle. There, live with deer; grow gray with the beard of the thiftle. Sleep in the fame mofly bed with them in death; thy fame unfung, thy tomb unknown, thy race unnoticed. One by one, they fall around thy tomb, unheeded; as ferns die in the deep cleft of the rock, where they grow in fecret. They grow, they decay, they die: no traveller fhall ever fay, Behold them!—From the defart comes a wintery blaft; on its cloudy wing fits Death, pale, grim, unlovely. Thoufands are his quivers; and many are his bows, always ftrung. Through the fecret vale as he paffes, he beholds in his bed the lazy man. He draws the ftring. The arrow filent flies. It ftrikes; it kills; but its mark is not feen in the breaft, like the death that is dealt by the fteel of the valiant, in the fields of fame. Heroes raife over the feeble no tomb: bards fing no fong: virgins touch no harp. The little foul now hangs in the bowels of cold, dark mift; like the fifh locked in the ice of Lano's ftream; and now, it is toffed on fenny clouds, the fport of rufhing winds. His courfe is often with the vapour of death, that hovers on marfhy lakes, and fends forth its blafts, like fecret arrows, to bring death to nations.—Never are his fteps on green woody hills, on funny plains with heroes [*].

" But fuch were not thy race, Ardan; the lifters of thy brown fhield in war.—Guard it on high, thou dweller of ftorms; frighten the feeble when they approach it in thy hall.—But the hall fhall

---

[*] This paffage alludes to the notion which the Celtic tribes had of a future ftate; the punifhment of which, in their opinion, confifted chiefly in thick darknefs and extreme cold. The utter contempt in which they held fuch as led an idle and inactive life, appears from their configning them to this region of horrors after death

one day be no more. Like a gray tree which the blaſt hath overturned in the flood, it ſhall fall; and its top ſhall be wet in the midſt of Alva. The crowded ſtream ſhall change its courſe. Through the ruin is its wandering way. The thorn had been lifting there its flowery head: the brier was green betwixt the moſſy ſtones. The heath and the fern ſhook there, in the breeze of night, their heads, and formed a bed for the dun roes.—The ſtream came. It waſhed away the mound of earth. In the face of the broken bank juts out the dark-cruſted ſhield. The hunter obſerves it, as he bounds over the ſtream in his courſe. ‘What dark orb,’ he ſays, ‘is that; dim as the circle within the new horns of the moon?’—He looſes away, with his ſpear, the earth: his ſoul travels, glad, through the ages that have been. Lifting his head he looks around, and ſees the palace of other years in its own green tomb. ‘The dwelling of heroes,’ he ſays, ‘has been here; the hall of kings in the years that are no more.’—Yes, ſtranger, thou ſtandeſt in the hall of kings: touch not their dark-brown ſhield, if thou art not of the race of heroes. For that was the ſhield of Ardan.—Ardan! thou dweller of the tempeſt's wing, deſcend from thy miſt: deſcend on thy ruſtling blaſt, and receive thy arms.—Guard them in the hall of Dunalva †.”

Such was the ſong of the bards, when they hung on high the arms of Murno. But the ſoul of the chief ſtill is ſad. The ſigh of his breaſt is heard, at times, like the ſound of a lonely wave, or the ſigh of the gale in the graſs of the tomb.—We bring him to Selma

† Beſides this ſolemn reſignation of arms made by the laſt perſon of any race to the ghoſts of his fathers or tutelar ſpirits of his family, it appears from ſeveral paſſages in the ancient Galic poetry, that every hero at a certain age was allowed to “hang up his arms in the hall,” and decline the toils of battle.

Selma in the silence of grief. Two tombs, as we go, lift their green heads before us on the heath. On earth between them Murno lies. None said unto the chief, Arise. All lie on the grass around, and listen to the mournful tale of his children.

" Morning rose on the isle of Croma, and the horn of my son was heard. Three gray dogs leap around him, and lift their ears with joy at the sound of his quiver. They bound in their skiff through the strait, and pursue the dark-brown deer of Croma. With evening we see the skiff return. The waves arise on the deep. The skiff is seen at times on their white tops: but, sudden-sinking, it disappears. In vain we look for it again; it is concealed in the sea, or in night.

" My soul trembled for my son. But old as I was, what could I do?—I bade the years that were past return; but they heard me not. The path of their course was distant, and the voice of Murno was feeble. My daughter too shrieked, and shook my aged soul, as shakes the blast the dry leaf of the desart.—' O my brother! my brother of love! in the storm art thou lost?—Art thou lost, my brother!'

" To the shore she rushed. Distracted, wild were her looks. The sea had shrunk from a dark rock. To its tops are the steps of the maid. Her looks and her cries are towards the deep. ' My brother, my only brother of love, dost thou not hear the cry of thy sister?'

" Dim appears a dark spot on the foamy top of a wave.—' Is that the wandering ooze; or is it thou, my brother?' He heard her voice; and with one faint note he replied. Fear and joy divide, by turns, her soul.—Two of the gray dogs had reached the shore:

the third, in the foam of waves, was loft. The two heard the voice of Finan fail. They bound again into the furgy deep. They return, with Finan, on the third wave; but one breathes on the beach his laft.

"Lorma bore her brother to the rock. 'Here,' he faintly faid, 'Let me for a little reft, for my ftrength is failed.'

"She wrapt her robe about his breaft, and made his pillow of the weeds that were drieft.

"He fleeps. The maid in filence bends over his face. She bids the waves be ftill, and the noify path of their whales be diftant. And diftant be your ruftling courfe, ye winds of the mountain; and foft be your gliding, ye ftreams from the vale of hinds. Quiet, through the bofom of woods, be the noife of your torrents: and filent, through ruftling leaves, be your fteps, ye dun-bounding roes. Let my brother of love fleep, for his eyes are heavy. Soft, Finan, on the dark rock be thy fleep; calm, my brother of love, be thy flumbers.

"But, ah me! his face is pale; it is wan, as the moon in her gray watery cloud. The countenance of my brother is unlovely. Perhaps he ftill dreams of the troubled deep; for his brow is dark. It is clouded as the face of children in their unfettled reft, when their dreams are of the coming of wolves †.— Mothers of the tender foul, do you then awake your children from their flumbers? Do you bid their fleep depart, and fcatter, as mift

on

---

† Mar ghnuis leinibh, 's e'n fuain gun fhois,
A bruadar air maddai' nan coilkean.

Some have quarrelled with Offian for not making mention of the wolf, fo frequent at that time in his country. But thefe gentlemen ought to remember, that a great part of Offian's works is loft, in which mention may have been frequently made of this and many other things which we now defiderate.

on the gale, the fear of their dreams? Yes, you do awake them: but I will not awake my brother of love till the morning come, for his ſtrength is failed; his ſleep is heavy.—But the flies of night diſturb thee, Finan. How ſhall I keep them away? Thy face, with my own, I'll ſoftly cover; but I will not diſpel thy ſlumber. —Ah! my brother, thou art cold.—Thou haſt no breath—thou art dead! my brother! O my brother!

" Her cries aſcend on the rock. As I approach they ſtrike my ear. The ſea grows, and ſhe perceives it not. She loads with her cries the wind. The beating on her white breaſt is loud; the howling of the gray dog is wild. My ſoul melts on the ſhore with grief. Often it bade me ruſh to the relief of my child. But the voice within me ſaid, ' Murno, thou art old and feeble; the days of thy cleaving the deep are over.'

" The gathering wave lifts my children from the rock: it toſſes them on its breaſt to the ſhore. There dark rocks meet them with their force, and the ſide of Lorma is torn. Her blood tinges the wave: her ſoul is on the ſame blaſt with Finan.

" Sad, O my children, have you left your father: the name of parent I will hear no more. I ſtand on the heath, a blaſted oak; no more ſhall my branches flouriſh. Autumn is dark on the plain. The trees are bare on the brown heath. Their leaves with the ſpring ſhall return; but no green leaf of mine ſhall lift, in the ſummer-ſhower, its head. The race of Alva is failed, like the blue ſmoke of its halls when the beam of the oak is decayed.— Great is the cauſe of Murno's grief; for one night hath ſeen him without a child. Thy tomb, O Finan, is here; and here thy grave, O Lorma!"

The soul of the aged was sad. The burst of his grief still arose. We remain silent in our place, like ghosts when the winds are calm; like a stream of ice when it sleeps between two banks of snow, and shews to the pale moon its glittering beard.

But who comes, wandering, wild on the mountains, like the roe that hath lost his companion among the woody streams. His yellow hair wanders on the dark breath of winds. Unequal are his steps. Frequent the burst of his grief: the sigh of his breast is mournful. It is like the voice of a blast in a cave, when the waves, before it, toss themselves in a storm.—It is Uran, the bender of the bow; the love of thy youth, O Lorma! He had come to Dunalva in the night of storms: but the halls were silent and dark. Two blue stars had used to shine there. But now he saw them not; set were the eyes of Lorma.

" Lorma, where dost thou rest? My love, where are thy slumbers? Has the night seized thee in the lonely chase; has darkness hid thy steps in the desart? Daughter of the bow, where dost thou rest? O that I knew thy place; then should I haste to find thee! Dost thou sleep at the foot of a gray rock; is thy bed of moss on the bank of streams? Ah me! if it is, the breasts of my love will be wet: they will be wet, and the night is cold.—It is cold: but peaceful be thy rest, dweller of the soul of Uran; let thy dreams of me be lovely.—

—" Disturb her not, ye spirits of the night on your blasts; ruffle not her hair, ye winds; blow not away that smile on the lips of my love.—My love is calm in the midst of storms; for the thoughts of her soul in the season of rest is Uran.—Glide smoothly by her, ye streams of the valley of roes: skip quietly, ye dun sons

of

of the mountain, through your bush. Eagles of the hill of hinds, let the rustling of your wings, in the desart, be distant. See that ye disturb not the dreams of my love; that ye awake not the slumbers of Lorma.—Sleep on, O Lorma; let not the murmur of the stream, nor the rustling of the storm in trees, affright thee. Sleep on; with morning, I will come and awake thee. I will awake thee, but my voice will be soft. It will rise in thy ear like the hum of the mountain bee, when he travels on the wing of the breeze at a distance. The voice is lost at times: the brown son of the wing is drinking the dew of roses, where they grow on their secret banks.—Sleep on, O Lorma; and if the slumber of night descends on the soul of Uran, rise thou in the dream of his rest, and let the look of thy eye be lovely!"

He rested on the mossy bank. Sleep half-descended on his soul. The murmur of Alva in his ear was less. The moon still looked through the windows of his rest; for only by halves were his eye-lids closed.—Before him twice arose the sighing Lorma. She was like a white cloud before the moon, when her light is dim, and her countenance sad. Uran knew the ghost of his love. He wandered, mournful, wild on the heath. The voice of Murno reached his ear: he perceived the two green mounds of earth. He dropped the bow. He fell. But why should I tell the grief of Uran?—Silence was long on the hill. The bard of Morven, at length, took the harp. We leaned forward our breasts upon its sound, and listened, as he sung with the voice of grief.

" Turloch lived at Lubar of streams. In deeds of fame his hair grew white. Strangers knew the way to his hall: in the broad path there grew no mountain-grass. No door had he to his gate,

gate. 'Why,' he said, 'should the wanderer see it shut?' Turloch was tall as the oak of his vale. On either side, a fair branch, lifted its green-growing head. Two green trees smiling in the shower, and looking through rainbows on the sun, were the two children of Turloch. Heroes admired the beauty of Migul; and virgins, with secret pleasure, beheld the steps of Althos. 'He is stately,' said the strangers, 'as the son of Turloch; and she is fair,' they said, 'as the maid at Lubar's rolling waters.'

"Long did the years of Turloch glide smoothly by. Their steps were silent as the stream of his vale. Joy smiled in the face of the chief, like the sun-beams on the brow of his hill, when no cloud travels in the road of heaven[*].

—" But ever-varying, as the face of the sky, are the days of man upon his mountains. The storm and the calm roll there in their course; the light and the shade, by turns, are there.

" Migul one day went forth to the chase. In her white hand was the bended bow; and two gray dogs bounded, through the morning dew, in her steps. Swift as mists that fly through heaven when the winds are high, they pursued on hills the deer. Migul drew the string. Her winged darts were unerring as death. On the brown heath the sons of the mountain, gasping, fell.

" The huntress sits on her rock. The thunder is heard on the hill. The clouds gather like night. The streams descending from the

---

[*] Where different images are used in the different editions of the original, they are often joined in the translation, when the sense and poetry admit of it. In other places, however, some of the original is omitted, as here, where a part of the passage seems to be borrowed from an encomium of Ossian upon his beloved Oscar in another poem.
Bha do chroidhe mar ghathaibh greine
S do spiorad mar chanach sleibhe
Be do nos bhi aoibheil failteach
Mar na rosaibh air gach faire.

the mountains are white, and Lubar rolls in foam. How shalt thou cross it to thy home, thou trembling maid?

" Althos saw his sister approach. He knew where two bending rocks almost met above the stream. An aged oak spreads its arm across: often had the trembling hunters of other times crept along its moss in the day of storm. Here stood Althos, above the deep. ' Give me, my sister, thy hand.'—Both shake upon the bending branch: it quakes; it cracks; it breaks; it falls!

" TURLOCH was kindling the fire in his hall. My daughter from the hill, he said, is wet.

" A CRY strikes his ear, as he fans the flame. Sudden-starting, he issues forth. He sees his two children shoot along the stream; they are clung to one aged branch.

" HE cried; but his cries were vain. Night, descending on the vale was dark. The rocks till morning heard his moan; and deer, awaking at the sound, leapt wildly from Lubar's banks.—Day found him wandering there; and night again overtook him in the same place. But his children at the dark stream he found not; and sad he returned to his empty house. Long did it echo to his sighs; and long did he wander at the dark stream, when the children of the vale had retired to rest.

" THE shield of battle, at length, was struck. Turloch heard, as he wept on Lubar's banks, the sound. He sailed with his people to Lalin; but they landed, as they passed, in Ithulmo.—There, two lovely beams met them on the rock; benders of the bow, when bounds before them the dun roe. The eye of Turloch darkened with grief as he beheld their beauty, in the midst of the children of the isle.—' Two such lovely beams were you once in my sight, my

chil-

children! Such was thy statelines, O Althos! and such thy beauty, O Migul!'

"They heard the voice of their father, on the isle to which they were borne, by the oak, on the wing of streams. They heard it, and sprang to his arms with joy.—The face of the aged again was bright; and gladness returned to Lubar."

"Thy children, O Murno," added the voice of age [*], "are, like those of Turloch, only lost for a season. They are only gone before thee on their own stream to the land of the happy. There thou shalt soon behold them lovely, lifting their young heads in the midst of heroes. Already, their course is in the fair mists that wander on the face of the moon; when she looks pale through clouds, and shines in the stream of Alva. Let, therefore, the grief of Uran be forgot, for there he will find his Lorma. Let the tear of the red eye of Murno be wiped off, for there he will find his children."

The grief of the mourners calmed by degrees. Uran was like a tree, which, though the storm is laid, still shakes its waving head: and the bosom of Murno still heaved above the sigh; like waves which toss themselves, at times, after the winds have retired.

CATH-

---

[*] The original of this passage is beautiful, and deserves here a place. The translation may appear somewhat fuller in one or two of the expressions, owing, here and in some other places, either to the abruptness of the original, or to the admission of an epithet or idea somewhat differently expressed in other editions. Such as will take the trouble of comparing any of the other Galic passages with the English, will please extend this remark to them also: it will account for a few inconsiderable variations which they may meet with.

Is amhuil sin air an sruthai' sein
Dh'imich, re seal, clanna Muirne;
Ach gheibhear iad ann Innse nan Treun,
Mar iurain aoibhin 's an doire uaine.
Cheana chitear an caoin-chruth
A' snamh doilleir seach Gealach na h oidhche,
'Tra shcallas i nuas sui' smal
Air Alva nan ceime ciuine.
Caisg, Urain, mata do bhron,
Sna biodh do dheoirs', a Mhuirne, co snitheach;
Sgach aon, air a steud-shruth sein,
Ann deigh's a chairdean ag im'eachd.

The ARGUMENT.

Annir, the daughter of Moran, having been loved by two intimate friends, Gaul and Garno, resolved to get rid of the last by a stratagem.—In the disguise of a stranger, she brought him a challenge from Duaran, who, she alleged, was his rival, and whose prowess she thought he would not choose to encounter. But being disappointed in this, and resolved to get rid of Garno at any rate, she delivers the same message to Gaul, confident that his superior valour would give him the victory.—The two friends met in the night, and fell by mutual wounds. The issue of her plot affected Annir so much, that she could not long survive it.—The poem opens with some reflections suggested by the scene where they were all buried, and concludes with their funeral song.

I HEAR the murmur of the brook; I hear its fall over the rock. Lead me, son of youth, to that oak which spreads its branches over the stream. At its foot, three gray stones lift through withered grass their heads, and meet the falling leaves. There sleep the friends of Ossian. The murmuring stream they hear not: the rustling leaves they heed not. In the chamber of their rest, the steps of our approach will not disturb them.

---

* In the district of Lorn in Argyleshire, there is a lake which is now called Loch-avich, but anciently Loch-luina, or Lochluana. Near it was probably the scene of this poem. Many places in its neighbourhood are still denominated from Ossian's heroes.

The *son of youth*, to whom this piece is addressed, is supposed to be the same with the *son of Alpin*, so often mentioned in some other ancient poems. Tradition relates many stories of him; among others, that he took down in writing all the poems of Ossian as they had been repeated to him by that old and venerable bard.

MANY, fon of youth, were the valiant on the hills of Morven, in the days of our joy. But the blaft came and fpoiled our wood of its leaves. It overturned our lofty pines on their green mountains. It whiftled with its wintery noife through our palaces, and marked its dark path with death. The feafon of our joy is a fun-beam that is paft; the voice of gladnefs in our hall is a fong that hath ceafed; and the ftrength of our heroes is a ftream that is no more. The owl dwells in our fallen walls, and the deer graze on the tombs of the valiant. The ftranger comes from afar to beg the aid of the king. He fees his halls, and wonders they are defolate. The cow-herd, carelefs, whiftling, meets him on the dufky heath, and tells him the heroes are no more. " Whither," he fays, " are the friends of the feeble gone; and where is Fingal, the fhield of the unhappy?"—They are gone, O ftranger, to their fathers. The blaft hath laid the mighty, like the tall pines of Dora, low; and the fons of the feeble grow in their place. Thou feeft on every hill the tombs of thofe who helped the unhappy. Thou feeft their ftones half-funk, amidft the rank ruftling grafs of the vale. The heroes have made their bed in duft; and filence, like mift, is fpread on Morven.

BUT the voice of Cona's harp, ye mighty dead, fhall be heard in your praife. The ftranger, as he paffes, may attend perhaps to the fong. Liftening on his fpear, at times, he ftands. The bard fees him not, but his fighs are often heard. Humming the tale he goes away, and, mournful, tells it at the ftreams of his land. Young bards fhall hear it as they bend, filent, over their liftening harps. On future times they will pour the fong.

WE are come to the place; but where are the ftones that mark

the

the abode of my friends? Lift your heads, ye gray mossy stones; lift your heads, and tell whose memory you preserve. Why shrink you in your moss, forgetful of the mighty below you?—But I will not forget you, companions of my youth. Your fame shall remain in my song, when these mouldering stones shall fail.—Often did we shine together in steel, and pour death on fields, like roaring streams. Mighty were ye then, my friends, though now so low! Mighty were your deeds when you strove together here. Listen to the tale, son of youth, and let thy soul be kindled to deeds of fame.

GAUL * and Garno were the terrors of the plain: their fame was in the land of strangers. The strength of their arms was unmatched, and their souls were steel. They came to the aid of Moran. They went to the hall of the chief, where it lifts its gray head, in the midst of trees, in the green isle of Inniſluina.—The daughter of Moran seized the harp, and her voice of music praised the strangers. Their souls melted at the song, like a wreath of snow before the eye of the sun. The heroes burned with equal love to Annir; but it was on Gaul alone that she rolled her blue eye. Her soul beheld him in the dreams of her rest; and the streams of Iniſluina heard, in secret, his name.—The daughter of Moran turned away her eye from the brow of Garno; for she often saw the fire of his wrath arise, like a dark flame when clouds of smoke surround it.

THREE days the heroes feasted. On the fourth they pursued the chase on the heath of Luina. The maid followed at a distance, like

E e 2   a

---

* Who this Gaul was is not certain. He is probably the same with him who speaks in that dialogue often foisted into the poem of Gaul the son of Morni, and beginning with

A righbhin is binne ceol,
Cluais gu malda 's na gabh bron, &c.

a youth from the land of ſtrangers. She followed to tell the words of fear, that Garno might leave the land *.

THE ſun looked down on the fields, from beyond the midſt of his courſe, and the panting roes ſtill lay in the ſhade of the rock. Garno ſat on Caba's rugged top. His quiver is by his ſide, and Luchos lies at his feet. Beſide him is the bow with the head of horn, unſtrung. He looks round for the deer; he ſees a youth. " Whence are thy ſteps," ſaid the dark-brow'd chief; " and where is the place to which thou art bound?"—

" I AM," replied the youth, " from the mighty Duaran, chief of the halls of Comara. He loves the daughter of Moran; but he heard that Garno wooed his love. He heard it, and ſent me to bid thee yield the fair; or feel, this night, the ſtrength of his arm in battle."

" TELL that proud ſon of the ſea, that Garno will never yield. My arm is ſtrong as the oak of Malla, and my ſteel knows the road through the breaſt of heroes. To Gaul alone, of all the youths on the hill, I yield the right-hand in battle, ſince he ſlew the boar that broke my ſpear on Elda.—Bid Duaran fly to his land: bid him retire from the daughter of Moran."

" BUT thou haſt not ſeen Duaran," ſaid the youth. " His ſtature is like an oak; his ſtrength as the thunder that rolls thro' heaven; and his ſword as the lightning that blaſts the affrighted groves. Fly to thy land, leſt it leave thy withered branches low, and ſtrew on the heath thy blue arms."

" FLY thou, and tell Duaran I meet him.—Ferarma, bring me my ſhield

* For moſt of this and the two following paragraphs, we are more indebted to the tale than to the poem, which is defective.

shield and spear: bring me my sword, that stream of light.—What mean these two angry ghosts that fight in air!—The thin blood runs down their robes of mist; and their half-formed swords, like faint meteors, fall on sky-blue shields.—Now they embrace like friends. The sweeping blast passes through their airy limbs. They vanish. I do not love the sign; but I do not fear it. Ferarma, bring my arms."

THE maid retires. She is grieved that Garno will not fly. But she heard him say that to Gaul he yielded in battle. To the hill of his chase are therefore her steps.—The hero leans on his spear: a branchy deer lies by his side, and his dogs are panting around. His looks are towards the green dwelling of Luina. His thoughts are of his lovely Annir; and his voice is heard in her praise.

"FAIR is my love as the bow of heaven: her robe is like the beam of the morning. Mild is the blushing of thy face, O Annir, as that sun, when he looks through the red-tinged clouds of the west, and the green tops of the mountains smile. O that I saw thee on the hill of deer, in all thy beauty; that I saw thee like the young pine in the vale of Luina, when it softly waves its head in the gale, and its glittering leaves grow in the shower of the sun!—Then would my soul rejoice as the roe, when he bounds over the heath in his speed; for lovely art thou in the eye of Gaul, thou daughter of car-borne * Moran!"

"AND

---

* Ait mar c:lid an aonaich,
Na deann air raon nan rua 'bhoc,
Tha m' anam fein, tra chi mi do dhreach,
Inghean Mhorain nan each 's nan carbad.

Car-borne is always a title of distinction in the poems of Ossian. That the ancient Britons and Caledonians used cars and chariots of various kinds, is a fact so well attested by Tacitus, Mela, Cæsar, and other authors of credit, that none has room to ask, Where could they drive them? Their chariots of war were generally armed with scythes, and called *cubh'ain*,.

"AND art thou Gaul," faid the approaching youth? "Thy Annir may be lovely, fon of Ardan; but dire is the battle thou muft fight. Duaran loves the maid: on that hill he awaits thy coming. Yield, Gaul, thy love to Duaran."

"My love I will yield to none. But tell thou that chief to come to the feaft to-night. To-morrow he fhall carry away the gift of a friend, or feel the ftrength of a foe."

"THOU mayft fpread the feaft but thou muft eat it alone, for Duaran comes only to lift the fpear. Already I fee his diftant fteps. He ftalks like a ghoft on that dufky heath. The beam of his fteel fupplies the departing light; and the clouds brighten their dark-brown fides around him. Hark! he ftrikes his fhield. Its found is the death of heroes."

GAUL covered himfelf with his arms, like a ghoft that clothes his dark limbs with meteors of light, when the mountain-heads are fhaking in thunder. He moved to the hill from which he heard the fign of battle. As he went he hummed a carelefs fong. He thought of his Annir, and the deeds of his former days.

HERE, fon of youth, the warriors met. Each thought his foe was Duaran: for night was dark on the hills, and this oak con-cealed the fky. Dreadful was the wrath of the heroes; dreadful was

---

rebh'ain, (the *covinus* of the Latin writers), from *co-bhuain*, a word which fignifies " to hew down on all fides." Of this kind feems to have been the famous car of Cuthullin in the 1ft B. of Fingal, and the 4000 which Cæfar afcribes to Caffibelanus.—Befides this, the ancient Caledonians, as they inhabited a mountainous and uneven country, ufed for ftate a fort of litter borne between two horfes in a line, and fomewhat in the fhape of a bier. Hence, in Galic, the word *carbad* is ufed either to denote " a bier" or " a chariot."

was the echo of their fwords, as they mixed on high, like ftreams of lightning, when they iffue from dark clouds of many folds *. The hills reply to their fhields. Luina trembles, with all its woods. The heath fhakes its head; the roes are afraid in their dreams; they think the chafe is already up, and the thought of their fleep is of danger.—Still louder grows the noife in their ear; they think the approach of the hounds and the twang of the bow are nearer. From their midnight flumber they ftart; their face is towards the defart.

TERRIBLE and long was the ftrife of battle.—But the fhield of Gaul is cleft in twain: and the blade of Garno flies in broken pieces. Its found is like the whirlwind on Ardven, when it tears the heath from its roots, and ruftles through the leafy oak.

GAUL ftands like a whale, which the blue waves have left bare upon a rock. Garno, like the return of a ftormy wave, rufhes on to grafp the chief. Around each other they clafp their finewy arms; like two contending fpirits of heaven, when all the ftorms are awake. The rocking hills fhrink with fear from the thunder of the fons of the fky; and the groves are blafted with their lightning.—Thus from fide to fide the warriors bound. Rocks with their earth and mofs fly from their heels. Blood, mixt with fweat, defcends in ftreams to the ground. It wanders through the green grafs, and dyes the paffing rill.

ALL

---

* Another edition of the poem defcribes this combat fomewhat differently, but with almoft equal energy, in the following lines;

 Bhuail iad ann fin air a cheile,
 Gu eruaidh cuidreach is do-bheumach,

Chaidh an leirg air chrith fui'n eafaibh,
'S chaidh teine da'n armaibh glafa.
Bhuaileadh iad gu neart'ar dobhidh
Mar dha bhuinne ri eruaidh cho'rag.
Cho-fhreagair na creagan 'fna beanntai'
Do airm nan Curine calma.

ALL night they fought. With morning light the fon of Ardan falls on earth, and his wide wound is expofed to day. The helmet falls from his face. Garno knows his friend. Speechlefs and pale he ftands, like the blafted oak, which the lightning ftruck on Mora in other years. The broad wound in his own breaft is forgot. The red current flows unperceived. He falls befide his friend.

"BLESSED," he faid, " be the hand that gave the wound! My body, O Gaul, fhall reft with thine, and our fouls fhall ride on the fame fair-fkirted cloud. Our fathers fee us come: they open the broad gate of mift: they bend to hail their fons, and a thoufand other fpirits are in their courfe. We come, mighty ghofts; but afk not how your children fell. Why fhould you know that we fought, as if we had been foes? Enough that you know your fons were brave. But why have we fought together; why have I heard the name of Duaran?"

GAUL heard the voice of his friend. But the fhades of death are on his eyes: they fee but dimly half the light. " Why did I fight," he faintly faid, " with Garno; why did I wound my friend; why did I hear of Duaran? O that Annir were near to raife the gray-ftone of my tomb!—Bend down, my fathers, from your airy halls, to meet me!" His words were heard no more. Cold and pale in his blood he funk.

ANNIR came. Trembling were her fteps: wild were her looks: diftracted were her words. " Why fled not Garno? why fell my Gaul? Why was heard the name of Duaran?" The bow dropped from her hand: the fhield fell from her breaft. Garno faw her, but turned away his eye. In filence he fell afleep.—She

came

came to her lovely Gaul. She fell upon his clay-cold corfe. There the fair, unhappy mourner was found; but she would not be torn from her love.

ALL day, the fun, as he travelled through his watery cloud, beheld her grief. All night, the ghosts of rocks faintly anfwered to her figh. On the fecond day her eyes were clofed. Death came, like the calm cloud of fleep, when the hunter is tired upon his hill, and the filence of mift, without any wind, is around him.

Two days the father of Annir looked towards the heath: two fleeplefs nights he liftened to all the winds. " Give me," on this morning he faid, " my ftaff. My fteps will be towards the defart." —A gray dog howls before him: a fair ghoft hovers on the heath. The aged lifts his tearful eye; mournful he fpies the lovely form. —But, Moran, I will leave thee; I cannot ftay to behold thy grief †.

* * * * * * * * * *

HERE, fon of youth, we laid the three. Here we reared their gray ftones. Our forrow was great for their fall; and our bards gave the mournful fong.

" WHO, from the dufky hill with his armour of light; who ftalks fo ftately over the plain; who ftrides in terrors over the heath; who rufhes into danger and defies the brave? Who is it but Garno the bold; Garno of the awful brow: the chief of fpears; the terror of the field; the ftrength of a thoufand ftreams?

" BUT who meets him, with ftately fteps and yellow locks? Like

F f   the

† Some editions enlarge here upon Moran's extreme grief on learning the death of his daughter; but as the paffage, though very tender, appears either to be not genuine, or not correct, it is omitted.

the fun, when he looks through a thin watery cloud, he fmiles in the hour of danger. Who rolls before him the ftorm of battle, and thunders through its wide-fkirted fields?—Hark! his voice is the found of waves in a ftorm; his fteps like the fhattered rocks, when hills fhake their heads on the heath of the defart.—It is Gaul of the fair hair and mild look; the fon of Ardan of renowned deeds: the chief is mighty, but lovely.—O why was the name of Duaran ever heard, or the maid of Luina ever loved? Why fought two fuch friends in darknefs?—Like angry ghofts in a ftorm, ye fought; like two green oaks, laid low by the ftorm of angry ghofts, ye fell.—The traveller paffed by in the night; he faw them raife their lofty heads in the plain. 'Fair trees,' he faid, 'your growth is ftately, and your leaf, on the bank of your own blue ftream, is lovely!'—But he returns in the morning, and finds their green heads low; he fees their roots torn from the earth, and their branches in the foam of the ftream.—The tear ftarts into his eye. 'Each of us,' he fays, 'will one day fall before the ftorm.'

" Low are your heads beneath the ftorm of night, ye warriors who were lately fo brave! And pale is thy beauty, lovely Annir, in the place of thy filent repofe! Mark, O maids of Morven's ftreams, the day whereon the lovers fell. Let it be a day of fadnefs on Luina. Let no youth, on that day, purfue the dark-brown deer.

" O GARNO, warrior bold! Gaul, thou lovely hero! and Annir, fair and unhappy!—Whether you ride on the filent clouds, or turn the courfe of the tempeft; whether you reft in the peaceful halls of your fathers; vifit the cloud-robed hills of Morven, or haunt

the

the green groves of Luina:—O let your love, your grief, and your wounds, be forgot; and liften with joy to your fame in the fong.— While harps remain, they will repeat your name; and the laſt voice of bards ſhall praiſe you."

Such was the fong of the bards when we reared the tomb of the heroes. Often I fung it in our halls, when the dark day of their fall returned.

I hear the murmuring of the brook: I hear its fall over the rock: lead me back, fon of youth, but forget not the fame of the heroes.

C A T H U L A*:

A P O E M.

The ARGUMENT.

Cathula king of Iniftore, having invited Fingal to a feaft in his palace of Carricthura, receives intelligence, at the time, of an intended invafion on his coaft. Fingal removes his anxiety on that head, by reminding him of the fame of their fathers; which they would tranfmit, he faid, to their children. Upon this Cathula laments his misfortune, in having loft, as he fuppofed, his only fon, when a child. The bard relates in what manner; and Fingal comforts Cathula, by telling him his fon may, poffibly, be ftill alive.—
Being informed in the morning, that Manos, a chief of Lochlin, had actually landed, they go forth to give him battle. The command is devolved upon three of their young warriors; but as they were like to be worfted, Fingal, Connal, and Cathula defcend to their aid. The laft, with fome mifgivings, encounters with a youth, whom he afterwards difcovers to be his fon.—
Manos, being overcome, is reprimanded by Fingal, and difmiffed on a promife of his never giving any further trouble to Fingal or any of his friends.—The poem is addreffed to a *Dweller of the rock;* either a fequeftered Culdee, or Druid.

O UR life is like the fun-beam of winter, that flies, between the fhowers, over the heath of Lena. The hunter, lifting his head upon his hill, beholds the beam, and hails the day of the fun.

He

---

* From the refemblance between the names of Cathula and Cuthullin, and both having a fon called Conloch, many who repeat this poem, in place of Cathula, fubftitute the more familiar name of Cuthullin, and call the poem by the title of " Mar mharbh Cuthullin a Mhac :"—tho' it appears that Cuthullin died under the age of thirty, when his fon was very young; and the other circumftances of the poem can relate only to the king of Iniftore.—See Offian's poems of *Carricthura* and *Death of Cuthullin.* The edition here followed begins thus :

He hails it; but it is already gone. The dun-robed clouds have drawn their shade over its path, and who can trace its footsteps? The leafless woods lament its departure; their branches sigh to every breeze; and the drooping herbs of the mountain wither.

THE sun, O woods, shall again return; and your green leaves, in his warm beam, will flourish. The season of your youth will come back, and all your bare boughs will rejoice. From the height of his beauty, the dweller of heaven will look down: he will smile through the thin sparkling shower, on the herbs that are withered. They also will come forth from their winter-house, and lift their green glittering head on the bank of their secret stream.—They will come forth from their dark house, with joy: but the dwellers of the tomb remain still in their place; no warm beam of the sun shall revive them.—But your memory, companions of my fame, shall remain; your deeds shall descend, a beam of light to future times, and be the tale of the years that shall come.—Hear, dweller of the rock, the tale of Iniftore. Dim-gleaming, it comes on the soul of the bard. It comes like a faint moon-beam on the distant wave, when Lumon † fears the storm.

THE feast of Cathula was prepared, and Fingal raised the sail. The wind came down with its rushing noise from our mountains. Beneath its steps is the groan of oaks. On the deep is the roar of waves.

Mar bhuisge greine 's a ghcamhra'
'S e ruith na dheann air raon Lea'na;
'S amhuil fin la'ith nam Fiann
Mar ghrian eid'r-fhrafach a' treigfin.
 Dh'aom neoil chiar-dhu' nan fpeur,
'S bhuin i.d an deo auibhin on t fealgair:
Tha loma-gheuga na coill a' caoidh,
'S mao' lufrach an t ficibh a' feargu'
Ach pillidh fathafd a ghrian

Ri doirre fgiamhach nan geug ur,
'Sni gach crann 'sa cheituin gaire
'G amharc ann aird ri mac nan fpeur, &c.

· As feveral parts of this poem are supplied from the tale or *fgeulachd*, the narration is more prolix than it is in the general run of old Galic poems.

† Lumon; the name of a bay.

waves. Iniſtore ‡, dweller of the ſea of whales, lifts through the low-hung clouds its green head, and beholds with joy our coming. The people ſpy our ſails through miſt, and gladneſs is in Carric-thura.

But who are theſe with the king, deſcending to the ſhore to meet us? One tall tree is gray; the other two young oaks are green, but their ſteps are ſtately.---Hail, Connal, from blue Togorma *, is it thou! Hail, yellow ſon of Rinama †, king of plains! And hail, thou ſon of Ruro, from the iſle of boars!

" Let the feaſt," ſaid Cathula, " be ſpread, and the ſhell go round. Let the voice of harps and the ſongs of bards ariſe, that the joy of my friends may be great in my echoing halls. Cathula, O bards, is in the midſt of his friends. This is the day of his joy. Let no ſhade obſcure its beams; let no dark cloud, in its wandering courſe, paſs over Carric-thura!"

Such were the words of Cathula. But how ſhort, ſon of the troubled days §, is the dream of thy joy! It is like the ſhort calm that comes between the inconſtant blaſts, in the night of the ſtorm. The hunter lays down his head in his booth. His dreams of joy are beginning to ariſe: white-handed virgins are coming towards him with their harps: bards are beginning to give his fame to the ſong: ſhields ſound, and his heart bounds with joy for the battle:

‡ Iniſtore, properly *Innis-orc*, or *Orc-innis*, " the iſles of whales," or Orkneys. The word *orc* is uſed in this ſenſe by Milton:

———————an iſland ſalt and bare,
The haunt of ſeals and *orcs* and ſea-mews clang.

* *Tonn-gorma;* " the iſle of blue waves."

† *Ri' na ma,*' " king of the plains," or Maiatæ. The Highlanders ſtill call the low parts of Scotland *a mha'-thir*, the plain country.

§ In this apoſtrophe the poet does not mean Cathula only, but man in general, whoſe chequered life he deſcribes thro' the whole of this beautiful paragraph.

battle: fields of fame rife before him; and he beholds, at times, the gleam of a thoufand fpears.---But the blaft, in the midft of this gladnefs, comes. It fhakes above the booth its terrible wing, and the dreams of joy vanifh. The hunter lifts his head amidft the ftorm, and fays, " Dreams of my love, why are you gone! or why did you come to deceive me?"---The virgins were of clouds! the voice of bards was but the wind of the heath! the found of the battle was the thunder; and the light of fpears the flame of heaven!

HUNTER of the heath, thy dream was fhort, but pleafant: and fuch a dream was thy joy, O Cathula!

THE feaft of Iniftore had ceafed. The blaze of the oak was paft its ftrength. Still, the heroes hear the fong around it; while Cathula views the night.

" THE fleeping fea is calm †. The fparkling ftars bend over it in the weft. They admire, in its fmooth face, their own beauteous form. They are like the young virgins, when they lean on the brink of their fecret ftream, and behold, with a fmile, the fhade of their beauty. A ruftling comes as, bent, they lie. They ftart. They look, confufed, around. They fee it is but the roe in the withered leaf; but the blufh is on their face of love.---Some of the ftars are likewife feen to blufh; it is the fign of blood, I fear.---But I will behold the face of the moon. She begins to lift, through trees, her half-unveiled head. Dim forms are on her beams. I perceive their limbs of fmoke.---I know thee, my father, in thy darkened mift. But tell me why ftirreft thou the leaf with thy figh?"

THE anfwer came only by halves to his ear. The wandering breeze,

† Cathula fpeaks.

breeze, in its fold, had rolled the other half away. He returns to the hall, but his face is sad. Fingal knew he had seen his fathers; and his were always the words of hope. His speech was like the sound of the harp, when the white-handed daughter of Toscar holds it.

" In the dark years that have passed, a silent stream, to their own sea, our fathers trod together in the path of fame. Sarno, Colgar, and Comhal, were three lights that shone in every danger. The battle was rolled before them, as the dark, dusty cloud by the whirlwind's blast, when some angry ghost sweeps it along the narrow vale. In broken columns it flies: it sinks behind the shelter of the woods, and hides its head in the moss of the desart.— The spirit careless rides through air, and pursues some other sport. —Thus strode the warriors. No concern was theirs in the day of danger. Thus they broke the ranks of Lochlin, when its hosts opposed them. And are not we their sons, Cathula; and shall our face be dark when dangers come? Our fathers would turn away their course upon their blast; no voice of theirs would descend into our dreams; nor would their hall open to receive our feeble spirit, when our gray head would fall, like the withered leaf in the unknown vale. We should fly, the sport of winds, in the dim, fenny mist of Lego.—No; chiefs of Togorma and Iniftore, our fathers have left us their fame; and the mighty stream, increased with our renown, shall, like growing Lubar*, roll down to our children."

" And long," said Cathula, " may the sons of Fingal rejoice in their father's fame. May they brighten in its beams, in the dark

---

* *Lubar*, " a winding river;" often mentioned in the old Galic poems.

dark ages to come, and the bard fay in his fong, ' He is of the race of Fingal.'—But to no fon of mine fhall my renown defcend, a bright beam, to fhine around him. Conloch, fon of my love! that fad night, which tore thy mother and thyfelf at once from my arms, rifes with all its ftormy horrors in my view, and wounds afrefh my foul. It rifes before me like the fea of Iniftore in that night of ftorms. The rocks hear the noife of its waves, and they fhake, with all their woods. The fpirit of the mountain roars along the fall of ftreams; and the dweller of Iniftore fears his trembling ifle may fink.—But grief ftops the voice of Cathula. His foul is a ftream that melts, when tender thoughts are warm within.—Let me hear the fad tale, O bard, from thee. It awakes my grief; but I love it."

* * * * * * * * * *

I HEAR the din of arms in Icroma †. I hear, through its woods, the echo of fhields. I fee the blaze of fwords, gleaming to the moon. I fee the fpear of battle lifted. The roe ftarts from his midnight reft, and Turlèthan * fears the danger.— But why art thou afraid, roe of the mountain? Why trembleft thou, Sgaro, in thy halls? Sora's king is ftrong, but the wind of the north is awake. Upon its cloudy wing Cathula comes, like a red angry ghoft of night, when hunters tremble on Stùca. The ranks

† *I-croma*, " winding or crooked ifle." The poem, which in this place is not entire, brings Cathula very abruptly to I-croma, in order to affift Sgaro; but the tales or *urfgeals* mention feveral previous circumftances, which it might be tedious, and not effential, to mention.---With the confufion and terror that attend war, as defcribed in this paragraph, the calm joy of peace is happily contrafted in that which follows. The narration of this expedition feems to be put in the mouth of Cathula's bard.

* *Tur-leathan*, " broad tower;" the name of Sgaro's palace in Icroma.

† This,

ranks of war are broken before him, as the mail of the spider before the blast. The mighty are scattered in his presence.—Sora, with the clouds of night, hath fled over the sea. He hath disappeared, as the path of his ship on the deep.—Sgaro, hang up thy shield; bring down thy harp; let the daughters of Icroma rejoice.

I HEAR the voice of songs in Icroma. I hear the echo of harps in its halls. The sword of war is sheathed. The shield is hung on the peaceful wall, a dark orb, like the inner moon; and the spear of battle rests beside it. The roe is glad on his rock. The virgins of Turlethan look, with joy, over their window. The sun shines bright. No cloud is on its beams. But the maids observe it not; their eye is on Cathula, moving in the light of his steel. They bless that beam of brightness, from whose presence the darkness of their danger retired. " Awake, our voice," they say; " awake, our harps: let our song be Caric-thura's king †!"

But who comes forth to meet the chief? Her steps are on the dew of the morning. The tear of joy hangs forward in her eye, like the tear of night on the bended grass, when it glitters in early sun-beams. Her face of beauty is half-concealed by the wandering of her fair locks. But the morning-beams look through them on the mild-blushing of her cheeks, as looks the sun on the budding rose, when its colour grows in the drops of dew.—Who can this be but Rosgala, the fairest of the maids

† This, of the maids of Icroma, appears to have been a chorus-song; a species of composition very ancient, and still much used in the Highlands. The time of these pieces is adapted to the various exercises of rowing, reaping, fulling, &c. They greatly alleviate the toil, and inspire men with ardour to go through with it.

of Icroma?—Sgaro gives her to the chief who scattered the cloud of his foes.—" Cathula, were ten daughters mine, Chief of heroes, I would say, be thine the choice."

Three years, on their eagle-wing, flew over the hills of Turlèthan. The hawk darting on his prey moves not with a pace so silent or swift. Cathula looks back on their course, as the awakened hunter on the space he travelled over in his dream. He wonders how soon they are past. " It is time to return to Iniftore; to the streamy groves of Carric-thura."

The sails of Cathula are raised. Rosgala, by turns, is glad and sad. " Adieu, thou isle of my love; adieu, thou abode of my youth! My friends are on the shore: the roes look forward from their bushy rock.—But why should the tears of Rosgala flow? she goes with Carric-thura's chief?"—Conloch, the young pledge of their love, is in her arms. Two streaks of light on a cloud are his fair brows. His little helm above them is of the fur of fawns. Lulled by the rocking of the waves, he sleeps. In the dreams of his rest, he smiles. He hears the buzz of mountain-bees, and thinks he is near their store of sweet. But it is not the buzzing bee, thou dost hear, O Conloch! it is the rising wind, whistling through the rattling shrouds.—But still thy smile is pleasant. Thou lookest like the flower of Lena, when the many-coloured rainbow adorns it in the day of the inconstant sun. The hunter, as, hastening to the shelter of some dark-bending rock, he strides along, beholds it with a sigh; for he sees the stormy shower, riding towards it on the blast: The pillars that support it are hail. " Flower of Lena, thou art lovely; but the tread of the storm is near thee."

The breast of Rosgala heaves under the broken sigh, white as the

the foam of the wave, when the storm uplifts it, and darkness dwells around. The bright drop is in her eye; it falls on the face of Conloch. With the pressing of her lip, she wipes it away. He awakes and sees the storm. He wonders what it means; and, shrinking, clings to the bosom of Rosgala. She, over him, spreads her skirt, as spreads the eagle of Lora her dark wings, wide, over her young, when they shrink in their head from the hail, and hear the voice of storms.—" Fear not, child of my love," said Rosgala; " for thy father is nigh us."—Nor be thou thyself afraid, said Cathula; I know the sea of Iniftore. Often have I rode its deep, when louder was the roar of its waves.---Rosgala asks for Iniftore; but it is distant. The sea hides it behind its hills of foam.--- Mixed with the noise of waves, rise, at times, the sighs of the fair.

Now descends, on the deep, dark-skirted night. The thunder is in her course. The streamy lightning bursts, dark-red, from her womb. Spirits feel its flames. Their shrieks are heard in mid-air. They rush to quench their half-burnt robes in the deep. The billows roar, with all their whales.---The moon hears the noise within her house of clouds, and she is afraid to lift her head above the hill. The stars wrap their heads in their mantle of Lano's mist [*]. At times, they look, trembling, through the window of their clouds; but, quick, draw back their wandering hair. —They are like the hunter on the heath, who shoots out, at times, his head, but will not venture forth from his booth till the storm

is

---

[*] *The mist of Lano* seems to have been a proverb for any mist of the thickest and darkest kind.

is over.---Hunter of the roe of the mountain, thou art on the heath on fhore; O that Rofgala were there!

But what voice did you hear that night, ye rocks of Icroma; when on the deep was fhe, to whofe harp you often echoed? Did you liften to the roar of waves at your feet, or to the thunder that rolled in the blafted head of your pines? Louder than either of thefe, rofe in your ear the cries of Sulingorma †. She is wildly-fad, for her daughter is on the deep with her child. She ftands on the dark rock, carelefs of the beating ftorm. White billows breaking on the diftant deep, deceive her oft for fails.—Mother of Rofgala, retire from the ftorm of night; thy daughter does not hear thy cries.

Retiring, fhe foon turns back to view once more the main. A wandering bark, defcending into the creek, is half-perceived. Oh! art thou fafe, my child!"

"What voice is that on the rock?" fays the mariner; "my mates take down the fails."

The voice of joy mixed with fear again is up: "Rofgala! art thou fafe?"

"It is the cry," fays the mariner, "of the fair ghoft that we faw upon the deep: behold it there!—Come, O ghoft, on moon-beams to our dreams, when the night is calm, and the ftorm is over!"

Sulingorma hears his voice, and fad retires. The rocks reply to the name of Rofgala.

But Rofgala is on the fea of Iniftore. The ftraggling ray of a di-

---

† *Sulin-gorma* fignifies " blue eyes;" *Rofgala*, " fair countenance;" *Cathula*, " eye of battle;" *Conloch*, (or *Ciun-laoch*), " mild or beautiful hero."

diſtant oak travels there over the deep. Cathula beheld his love, like a fair virgin-ghoſt in its beam. In her arms he beheld his ſon. He looked like a ſtar in the boſom of the bended moon, when her face is almoſt hid in grief, and the darkneſs of her countenance growing. He beheld them; but he was ſad, and his half-ſtifled ſigh aroſe. The paſſing breeze bore it to the ear of Roſgala.

"Why that ſigh," ſhe ſaid, "my love? The night on the deep is dark, but the ſtorm will ſoon be over. The moon will come forth in her ſilent beauty; her ſteps on the mountain will be lovely. The ſtars will ſhew their blue-ſparkling eyes in the clouds, and the winds will retire from the ſea of Iniſtore. Nor is Iniſtore far diſtant: is not that the light of its halls?"

"LIGHT of the ſoul of Cathula, the ſtorm will ſoon be paſt; and the light of Iniſtore, amidſt blue, calm waves, ariſe. But what is night, or ſtorm, or diſtance of Iniſtore, to Cathula; while he beholds the face of beauty, with all thy calm of ſoul?—Let me behold the face of my love, O beam! and I will bleſs thee, tho' thou doſt come from Sora's hall; though thou haſt brought me ſo nigh his ſhelving rocks."

Too nigh them art thou brought indeed, O Cathula: on their edge thy ſkiff, in two, is divided. The chief climbs the oozy rock. Roſgala and his ſon are in his arms. But no ſhelter, ſave from cold ſea-weeds, is there. It is, at times, the habitation of ſeals.

"THE land, my love, is nigh. My ſtrength, I know, can reach it. On its ſhore I may find ſome boat that ſhall convey us from Sora's wrath *, before the light ſhall ariſe. Reſt thou here, Roſ-

gala.

* The ſituation of Cathula was the more alarming, as he had formerly incurſed the diſpleaſure of the king of Sora, by aſſiſting Sgaro againſt him.

gala. The storm is lower. The stars look over the edge of their broken clouds, and the moon lifts her pale head through the distant tree. They will soon shew thee the path of my return. Rest here, my love, Rosgala!—Ye lights of heaven, shine on my love; ye spirits on their beams, dwell with her on her rock. When you hear her say, 'Cathula, what delays thy return?' tell her you behold the steps of my coming.

"Come, thou mayest," said Rosgala; "but ah! I fear the billow's roar. Some blast may raise it high; or some angry ghost may, again, embroil it in his course. But thou shalt come, my love: and yet I fear.—The sea may grow; the shades may depart; or Sora awake ere thou dost come. But no; my love shall return soon. Spirits of my fathers! guard Cathula."

He went; he reached the shore: but no boat is nigh. He runs in search of it far. The thought of his soul is on the oozy rock with Rosgala.

What shall that helpless mourner do?—Her eye is towards the darkly shore; but no Cathula comes. The waves grow upon her rock. They gather about her feet. But, Conloch, thou art not wet; thou art lifted high in her arms.

"What detains thee, my love? Have the waves stopped thy course to the shore; or have the boats of Sora been distant far?—O that thou wert ashore, my child! 'Tis for thee that trembles thus the soul of Rosgala."

She ties him on Cathula's shield. A withered tree comes, wandering on the wave, to her rock. On its top she fixes Conloch.

Shall I awake thee, Conloch? No, thy cries would pierce my soul, like darts. Safe thou mayest reach the shore; and So-

ra's

ra's king may have pity. Or, thy father perhaps may find thee. But ah! my child, thy father I fear is not. On that cloud his spirit waits for mine.—Stay, Cathula; thy love is coming.

A HIGHER surge comes, white-tumbling, over the rock. In its cold bosom it folds Rosgala. " Farewel, O my Conloch!"

Too late, Cathula comes in the boat of Sora. He looks for the rock: but no rock, dark-rising above the wave, is seen.—" The growing sea hath covered its oozy top! No Rosgala; no Conloch is here! O that the same wave had inclosed Cathula! Then, Rosgala, would we smile in death; Conloch we would clasp in our arms; his tender frame should not be hurt by rocks.—Shall Cathula die or live?"

THE light, half-mixt with darkness, breaks on Sora's hills. A small isle is near. A watery cave is under its rock; and over its mouth there bends, in its own gray coat of mofs, an aged oak. Five generations saw the ocean shrink and grow since this oak had given the king of Sora shelter. In the cave below it he once hid his spouse, as he moved to war. ' To-morrow,' he said, ' I return, and bring the head of Lanfadda.' He went; the spear of Lanfadda travelled through his side, and forbade to fulfil his promise. Two days, with their nights, returned. But no word of thy return, red-haired Ulan-orchul. Oi-dana is sad in her cave. Her dark hair wanders on winds; and her white hands beat, like foamy waves, her breast.—Mournful through night is her voice of grief. The mariner hears it as he passes by. He turns to see if it may be the music of a spirit of the deep. And thus was discovered the secret cave.—It is here Cathula waits for night. It comes with all its stars. Rosgala descends on the soul of her love. She comes, soft-gliding on the face of the deep. Her robe is of the white mist that rises on Cona, when morning-dews are melting in the beams of the sun. But her tresses still are wet: they drop like the dew of roses on the bank of their slow-rolling river.—She tells him of her fate; she tells him how she laid Conloch on his shield. 'But let Cathula,' she says, ' awake, and fly safe to Iniftore."

He rose. In silent grief over the waves he came. But since, he is often sad. His tears in the morning flow for Rosgala; and his sighs in the evening are heard for Conloch †.

GREAT, said the king of Morven, is the cause of Cathula's grief. But Conloch perhaps may live. Thy shield may have carried him to the shore, and the people of Sora might have pity. " He may one day," they would say, " lift this shield to defend us." Yes, they may have spared him; and the warriors may one day say of him, " His arm is like the arm of Cathula: his spear is like one of the spears of Morven." Why then should darkness dwell on the soul of the mighty? Cathula is not alone when the clang of the shield arises.

THUS passed the night in Carric-thura's halls. Gray morning at length arose in the east. His eyes are half open like the weary hunter on the heath when he is scarce awake. Dark waves begin to roll in light. Hill's left half their head in day. Stars hide in caves their dim heads; for they see the son of the morning lift his yellow head behind his hill, and looking, with his broad eye, farther than

† Here Cathula's bard ends his narration.

than ever travelled the reſtleſs kings of the world †. They ſee him, and retire from his preſence; as the daughters of ſtrangers when they ſee Malvina.

NOR did the beams of the ſun, that day, bring gladneſs to the ſcout of Iniſtore. From the height of his rock he looks on the ſea. Dark ſhips are on the ſhore. Like bees iſſuing from the trunk of their oak, when the ſun is on the vale of flowers, they pour on the beach their men. The ſteps of his return are quick. " Cathula! Lochlin is on thy ſhore."

AND let them come, ſaid Cathula; for my friends are nigh. But why didſt thou not ſee them ſooner? Why, O ſun, didſt thou not ſooner riſe?—But perhaps thou haſt been hearing the tale of wo, like Cathula; or mourning for thy ſpouſe and ſon.—Yes, great light, for thou moveſt in thy blue field alone: no beam, like thyſelf, attends thee in the glory of thy courſe. Thy ſpouſe has been torn from thy ſide in heaven, by the ſtorm: thy ſon has been torn from thee, as, ſome night, thou haſt been travelling through the troubled deep*. Yes, fair light, thou haſt met in thy courſe ſuch a night as ſeized Cathula; and thou art now the huſband of no ſpouſe; the father of no Conloch.—Yet thy grief is only for a ſeaſon. Thou moveſt forth in the ſteps of thy majeſty, and thy dark foes vaniſh. The ſpirits that ſpread death over the plains in thy abſence, hide themſelves in the caves of the mountains when thou doſt come.—So ſhall the fame of Cathula, in the interval of his

† When the ancient Galic poets uſe this expreſſion, they are ſuppoſed to mean by it the Roman emperors.

* The mind, when under the influence of any ſtrong emotion or paſſion, is apt to aſſimilate every other object to its own ſituation. This figure, when properly uſed, has a fine effect, as we are pleaſed to ſee life and ſentiment aſcribed to inanimate objects.

his grief, arife. No cloud of forrow fhall hide the battle from his fight. His foul fhall grow like a mountain-ftream when its courfe is ftraitened; it fhall fwell in danger like a flood, when dark rocks oppofe it.

The fhield of Iniftore was ftruck. Connal took his fpear; and the hand of Fingal is on the blade of Luno.—The ftandard of Rinama ftreams, like a rainbow, in air: the fon of Ruro and myfelf ftand like two pillars of fummer's fultry cloud: they are fair without; but they hide the lightning in their fold, and the roar of the thunder is around.

As a ftorm of hail comes rufhing over ocean*, and drives the furge before it, till it breaks its force againft the fcaly fide of a whale or oozy ifle; or as the fpirit in the ftorm lifts the white billows in his wrath, and heaves them, with all their foam, hoarfe-roaring over a rock; fo rufhed our hofts, in all their terrors, to meet the war.—We faw the crowded ranks of Lochlin gathered around Manos, like flights of fea-fowl round their own rock. Its dark fides are covered with their thronging wings; but its head rifes, with all its fhaggy brows, above them, and fhrinks not at the roar of the coming ftorm.

It was then Fingal fpoke to Connal, and to the chief of Iniftore. All the youths bleffed the king of Morvan, as they liftened to his words.

" Our names, chiefs of the battles of the fpear, are already in the

---

* In the original, this paffage is no lefs terrible than the fcene which it defcribes.

 Mar ftoirm ghailbheach mheallain
Na fleud-ruith thairis air cuantaidh,
A' fguaba' nan tonna ftuadhach,
'S gam buala' ri † uchd nan ard-bheann;
  † *al. biafta gabhuidh.*

—No mar fpiorad na doininn a' feide'
Nam beanntai' eitt' faile
Le'n cobhar ceann-ghlas, a' flairirich
Meafg chorraige cruaidh a' ganraich;
—B' amhuil fin farum ar feachd
Dol an cinnfeal gleachd do'n araich.

the fong, while others want their fame. Let the fons of youth have the honour of the battle of Iniftore. We ftand on the hill, rocks ready to rufh into the vale, if they need our aid."

THE hand of Ogan is on his fword: the fon of Ruro half-exalts his fpear; and the eye of Offian is on Fingal.

I SEE, faid the king, three chiefs before the three columns of Lochlin's fpears. One fhines a beam of light, perhaps, in the firft of his battles. Nor is he of the weak in arms. Thine, Offian, be the lot to contend with the chief; but quench not at once his fame. The tear, perhaps, is in the eye of his fpoufe; and his father may now be dim with years. No fon befide, perhaps, has the aged chief: Offian, fpare the beam.---Thine, Ogan †, be that other dark leader of the war. "And mine," faid the fon of Ruro, "fhall be Manos, king of fpears."

THE kings remained upon their hills. Like three whales, with all their billows of foam, we rolled to battle. But the hoft of Manos withftood our affault, firm as the rock in the fea of Iniftore. Whales ftrike againft its fides, and waves climb up its face. But it remains fixed; all their force cannot move it.

NOR ftood the fons of Lochlin harmlefs in their place, when the fury of the battle rofe, and the ftrife was kindled by the fongs of the bards *. Ogan is bound with a thoufand thongs, and the fon of Ruro fhrinks back from the fpear of Manos.—The young lifter

of

---

† Ogan: the name of Rinama's fon.

* It was part of the office of the bards to animate the combatants by their fongs during the action. The old Perfian Magi are faid to have done the fame; and Homer alludes to the like cuftom in the time of the Trojan war:

———thro' the Grecian throng
With horror founds the loud *Orthian fong:*
The navy fhakes; and at the dire alarms
Each bofom boils, each warrior ftarts to arms.

Il. xi. 13.

of the spear preſſed upon Oſſian. I defended myſelf from his ſtrokes, but ſought not his early fall.

"Doſt thou deſpiſe my youth, ſon of ſtrength," he ſaid, as the big tear ſwelled in either eye; "doſt thou deſpiſe my youth, when thou doſt not lift thy beamy ſpear? Shall I, all day, beat thy ſhield, as does the harmleſs boy a rock? Shall I reap no ſhare of fame, while my friends hew down the ranks of war?—But I will elſewhere ſeek renown."

His people followed him as he went, and my ſteps purſued him ſlowly behind. I ſaw the chiefs come down from their hills, like three mountain-ſtreams when they leap, white, from rocks, and meet with all their earth, and ſtones, and trees, in ſome green vale below.—Manos meets the king of Morven, and the clang of their ſteel is terrible.—But who could ſtand before Fingal? The ſpear is wreſted from the hand of Manos, and the thick thongs confine him. Connal ſtands in the place of Ogan; nor was his ſtrength in battle ſmall.

CATHULA met the beam of youth that fought with Oſſian, as o'er the field he wandered in ſearch of fame. His heart warmed to the ſtranger, as he ſaw him brightening before him in all the ſtately beauty of youth. What pity, ſaid his ſoul to him, this light ſo ſoon ſhould fail! "Why, warrior of youth, ſhouldſt thou ſo early fall, like a young tree in the vale? the ſummer breeze creeps thro' its bloſſoms, and ſpreads its fragrance on the fields around. Retire, ſon of youth, leſt the maid of thy love ſhould mourn. Retire, for her ſake; that thou mayeſt fight thy future battles."—" But I will be famed in my firſt," ſaid the youth, as on he ruſhed.---" Thou

mayeſt,

mayeſt, in falling by the mighty," replied the chief, as he lifted on high his ſpear.

Like the force of two warring ſtreams †, or two waves driven on by contrary winds, they fought. Like the breaking of thoſe waves on the rock between was the ſound of the ſhields of heroes. Their broken ſpears fly, glancing, through air; but their ſwords, like meteors wielded by two contending ghoſts, are in their hands. The ſhield of the youth is pierced in the midſt. The ſword of Cathula paſſes through its folds. Nor ſtops it then. Its return is ſtained with blood; and the red ſtream follows it through the cleft in the ſhield.

As falls a green lofty pine by the mountain blaſt *, when the ax hath half cut it through, making the echoing rock ſtart, and the earth tremble around; ſo falls the youth on his ſounding arms. His foot is bathed in a little rill, and his blood is mixed with its gurgling ſtream.

" I

† The Galic language abounds in epithets, which give it often a peculiar energy that cannot always be transfuſed into a tranſlation. Of this we have here a ſtriking inſtance.

'N ſin chuaidh iad an dail a cheile,
Mar dha bhuilune ri treun-cho'rag:
'S gach gaoth a' neartach an faothreach—
Duillean bao'bhi', beucach, do'bhidh.
    Gu cuidreach, cuidreamach, beumnach,
Bha na Trein mar thuinn tigh'n da thaobh,
Gan ruaga' le ſtoirm, toirt nualan
Air carraig chruaidh meadhon-barach.

* The ancient Galic poets were peculiarly happy in their choice of ſimiles. They always drew them from objects ſo ſtriking and familiar, as to make a powerful impreſſion on the fancy; while a certain combination of harmonic and correſponding ſounds, peculiar to the Celtic poetry, took the firmeſt hold of the memory and ear. This livelineſs of images, and arrangement of ſounds, greatly contributed to the preſervation of their poetry by oral tradition. It was probably with a view to facilitate this, that they uſed ſuch a profuſion of tropes, as may rather dazzle than pleaſe in a tranſlation, while in the original they always charm. The compariſon before us is both grand and beautiful.

Thuit e mar chrann giuthais ard-ghom
Le gaoith-fhaſaich, thun a ghearraidh;
Le geilt thug a charraig fuaimneach;
Chrithich agus ghluais an talamh.

"I fall [†]," he said as the strife ceased along the plain, "I fall in the first of my battles; and my fame shall not be heard. But I fall by the mighty, and my name may remain, with his, in the song. ' It was the sword of Carric-thura's king,' the bard may say, ' that pierced the side of Anal! I will hear thee, O bard, on my flying wind, and with joy I will ride on my cloud. Cathula, raise in this green spot my tomb. Place that gray stone at my head: but the son of future times will not know it. He will make it the bridge over some little stream which he cannot bound across. Some gray bard will miss it from its place, and say, ' Where is the stone of him that fell by Cathula?' And thus my name may be heard.— O that thou hadst this sword, Annir of Sora! thou wouldest shed over it a tear; though without fame thy youth is fallen.—Cathula, hang that shield in thy hall. Though it did not defend me, I love it. Once it bore me on the stormy billows."

His last words were darts of death to the soul of Cathula. He stood in his place, like the tree which is blasted by the lightning, for he knew the shield of his fathers. He falls on the face of his son.

OUR heroes gather around them. We stand, silent in our grief, like the pines of Gormla, when they behold the fall of their companions by

an

[†] In the original, this speech of Conloch is very affecting, and has a melancholy tender cast which cannot be so easily conveyed into another language.

Thuit mis· ann tus na t eug-bboil ;
'S chon eirich mo chliu fan dan.
Ach thuit mi le lamh nam buadh,
'S blaidh luadh air mo ghaifge le chliu'fan;
—" Si Iann Ri' Innse-torc
A lot 's an araich an t Aineal."
Beannachd do t anam, a bhaird,
Cluinneam fein gu h ard do ghuth,
-S Liom ait a marcachd na fine,

'S glas-cheo na fri' gam eide'.
—An leac ud 'san lonan uaine
Togaibh afuas aig mo cheann ;
Gus an leagar thar fruthan faoin i,
'S an dean an t Aos-dan a h iontrain.
Ainnir Shora mo ghraidh!
Ged' thuit 'fan araich fo t annfachd,
Shille' do dheoir gu bras
Nam faighe' tu Ghaoil mo chloidhe.
A fhuil cholgach nan dearg-chath
Crochs' ad thalla mo chaomh-fgia ;
Sgia' mo ghraidh (ged'rinn i mo leon)
Air 'n do fheol mi ro fleuda faile!

an angry spirit of night, that had laid their green heads low. We hear, at times, the broken words of Cathula, and echo to his grief with our sighs.

'AND art thou fallen, son of my love*! art thou fallen, Conloch, by thy father! Was it for this I unsheathed the sword? O that in thy place, my Conloch, I had been low! Let The man of wo be the name of Cathula!"

FINGAL saw the grief of his friend, and long descended his tears in silence. At length he bade the tomb of Conloch rise, and the bards pour the mournful song. He bade the thongs be loosed from the hands of Manos; as thus he spoke to the king of spears.

" Why, chief of Lochlin, dost thou delight in war? why dost thou deprive the warrior of his future fame; and bid his days, like that early-fallen flower, to cease in the midst? Why dost thou darken the days of the aged, and add sorrow to the burden of years, with which their gray head is already bended. Why dost thou cause the eye of the virgin to weep, and take pleasure in the tear of the orphan?---Are their sighs to thy ear as the music of harps, when thou dost bid them so often rise? Are their tears a stream to thy soul, when thirsty? Or canst thou smile, when they weep, because the pursuer of their deer on the mountain is fallen †?---Are not

---

* The original has here several lines which consist almost entirely of interjections. As this sort of natural language does not always admit of a translation, it will suffice to give the words in their Galic garb.

Och! is ochain! a mhic dhileis!
Gu dilinn cha duisg thu tuille!
Och! agus Och! nan Och eithre!
'S truagh gur m..iri mn inis' ad'dhiaigh!

† This image is beautifully pursued in the following extract of a St Kilda lament. True poetry is confined to no time or place. It is the offspring of nature, and extends as wide as her dominions. It is the genuine language of every feeling of the human heart when strongly agitated by any emotion or passion.

" Be hush'd, my tender babes! Your father will soon come with the spoil of the rock.—What detains thee, my love; why

CATHULA:

not the thousand ills which grow on every heath, and which the son of the hunter is heir to, a sufficient toil to go through?---Why shouldst thou scatter more evils in his way, and strew his path with swords? Canst thou not walk the few steps to the tomb without treading in blood; may not the deer of thine own woods suffice thee?---Like that shadow, must thou fly unsettled over every field, though the squally wind, that shall scatter its dark mist, is so nigh it?---Behold the blood of Conloch: behold the grief of Cathula: and behold the sword of Luno.---But my sword, Manos, seeks not thy blood. Go; return to thy spouse, and pursue thy deer; but let thy ship bound no more towards Morven, or the stormy sea of Inistore."

" If it shall; then may this broad shield, by which my father swore, no longer defend the breast of Manos!---O that I had not done so much; for dear to my soul was he that is low!"

He sailed in his dark ships on the wave. Mournful, we go with Carric-thura's chief. The steps of his silence were slow: and often, in the midst of his troubled sigh, he stood, and looked back on the tomb of his son.

MANOS:

why so long this day is thy absence? Hast thou forgot thy spouse and children of youth; thy sister of love, and mother of age? No: but perhaps the fowls have been shy, or scared away; or, ah me! perhaps the string has been weak, or the rock been slippery.---What detains thee, my love? I will look for thy return from this peak of the rock.

" I see none move through the gray cliffs.---But ah! who is that, dash'd at their foot by the waves? O! 'tis he; 'tis my love! he fell from their terrible height!

O my love! dost thou not hear; dost thou not pity the tears of thy spouse and orphans? Thy sister, too, calls; and thy mother, in all her feeble years, is sad. But thou hearest not; neither shalt thou any more arise!---My love, thou hast left us helpless indeed!---Our fishes from henceforth shall sport, safe, in their sea; our fowls shall roam, free, through their air: our eggs shall remain in the cleft of of their rock.---He that could bring them home is gone! My love, thou hast left us forlorn indeed!"

MANOS[*]:

A POEM.

THE ARGUMENT.

FINGAL, returning from his expedition to Iniſtore, mentioned in the preceding poem, finds an old man in great diſtreſs in Icola, a ſmall deſart iſle. His ſtory is told. Fingal and his men bring him with them, and promiſe to redreſs his wrongs. On their arrival on the coaſt of Morven, they find Manos, notwithſtanding his promiſe, had taken advantage of their abſence, and landed there before them. They offer him peace, which he rejects. After a ludicrous duel between two of their men, Fingal and Manos engage in ſingle combat, in which the latter is worſted, and mortally wounded.---After the fight, Umad, the old man who had been found in the cave, meets unexpectedly with his daughter, and obtains relief from Fingal.---The poet begins this piece with an addreſs to his harp.

DESCEND from thy place, mournful harp of Cona; deſcend, thou dweller between the dark-cruſted ſhields of my father. The winds are abroad: ghoſts ride on their bluſtering wings; per-
haps

---

[*] This poem is called in the original *Cath Mhanuis*, " the battle of Manos;" and ſometimes, from the ſcene of it, *La eas Lao'ire*, " the day of the water of Lora." Several circumſtances in it are ſo calculated to lay hold of the memory, and ſtrike the minds of *The many*, that it is ſtill one of thoſe that are moſt generally repeated by the lovers of ancient poetry; though the correct editions of it are not the moſt common.

That part of it which relates to U-mad and his dog, is often repeated by itſelf, and well known by the title of " *Laoidh 'n Amadain mhoir's a ghaothair bhain;*" or " *Laoidh 'n Umaidh gan geille' na ſloigh.*" *Amadan* and *Umaidh* are ſynonimous names: they ſignify " a fond," or " fooliſh man." It begins with theſe lines;

Tuirling a chlarſach a bhroin,
Tha cho'nuidh meaſg ſglathan mo ſhinnſear;
Tuirling

haps when they hear thy voice, they will bid their airy courfers
ftop, that they may liften to their praife.---Yes; for the night is
already calm: the blue face of the fea is fmooth; no breeze moves
the withered leaf. The thiftle's beard hangs in mid-air: the moon
refts on the hill, its beams are on the low mifts of the vale. In its
gray fkirts are the habitation of ghofts; they hover in filence over
the bard, for ftill they retain their love to his fong.

AND the fong of Offian fhall not be with-held, fpirits of my
love: neither fhall the harp of Cona, when you are nigh, be filent.
It is not fweet as the harps of clouds, for its voice of age is mourn-
ful. But you love it, becaufe it awakes the memory of the paft, and
brings back the days of your joy. You bend from your clouds to
hear it, as liftens fome bard in the funny vale to the weak lay of
the grafshopper. I liften, he fays, for I heard it when I was
young, and loved it. Thus you ftill love the fong of Offian.—
But are there no bards that attend yourfelves on your dark-wing-
ed courfe; who pour their nightly fong in your dufky hall? Where
is Ullin, the gray bard of other times, with his fweetly-trembling
harp? Where art thou, Alpin, with thy pleafant voice? And, tuneful
Carril, where art thou? Have you forgot all the fongs of Selma; are
you filent in praife of the heroes of Morven? No; fons of the fong,
you ftill tune your airy harps to their fame. The found mixes with
the figh of the mountain: the hind, liftening beneath the tree of
her ftream, hears it, when moon-beams glitter in the vale, and all
is calm around. Sometimes alfo, I hear your foft voices in the
breeze of night, when fcarce moves the edge of the light wither-
ed

Tuirling 'fgu cluinnte' le taibhfean
Air itte' na gaoith do cheolan,

'S iad a' eofga fion-fteuda dan fpeur
A dh'eifdeachd i fuaim do thormain.

ed leaf of the oak. The thousand ghosts, with their dim joy, gather around you, to hear the voice of their praise *. They bend forward, leaning on their deathless spears. Their shields, like the broad mist of the darkened moon, hang on the half-viewless belt; and the meteor-sword is in the dark, shadowy sheath beside it.

But how feeble are you become, my friends, who once have been so mighty! A rougher blast, on the wing of its whirlwind, comes: the harp and the bard are driven before it; and the heroes are rolled, a mixed cloud, together.—The sound of their music still spreads along the silence of Morven; themselves are rustling in the distant blast, and mixing their voices with the stream of Lora.

It was not so I beheld you once, heroes of woody Morven! It was not so I beheld you, when you followed the king, like the strength of his thousand streams to battle, when the strife of Manos rose. It rose on Lora, like the sudden storm of Lumon, which overtakes the mariner when he lays down his head, and says to his mates, We shall now have calm.

WE

---

* The fancy of this passage ought, perhaps, to procure it a place in the poet's own words:

Ullin aos-lia nan teuda binn.
Ailpein ghrinn, 's a Chaorril cheol'air,
'N do chaill sibhs' orain na Feine,
'S ar speis do chleachda nam Mor-bheann?
Ni hamhluidh; a chlunna nan dan,
'S tric fonn ar clarsach 'sa cheo,
'Se taosga' le ossun an aonaich
(Feadh ghleanntai 'saoin nam fasach,)
Gu cluas na h eilid 'si 'g eisdeachd,
Fu' shruth-gheugan 'f an oidhche shaimhe.
'S ni'n tearc gum chluasa fein
Fuaim ea'trom ar cuil bhinn,

Tra 'f gann air guala na daraig
A gluaiseas an duilleach tha feargte.
—Chi mi doilleir mile tannas
Ag ia'adh, nam pannal, man cuairt duibh,
A chlaisdin am molaidh fein
'S an taic ea'trom ri sleaghan gun bhuaire.
Tha'n sgia, mar chruth dorcha na Gealaich,
Air crios leath sholuicht nan nialuibh,
'S an cloidhe dealain na thruaill fein,
Ri slios doilleir nan treun-churaidh'.
  Ach c'ait a bheil ar treise anois,
Tra dh'fhogras an ossag na cuairt sibh?
'N a luib dh'fhalbh 'm filidh 'f a cheol,
'S na fir mhora nan neula duaichni'.
Tha 'm fonn a' sgaoile fea' ghleanntai' tosdach;,
'S iad fein ann osnaiche Laoire.

We failed from Carric-thura's bay. Night tumbled in her reſtleſs bed from wave to wave; and the thick-woven clouds, with their many folds, concealed the ſtars. Night, thou art dark indeed.—Lift, Morven, ſaid the bards, thy head through clouds. Selma, pour thy beam. Tonthena †, ſhake thy red hair above miſts; Uloicha, let the travellers of Ocean ſee thy beam. And thou, broad moon, lift on the wave thy face, and ſpread in clouds thy white ſails.

—But what faint light is that, which ſhoots its feeble ray thro' the gloom? It is like the eye of a ghoſt, when it darts a dim flame from his face, when the duſky winds lift, at times, his miſty hair. It is ſome friendly ſpirit that guides us on the nightly wave: in its path let us ſteer our courſe.

We reached the flame, dim-ſhining in its place; but no ghoſt was there. It was the light of the cave of Icola *. The beam had been dying away, after its flame had meaſured half the night. The burſt of grief, as we approached it, met our ear. It ſighed frequent in the gale of reeds. It came, pouring, from the hollow womb of a rock, and whiſtled mournful in its moſſy beard. We ſtood and liſtened to its ſound. It melted our ſouls of war.

" Thou art fallen, friend of my age! and I remain alone in the cave of my rock. I groan beneath the load of ſorrow, and of years.

† *Ton-thena*, " fiery tail;" *Iul-oiche*, " guide of night;" the names of certain ſtars.

* One of the Hebrides ſtill goes by this name, but it is uncertain whether it be the ſame; as almoſt all theſe iſles have loſt their ancient names, and retain only thoſe that have been given them by their foreign invaders, when ſubject to the crown of Norway. Hence the names of theſe *Innſe-Gall*, or, " iſles of the ſtrangers," cannot be traced to any Galic etymon; while thoſe of every country, promontory, &c. on the continent, have generally a ſignificant meaning, and an obvious etymology.

years. O thou laſt of my friends, why haſt thou ſo early left me! O that I had died before thee! Then wouldeſt thou have ſhed on my corſe the tear; and ſpread on my cold clay the duſt. But thou couldſt not ſurvive me long. Thou wouldſt waſte in thy grief, like the flower of Etha, when its root is conſumed by the ſecret worm. I remember thy ſorrow when my foot had failed. Untaſted beſide thee lay thy food. Had I died; for very grief, thou wouldeſt go with me to the tomb. For thee can I do leſs?—But ſhould I wiſh to live, can I, on one foot, purſue Icola's deer, or have I another friend to bring them to my cave in their chace? O that the laſt had never come there! It was with it thou didſt fall over the rock in death.

" BUT thou wouldſt not leave me, O Gorban †, alone: I think

† *Gao'r-ban*, " a white hound." The lamentation of Umad for his hound will not appear unnatural or extravagant if we conſider the ſituation of the mourner. Lame, old, in a deſart iſle, and deſtitute of all other means of procuring ſubſiſtence; his hound to him was every thing. The attachment and ſagacity of the animal himſelf ſeem alſo to have been remarkable. Two days and nights he had lain on the tomb of his maſter's murdered ſon, as if he had meant to expire on the grave where his duſt had been repoſited, if the neceſſity of the old man had not called him away to a voluntary exile. His uſefulneſs and ſagacity there, we have already ſeen.

If we form our opinion of what theſe animals were at that time, from what we now find them, we may perhaps be not a little miſtaken. Their uſefulneſs to ſo-

ciety at that period, raiſed them to a rank which now they have no title to hold. Their education and occupation were the ſame with thoſe of man; and they conſtantly enjoyed both his company and his friendſhip, which muſt have greatly improved their nature, ſo ſuſceptible of imitation and of gratitude. Strangers to the kennel, man late and early was their only companion; and man, the faireſt copy they knew, they ſtrove to reſemble. By man they found themſelves raiſed above their proper place in the ſcale of being, for which they ſhewed their gratitude by exerting themſelves to ſerve and to pleaſe him. This mutual friendſhip became at length ſo perfect, that almoſt all nations in the hunting ſtate, or firſt ſtage of ſociety, allowed, that even in their paradiſe, or that " humbler heaven" which they expected beyond this life,

" Their faithful dog ſhould bear them company."

" It

think I hear thy spirit's tread. Till Umad be there, thou carest not for the deer of clouds. Soon shall the stag thou hast left me fail; and then shall I ascend to meet thee in midst. Be thy steps nigh my cave till then; at its shadowy side shall thy grave be dug. O that some wanderer over the wave would make beside it my narrow bed!"

Why, said Fingal, dost thou weary for the narrow bed, dweller of the cave? Is not the night of the tomb long enough, although thou shouldst not bid its darkness hasten. Thou art not destitute; tho' time shakes in all thy limbs, and thy friends, like the years that are past, have failed. They are not the foes of the feeble, dweller of the rock, who are now around thee.

" I know, children of night, you are not foes to the feeble, but you are of the feeble yourselves. You cannot pursue the deer for Umad; neither can you dig, when he is no more, his grave. But you are not of the sons of the wind; I see your arms of steel. Come, stranger, into my cave; come, from the wanderings of night. Often have I spread the feast, and rejoiced in the presence of the sons of other lands. But now, no stranger do I see, though my cave is still open, and my nightly beam is kindled to guide them. Come, from the wanderings of night, and partake of my feast. It is the last gift of my low-laid friend; for there you behold the fair Gorban dead. No more wilt thou rise, my Gorban!"

We entered and saw the white hound for which the aged

mourn-

It cannot be thought that too much stress is laid on the circumstances to which this attachment has been ascribed, if we consider, that even the ox of the Hottentot has acquired almost as much sagacity as has *now* the dog of the European. And this is imputed, by *Buffon*, to his having the same bed and board and lodging with his master.

* It

mourned. Over it he leaned on a pointlefs fpear; on the end of it refted his tearful cheek. The wind of the cave fpread over his breaft his white beard, and toffed his few gray hairs about his neck.—" But thou wilt not rife," he faid with a figh; " thou wilt fpring no more with joy on the heath, nor bring the wearied fon of the mountain to my cave. No; but Gorban, on our clouds we shall meet *."

We partook of Ulmad's feaft, and liftened to his tale.

" He whom you here behold, in all the trembling of age, was once no dweller of a lonely cave: he was the chief of Stramora's echoing vale. Stramora, vale of my love! blue at the foot of thy gray rocks were thy ftreams; and green, on thy lofty hills, thy woods. Many were the heroes who feafted in my hall in peace, and ftood behind the ftreaming of my banners in the day of war. My deer wandered over many mountains, and drank of diftant ftreams. The morning fun rofe on my dwelling with joy; and the evening fhades were, to my halls, no harbingers of darknefs. Two glad lights fhone, in their brightnefs, there: the growing ftrength of Morad, and the mild beauty of Lamìna. But they were beams that fhone in the glad vale, only for a little. The ftorm came, and they hid themfelves in fecret.—Calmar beheld the beauty of my daugh-

---

* It has been already obferved, that the ftory of Umad and his dog is among the moft common of the fragments of Offian. As the ancient Caledonians lived by hunting, it was natural for them to have a particular attachment to their hounds, and likewife to put a high value upon poems that celebrated this attachment. Hence a peculiar regard has al- ways been paid to this piece, as we learn from an old proverbial diftich (feldom forgot when the poem is repeated), in which we find it claffed with Dargo, as deferving a very particular attention. See firft note on Dargo.

Gach don gu dan an Deirg,
'S gach luoidh gu laoidh 'n Amadain mLeir.

daughter, and fought her love; but she followed Morloch to the streams of Glendivar. The rage of Calmar grew. He came with war from Borba. Age was on the arm of Umad, and my son was young. The spear which he could lift was still but light; and thin was his youthful shield. He heard of the fame of that friend of strangers, the king of hilly Morven. He went by night to seek his aid. But Calmar heard the tread of his feet.—My son untimely dies!—The cry of death reached my ears. I took the shield of my strength in my hand: but I found it heavy. I put on the mail: but my knees trembled under its weight. I tried in vain to unsheathe the sword. Calmar sent me to this desart isle. Gorban heard my steps, where, for two days, he had sat on the tomb of my son. His tears were a stream on his grave; but his dreams of night were not of dark-brown deer. The thoughts of his sleep are of Morad: for him are his frequent sighs; for he will no more lead him to the chase, nor bound with him through the desart.—He heard my tread, and followed me. But his steps were heavy, like mine, when pensive I bore to his narrow bed the sleeping Morad.—Three years have since, with all their lingering days, failed by me on the deep. My foot too, by a fall in the chase, hath failed. But the burden of life, though heavy as the arms of his strength to the warrior of age, I still could bear, if thou, my Gorban, hadst remained with me. But now that thou art gone, I soon expect to follow."

We felt for the aged chief. The king promised to restore him to Stramora. He looked to Gorban; and we heard his sigh. " O that thy tomb were near the dwelling of Umad!"—We promised it should; and glad was the face of the aged.

THE winds whistled through the withered grass, and shook the waving tree. A louder blast descended from the mountain. Its tread was like distant thunder on the hollow stream. Half-viewless sat on its breast a ghost. He waved, as he passed, a meteor like a sword. The moon half-looked upon it over the edge of the heath, and shewed its dark-red stain. His words came to some of our ears, as rolling by in his blast he said, " Warriors of Morven, haste!"

WE opened our sails to the wind. We flew over the deep. Our speed was like the whale of Iniftore, when she is pursued home by the storm of Lochlin. In silence we reached our coast. Manos was already there. He knew the king was absent; and he gave his oaths to the wind.

MORNING pours from the gates of the east. Morven lifts its head in gray day. The white mist ascends from Lora's stream. It climbs up half the hill, and exposes to our view the sleeping host. " I will ascend," said Connan, " and kill their king; why should he again deceive us with his words?"

SOUL of the small renown, said the king, dost thou think, because Manos is false, Fingal will be base? Did ever warrior of mine fly, like the shaft of night, without striking first his shield? —Young Fergus, where art thou? Go to that host: tell them, Fingal never draws his sword till his peace is first refused *.

FERGUS went; mild as the morning sun on the mountain, when its beams are bathed in dew, and a thousand trees, with all their flowers,

---

* This line (in the original, " *Cha d' thug Fionn riabh blar gun chumha*") has passed into a common proverb, importing, That the strong should always be merciful;—or, That quarrels, if possible, should be avoided.

flowers, are feen below in their fmiling lake †.—But the breeze foon comes, and fpreads a momentary ruffle over the face of the fmoothed wave. The yellow hills, and the trees in the deep, are vanifhed; and all their beauty, for a feafon, is failed. Thus ruffled was the mild face of my brother of love, in his return from the hofts of Lochlin. Fingal knew he muft fight. " Manos demands the combat of heroes."

THE combat of heroes he fhall have, faid the boaftful Connan; I will bring to my king the head of the chief.

WHY fhould not Connan be allowed to know the weaknefs of his arm? He went: but Manos would not fight with the feeble. He bade the vaunting Fuathas come forth, to meet the boaftful Connan.—In the battles of Lochlin Fuathas ftood always behind; nor even there was he void of fear. One night as they had fought to the moon, too far behind, by the fide of a little ftream, was Fuathas. A tall hero appeared on the other fide; and taller ftill appeared his fpear. Fuathas flew: the other purfued him hard. In the midft of his fear, as he leapt the ftream, he fell. Beneath him, to his joy, fell the foe. In vain doft thou plead for mercy, he cried, as he drew his fword. But none, fave his own fhade, had Fuathas.—Not fmaller is now thy caufe of fear, when thou defcendeft to engage with Connan.

WE faw him come forth from their hoft: but the ruft was on his

---

† The beauty of this paffage in the original claims here a place.
Dh' imich Fear'as mo bhrathair fein,
Mar orra'-fhleibhte bha chruth,
Tra bhios dearfa na maidne 's an drinchd,
'Sa choill fa bla fan lochan fhe'ar.
Ach thuinling oiteag on aonach

'S mhill i caoin ghnuis na tragha;
Threig na coillte,—threig na fleibhte
Bha 's an lochan fheimh ri gaire.
—B' amhuil fin caochla cruth
No bhrathar teachd dubhach nar co'ail,
O fheachd Lochlan bha fiar uainn.
" Tha Manos ag iarruidh cu'raig."

his spear, It sounded on his shield like the screaming of fowls, when they prepare to fight the battle of the wing on the watery ridge. Connan feared; but he remembered the eye of his king. He rushed on with his sword, and wounded the gray feather in the crest of Fuathas. At the stroke the man of Lochlin falls down with fear. He thought the wound he had received was in the head. Connan turns to see if his king beheld. The sword of Fuathas comes behind, and hews his two ears from his head of pride. The valley echoes to his cry as back he runs to our host. At the foot of the king he falls. " I bravely die," he said; " Fingal, revenge thy hero's death *."

THE host of Manos came on with all their steel. Many were their shields and spears; many their rattling mails and swords of light; many their axes of war † to hew down the battle.—The joy of our people arose, as slowly we moved to meet them ‡.

—BUT

---

* The heroism of Connan, unlike all the rest of Fingal's warriors, lay chiefly in his tongue. For this reason he is upon all occasions ridiculed and exposed. Perhaps some mischiefs too, of which he had been the author, particularly the death of Dermid, had helped much to draw upon him this odium. In one of Ossian's poems he is called, *Mac mor na bha riabh ri ole;* " The heir of all who ever did evil." He is often called *Crionach nam Fiann;* " The blemish of Fingal's heroes." And from the above adventure he derived his common title of *Connan maol;* or, " Connan without the ears."—It is a strong proof not only of the valour but of the virtue of these heroes, that a single instance who failed in these qualities was looked upon as a rare phenomenon, and branded with such marks of infamy and disgrace.—The name of Connan is become a proverbial appellation in the Galic, for *a peevish ill-natured person.*

† We find no mention of this weapon among the arms of Fingal. It was, probably, peculiar to the Scandinavians, and the same with the Lochaber-ax afterwards adopted by the Caledonians.

'B iomad cloidhe 's b' iomad sgiath,
B' iomad triath le luirich aigh
B' iomadach ann clogaide cruaidh
B' iomadach ann *tuagh chum sgath.*

‡ A general engagement is sometimes related here, but so defective and incorrect as not to admit of a translation.

* * * * * * * * * *

—But who comes in his speed from our hills, tall in the beauty of youth? His spear in his hand is like a tree: and his shield is like the moon of night. He is from the land of strangers; he asks if he may fight the battle of the king. Fingal beheld the warrior with joy, and blessed the strength of his youth. But Manos demanded the combat of kings: for he remembered the thongs of Iniftore; and his pride arose like a whirlwind on dark waves, when mariners fear the danger.

We stood in our place †. Fingal went forward in his strength. The sound of his arms was like the noise of the spirit of Loda, when he spreads his blast over the land, and marks his path with death and terror. He struck with his spear the broad shield. His mail rung with the sounding of his steps: its noise was like the roar of a thousand waves, lifted by the rage of a storm against the dark side of a rock. The gathering of the tempest on the hero's brows is terrible. The son of Luno gleams high in his hand. His hair is tossed on the blast of winds, like the foam of a stream white-

† This passage is much admired in the original, and is therefore inserted for the sake of such as may understand it. It has indeed a native grandeur in its own dress, which will not sit so unaffected and easy on the idiom of another language.

Chuaidh Fionn afios le tartar uamhann,
'S fuaimneach arm mar fpiorad Lodda,
A' fgaoile gioraig is crith-chatha
Feadh an rathaid gu grad cho'rag:
No mar mhilte tonn a' beucaich
Ann fiolim eiti ri flios earraig;
Mar fin bha fuaim arm fa luireich.
S air a ghnuis bha dulachd catha.
Bha chloidhe liùhi' a dealradh,

Togt' ann aird an laimh a churaidh:
Sna gaoithe' ftrannar a' gluafad
A chiabh, air fhnuadh freotha luinne.
—Na cnuic air gach maobh dheth chrithich,
'S chlifg an t flighe fui' a chofan;
Las a fhuilean:—dh'ait a chroidhe;
B'ann fheilidh a chith 's a choflas!
• • • • • •
Chuaidh an fgiathan breac nam bloide';
Chuaidh an chloidhean gorm a bhearna;
Chuaidh an fleaghan fada libhidh
A chabba' 's a ghniomh bu ghabhaidh:
Fhreagair na creagan don fhuaimneach
Thug gathana cruaidh gan ftrachda'
Thall fo bhos,—air corp nan treunluoch;
Cho' fhreagair na fpeuran ard dhoibh.

* This

white-tumbling from the mountain rock. The little hills shrink before him, and the earth trembles under his steps. Lochlin see the awful terrors of his face: they see in it the flames of battle; and the beating of their hearts is high.

THE chiefs meet in battle: their two hosts look, with trembling wonder, on the dreadful fight.—But its terrors who can describe? Their varied shields are hewn, piecemeal, down. Their blue swords are broken; and their long tough spears fly, through the whistling air, in pieces. The echoing rocks answer to their strokes; and the skies resound with the noise.—Manos at length is bound.

HOLD, said Connan, Manos of spears, till I cut away his head of lies.

I AM, said Manos, in the hands of Fingal; his wrath burns not, like thine, a deadly flame.

YES; thou art in my hands: nor shall Fingal stain his fame, with the blood of a low-laid foe. Once more thou mayest go: But thy spouse must mourn, if thou dost again come back.

HE spoke; but the face of Manos is pale. The spear trembles under his weight as he moves. The thistle comes across his foot. Stumbling, on earth he falls. The broad wound is in his side. —His shield had opened its bosom to the spear of the king; for it had heard his former words*.

HIS

* This refers to his swearing by his shield, in the end of the preceding poem, that he would not for the future trouble Fingal or any of his friends. The abhorrence of the poet, or rather of the people whose sentiments he spoke, to such falsehood, is strongly marked in his making the very shield of Manos resent it. Even Connan, low as his character appears, had such a sense of the enormity of the crime as to think it deserving of instant death;

Cumaibh rium Manos nan lann,
Sgu sgardinn a cheann s'a chorp.

As every stage of society has its own virtues and vices, it may be observed, that lying, perjury and deceit, are refinements that belong to civilized life, rather than
to

His tomb was raifed. But what could the bards fay†? Manos remembered not his words. When he was afked what he had done with his oaths? " Alas!" he faid, " where I found, I left them."—Manos, thou wert generous; but wrathful and bloody was thy darkened foul.

We came to Selma's halls. The young hero who came to our wars was with us. But his countenance was fad, and often he looked to the hill.—" On its heath," he faid, " I left the fpoufe of my love.

to that period which we call barbarous. The barbarian feldom acquires the art of difguifing his fentiments, or the virtue of fneaking through the winding paths of infincerity and circumvention.

† Of all poffible evils, that of being denied the funeral-fong was thought, by the ancient Caledonians, the moft dreadful. On the fong of the bard depended not only their fame in this world, but their happinefs in the next. This perfuafion could not fail to have a happy influence upon their conduct, as it would be a continual fpur to good and great actions. Even till fome time after the extinction of their fuperintendants the Druids, the bards maintained their dignity, and difcharged this part of their office without any refpect of perfons. In the cafe before us, we fee the impartiality of Offian in drawing even the character of an enemy. His generofity is celebrated, both in this and fome other fragments; but unfortunately his delight in blood is always joined to it: He is ftill

And —Manos, fuileach, corrach, fial,
—Manos, Ri' fuileach nan cuath.

The Celtic bards did not, like the poets of Greece and Rome, punifh any man in the other world becaufe he was unfortunate in this; as was the cafe with every one whom they forced to wander " A hundred years a melancholy fhade!" (Æn. 6. 329.), for the want of burial. For their own faults only, the bards called people to an account: And then, as vice was never to be allowed quarter by them, they condemned the guilty to an adequate punifhment, not only for a hundred years, but for ever; or at leaft till the *brath* or *dilinn*, when the world was to undergo a general revolution by fire or water. The morality which they inculcated was not the leaft valuable property of Offian's poems. And it is remarkable, that his moral paffages are in the original always fhort and ftriking; as if they had been intended to take hold of the memory, and to pafs, as moft of them have done, into common proverbs.---When any perfon fails in a folemn promife, nothing is more common than, by a diftich of this poem, to remind him of the guilt and fate of Manos.

" Cait a bheil na mionnan mora Mhanuis?
Och! dh'thagas far an d' fhuaras."

love. We fled from the ſtrength of Calmar; for his heroes from the ſtreams of Borba were many, and the friends of Morloch failed.

His words reached the ears of Umad, as, bended, he leaned on his ſtaff, like a tree half overturned on Lena. The joy of the aged aroſe. He aſked for Lamina. She came. She flew to her father. We ſaw the mingled joy of their ſouls. We wondered why we wept in the midſt of our gladneſs. Our tears of joy were pleaſant; like the ſweet drops that fall from the oak of Morlia, when its green leaves rejoice in the day of the ſun.

To-day, ſaid Fingal, we ſpread for the ſtrangers the feaſt: to-morrow we give the children of diſtreſs our aid. The ſhield of Morven will ſtretch itſelf wide to cover the unhappy; and this ſword is bright with joy when it is drawn to defend them. Then only the ſon of Luno † ſays, " I long to be bathed in blood."

The night was ſpent in the feaſt and the ſong. Nor was thy voice

---

† The ſword of Fingal had this name from its maker Luno, a ſmith of Lochlin, who had likewiſe fabricated arms for ſome more of the Fingalian heroes. In return, Oſſian tranſmitted his name to poſterity in a poem compoſed on the ſubject, and known by the title of (*an Gobha*) "The ſmith." Some fragments of this piece which ſtill remain are very characteriſtical of the manners of the times. In the following lines the poet, with the ardour natural to a warrior, deſcribes the tranſport of their joy on receiving theſe implements of war; " O how glad were we the next morning on receiving our arms from Luno!"—He alſo tells the different names or epithets given to their reſpective ſwords: ſuch as, " the ſon of Luno;" " the flame of the Druids;" " the raven, or bird of prey;" &c.

O b' aighearach finn an dara mhaireach.
Ann an ceardaich Loin 'ic Liomhain!
Gum bu mhaith ar n ur chloidh'ne
S' ar deagh ſhleaghan fada righne.
B'e mac-an-Loin lann mhic Cu'il,
Nach d'fhag fuigheal riabh dh'fheoil daoine;
Gum bi'n Drui'lannach lann Oſcair,
'Sgum bi Choſgarach lann Chaoilte.
Gum bi 'n Liomhanach lann Dhiarmid,
B'iomad fear fiadhaich a mharbh i;
'S agam fein bha Gear-nan-calan,
Bu gharg, farum 'n am nan garbh chath.

* The

voice filent, my foftly-trembling harp*. Thy found was not then fo mournful. Thou hadft, like me, thy companions about thee; and the king with his heroes heard thee. From their feats they leaned forward to liften; their faces were fidelong-bending. —No filent mift on the vale were then our friends, my harp.—No mournful voice in the hollow tree of the mountain was, then, thy found: no mofs-gray blafted tree, ftript bare of all its leaves, was Offian.

* The bard had in the beginning of the poem addreffed himfelf to the folitary companion of his wo, the harp; and here he again returns to it.

TRATHAL*:

A POEM.

THE ARGUMENT.

OSSIAN, feeling the fun warm on the tomb of Trathal, addreſſes that luminary, and relates an adventure of the hero on whoſe tomb he ſits.—Colgul, having been worſted by Trathal at the chace and tournament, contrived a ſtratagem to reſent the ſuppoſed affront. He lands a number of his followers on the coaſt of Morven; and ſends an old man to Trathal to counterfeit diſtreſs, and aſk his immediate aid. Being thus enſnared, he defends himſelf with great bravery; and kills many of his opponents, with their leader, before he is miſſed by his people, who at length come to his aid.

SON of the morning, the ſteps of thy riſing are lovely; the lifting of thy yellow hair above the eaſtern mountain. The hills ſmile when they behold thee; and the glittering vales, with all their

blue

---

* The hero of this poem was grandfather to Fingal, and generaliſſimo of the Caledonian army in their wars with the Romans. There is frequent mention made of him in the other poems of Oſſian, and in tradition he is famous on account of his wars with the Druids. This piece, which could not be got altogether complete, goes by the title of

Sgeulchd air Tra'ul nam buadh
'S air Colgul nan tual bheart;

" The ſong of Trathal the brave, and of Colgul of the baſe deeds."...The addreſs to the ſun, with which it opens, is extremely beautiful; but, towards the end, reſembling ſomewhat that grand paſſage of the ſame kind in Carthon. It was natural for ſightleſs Oſſian, as well as for Milton, to make frequent addreſſes to this luminary. It is probable, however, they had at firſt no idea in common, tho' they may have been afterwards confounded by the careleſſneſs of thoſe who recited them. The opening of the poem, as correctly as it could be obtained, is ſubjoined in the Galic.

'S a Muhic na h og-mhadain! ag eiridh
Air ſleibhte foir, led' chiabhan or-bhuidh;

'S

blue ſtreams, are glad. The trees lift their green growing heads through the ſhower to meet thee; and all the bards of the grove ſalute, with their morning-ſong, thy coming.—But whither does the night fly, on its dark eagle-wing, when it ſees thy face; and where is the place of darkneſs? Whither do the ſtars retire from thy preſence, and where is the cave in which they hide their trembling beauty? Into what deſart doſt thou chaſe them, when thou climbeſt the mountains of heaven, and purſueſt them, like a mighty hunter, through the blue fields of the ſky?—Son of heaven, the ſteps of thy courſe are lovely, when thou travelleſt above, in thy brightneſs, and ſcattereſt from thy face the ſtorms. The departure of thy yellow hair is lovely, when thou ſinkeſt in the weſtern wave; and lovely is the hope of thy coming. In the miſts of night thou never loſeſt thy courſe; and tempeſts, in the troubled deep, in vain oppoſe thee. At the call of the morning thou art always ready, and the light of thy return

is

'S ait ceime do mhais air ᴁn aonach,
'S gach caochan gorm 's a ghleann ri gaire.
Tha croinn uaine, ro dhriuchd nam fras,
Ag eiridh gu bras ad cho'ail;
'S filidh bhinn nan coillte fas
A' cuir failt ort le 'n oran maidne.
 Ach c'alt a bheil ciar-im'eachd na ha oiche
(Rod' ghnuis) air fgiathan an fhirein?
C'ait' a bheil aig duibhre a co'nuidh,
'S uaimh chofach nan reulta foillſe,
Tra leanas tu'a ceime gu luath,
Mar ſhealgair gan ruaig 's na ſpeuran;
Thuſa' dire' nan aonach ard,
'S iads' air faoin-bheannta fas a leimuich?
 'S aoibhin do ſhiubhal a ſholluis aigh,
A fgaoileas le d' dhearfa gach donionn,
'S is maiſeach do chleachdan oir
A' inamh fiar 's do dhoigh ri pille'.
Le feachran ann dalla-cheo na h oi'che,
Cha ghlacar thu choidh' ann ad churſa;

'S doinionn nan cuanta gabhaidh
Cha feid gu brath a s t iul thu.
Le gairm na ciuin-mhadain bidh t eiridh,
'S do ghnuis fheilidh a' dufga' gean;
A' fogra' na h oich o gach ait'
Ach fuil a bhaird nach fâic do ſhollus.
 Ach amhuil fo aos-lia lag
Bidh tufa fathafd a' d' aonar;
Do ſhiubhal 'sna ſpeuran mall
'S tu dall mar mis'air an aonach.
Doilleir mar ghealach nan tra,
Bidh t anra 's tu ſiubhal nan fpeur;
Caiſeamachd na maidne cha chluinn thu;
Mar na fuinn gun luadh ri eiridh.
An fealgair feallaidh fo'n raon
Ach chon fhaic e t aogas a' ti'can;
Bruchdai' a dheoir, 'se pille' fu ſmalan,
" A mhadai' mo ghiaidh! threig a gh·iun fn,"
—Bidh aibhneas ann fin air folluis na h oi'che,
Tra bhios Mac na fuillfe mar Thra'ul.

is pleafant. It is pleafant; but I fee it not, for thou doft not difpel the night from the eye of the bard.

—But the mift of years, one day, may dim thy own countenance; and flow, like mine, may be thy fteps of age on Morven. A dim circle, like thy fifter, thou mayeft wander through heaven, and forget the time of thy rifing. The voice of the morning will call, but thou wilt not anfwer. The hunter from his hill will look for thy coming, but he fhall not behold thee. The tear will ftart into his eye. " The beam of heaven," he will fay to his dogs, " hath failed us!" He will return to his booth in fadnefs. But the moon will fhine in her brightnefs; and the blue ftars, in their place, will rejoice.—Yes, O fun, thou wilt one day grow old in the heavens; and, perhaps, fleep in thy tomb, like Trathal.

Dost thou not remember, O fun, the car-borne chief? His fteps before thee on the mountain were lovely. One day as he wandered on Gormal's heath, the beauty of youth, like light, was around him. A fpear was in either hand; and the fhield of his father was broad, like thy face, before him. His ruddy cheeks rofe beneath a dark helmet, and his hair defcended in ftreams upon his neck. As he went, he whiftled, carelefs, the fong of heroes. A fon of age rifes before him on the heath. His eye is red: on his cheek there refts the tear. Sad is his voice of grief, and mournful fings in his gray hair the mountain-wind.

" I come," he faid, " to afk thine help, if thou art Trathal king of fpears. On the banks of the diftant Dula, many heroes heard once the fhield of Tual-arma, and many ftrangers in his hall have feafted. But heroes hear now the found of my fhield no more; and my halls, where blazed in the midft of fongs the oak, are fi-

lent

lent, cold, and desolate. Mor-ardan saw the beauty of my daughter. No other child was mine. He loved her; but she heard him not. The wrath of his bosom was a fire that was concealed. He came on the sea with his skiff. Four rose upon his oars. Slisgala and her father stood upon the shore. We are forced to go in the boat. The storm detains them now on thy coast. Give me, Trathal, one of these spears; and lend, thou first of men, thy aid."

Trathal heard the tale of grief. Joy and rage burned at once in his soul. He gave the spear, and fearless went: the murmur of his course was like a stream that is concealed. An host arose before him. The son of age behind them sunk. The king, in his wrath, half-lifted the spear; but his soul bade him spare the age of the feeble. " Stain not, Trathal," it said, " with his blood thy spear."

Fifty spears are lifted; fifty swords shake their flames, like lightning, around him. Colgul rises in the midst. The joy of his face is dark; as fire in the pillar of smoke; as a meteor that sits on a cloud, when the moon of night is dark, and the woody mountains hear the storm.

—In Dorinessa he had once pursued with Trathal the chase, and lifted with the king, in sport, the spear. But who could pursue the chace, who lift the spear with Trathal? The brown-eyed maid of Dorinessa sighed, as she beheld the king; and turned away her eye from Colgul. The chief in the darkness of his wrath retired, as retires a ghost on his sullen blast when he cannot tear the oak. He waits in the cave of clouds, till he come again in the roar of winds.

winds. Thus waited for a feafon Colgul; but now he comes with his thoufands, when Trathal is alone.

THOU art alone, O Trathal; but thy thoughts are not of flight. Thy ftrength, like the contracted ftream of Inar, grows. Thy foul, like the heaving ocean, fwells in the roar of ftorms. Thy joy is terrible, like a fpirit of night when he lifts his red head in the midft of meteors, and ftrides, in his dark-growing cloud, from hill to hill.

* * * * * * * * * *

As the rolling of rocks from the top of hills; as the noife of waves when the tempeft is high; or as groves when their dry hair is feized by flames through night,—fuch was the terror of the path of Trathal. Colgul and he were two mountain-ftreams in the ftrife: the found of their fteel was like the echo of the narrow vale when its green pines are felled.—Dreadful is their battle! Trathal is a ftorm that overturns the grove, and a wave that climbs the fhore is Colgul †. But the eyes of Colgul reel in mift, as lights on his helmet the maffy fpear. Corran ftands without his fhield, like a rock which the lightning has bared. Duchonnis ftops with his hand the red ftream of his breaft, and leans his back to a broken tree. The helmet of Crufollis glitters between his feet, with one half his head, before he falls: and the gray hair of Tual-arma is trampled in blood and duft, by the crowding feet of heroes.

COL-

† The original of this paffage is fo truly grand and terrible, that the tranflation gives but a very inadequate idea of it.

    Chaidh Tra'al a fios na cide,
Mar fgarnaich o mhullach fleibhte;
Mar bhuinne-fhruth fuaimneach oillteil,
No mar theine 'm falt nan coillte an.

Bha Colguil 'f e fein mar dha fhruth aonaich,
Chluinnte air gach taobh am beucaich;
B' airde fuaim am faobhar geala
Na toirm mhic-thalla 's croinn gan gearra.
Bha Tra'al mar neart na gaoithe
Leagas giuthas Mhor'ainn aobhach;
'Shha Colguil mar luas nan fleud fhruth
Bhios ri aodan fhliabh ag tiridh.

TRATHAL:

COLGUL scatters from his red eyes the cloud. He sees his people in their blood around. Like the dark shadow of Lego's mist, he comes in silence behind the king. But he comes not unperceived. Trathal turns. Colgul flies. His steps are to the boat, and Trathal in his strength pursues him. A thousand arrows aim at the king. By one of them Colgul is pierced. He falls upon the shore, when one hand hath got hold of the boat. Trathal leaps into its dark womb, and turns upon the people of Colgul. He turns; but a blast drives him into the deep, and he bounds in the midst of his fame with joy.

THE spouse of Trathal had remained in her house. Two children rose, with their fair locks, about her knees. They bend their ears above the harp, as she touched, with her white hand, its trembling strings. She stops. They take the harp themselves; but cannot find the sound which they admired.—Why, they said, does it not answer us? shew us the string wherein dwells the song. She bids them search for it till she returns. Their little fingers wander among the wires.

SULANDONA looks for her love. The hour of his return is past. —" Trathal, where dost thou wander among streams; where has thy path erred among woods? From this height may I behold thy tall form; may I see the smiling joy of thy ruddy face. Between thy yellow locks of youth, thou lookest like the morning sun."

SHE ascended the hill, like a white cloud of the melted dew, when it rises on early beams from the secret vale, and rushes scarce wave their brown tufted heads. She saw a skiff bounding on the deep: she saw on the shore a grove of spears.—" Surely they must

be

be foes that lift them; and Trathal is alone. Can one, tho' strong, contend with thousands?"

HER cries ascend upon the rock. The vales reply with all their streams. Youths rush from their mountains, and wildly tremble, in their steps, for their king. They thought of rushing on the people of Colgul in their wrath; but Trathal raised on the deep his voice, and bade them stop the spear. They rejoiced when they heard the king, and saw him turn to the shore his ship.

THEY gathered about Colgul; but his face was dark, and the flame of his eye had failed. His people stood mournful around; but many of them had strewed the brown heath, like dry leaves on autumn's dusky plain when tempests shake the oak. We help them to raise their tombs; and first we dig the grave of Colgul.—A youth stoops to place beside him the spear. The mail, in rising, drops from two heaps of snow. Calmora falls above her love.—Sulindona, as she came, beheld her pale. She knew the daughter of Cornglas. Her tears fell over her in the grave: she praised the fair of Sorna.

" DAUGHTER of beauty, thou art low. A strange shore receives thy corse. But thou wilt rejoice on thy cloud, for thou sleepest in the tomb with Colgul. The ghosts of Morven will open their halls to the young stranger, when they see thee approach. Heroes around the feast of dim shells, in the midst of clouds, shall admire thee; and virgins in thy praise shall touch the harp of mist. Thou wilt rejoice, O Calmora †; but thy father, in Sorna, will be sad.

His

† The whole of the song over Calmora is beautiful; but the following verses are exceedingly soft and tender.

Biaidh gean ortfa a' d' neoil,
Ach t Athair ann Sorna biaidh dubhach;
Ag im'eachd air bile na tragha,

His steps of age will wander on the shore. The roar of the wave will come from the diftant rock. ' Calmora,' lifting his gray head, he will fay, ' is that thy voice?'—The fon of the rock alone will reply. Retire to thy houfe, O Cornglas, retire from the ftormy fhore; for thy Calmora hears thee not. Her fteps with Colgul are high on clouds. On moon-beams fhe may come, perhaps, to thy dreams, when filence dwells in Sorna. Daughter of beauty, thou art low; but thou fleepeft in the tomb with Colgul!"

Such was the fong over Calmora; but who could fpeak in praife of Colgul? He and his people came, like the cloud of death that rifes from the cave of Lano, and creeps through night into the booth of the hunter, when his eyes are clofed, and all the winds are quiet. Often have their ghofts fighed on the mournful mifts that lowly creep along the tombs: often has their voice been lonely there.—But thou feeft them not, O fun: they only come when darknefs robes the hills; when all thy beams are away. But thou feeft the ghoft of Trathal; often does he ftalk in thy beams at noon, when the hills around are covered with mift. Thou delighteft to fhed thy beams on the clouds which enrobe the brave, and to fpread thy rays around the tombs of the valiant. Often do I feel them on the bed of Trenmor, and even now thou warmeft the gray ftone of Trathal. Thou rememberest the heroes, O fun: for their fteps in thy prefence were lovely; and before their time

thou

Thig ganraich nan tonn ga chluafan,
" An e fo do ghuth, inghean mo ghaoil!"
—Tha ula aofda ri fiontai' arda.
 Pill gu talla nan corn-glas,

Pill o floirm alluidh na tragha,
'S gun neach a' freagra' do ghlaoidh
Ach Mac-thalla † nam faoin-fhafach.

† *Mac-thalla*, " the fon of the rock," is the Galic name for Echo.

thou haſt ſhone on Morven. And thou wilt remember them in the time to come, O ſun, when this gray ſtone ſhall be ſought in vain. Yes: for, " Thou wilt endure," ſaid the bard of ancient days †, " after the moſs of time ſhall grow in Temora; after the blaſt of years ſhall roar in Selma."

† What bard Oſſian refers to here is uncertain. He was poſſibly ſome one who had, by way of eminence, the title of " The bard of ancient times." It appears from the paſſage, that the art of poetry was by no means in its infancy in the days of Oſſian. The excellency of his poems proves, that it had been long practiſed, and had then made a conſiderable progreſs. Some have ſuppoſed, that a great number of the Galic tales, which are in a language highly figurative and poetical, but not confined to numbers, have been the firſt eſſays in poetry, and long prior to the æra of verſe. This is not improbable, as the warmth of the uncultivated imagination and the barrenneſs of language would naturally give riſe to all the figures of rhetoric before art could reduce words to meaſure or numbers. As many of the tales which accompany the oldeſt of the Galic poems are of this figurative and poetical caſt, they are a ſtrong preſumptive proof of the antiquity of the poems which they explain: They likewiſe afford a curious view of the Galic poetry in its moſt early ſtages.

DARGO THE SON OF DRUIVEL:

A POEM *.

The ARGUMENT.

DARGO, the fon of a chief Druid, having obtained fome help from Scandinavia, is difcovered landing by night on the coaft of Morven. Two of Fingal's fcouts, who had gone to watch his motions, are worfted by him in fingle combat, and then fent to challenge Fingal to battle. Fingal devolves the command that day on Curach, a chief of Innisfail. His father examines his arms; and relates to him an adventure of his early days to Iforno, which prepares us for the ftory of Ulan-forlo, near the end of the poem. In the engagement, Dargo is flain; and Curach, after lofing one hand, and behaving with uncommon bravery, dies as he is retiring from the battle. Some reflections, fuggefted by a Druidical grove, and the poet's notions of the ftate of the dead, begin and end the poem. The fcene is around the ftream of Moruth; and the time feems to be the end of fpring, or beginning of fummer.

A SOUND comes by halves to my ear. It is like the voice of a wave that climbs, when it is calm, the diftant rock. It is the voice of Struthan-dorcha's ftream, murmuring, deep, in the vale of

---

* As the name of Dargo is frequent in the poems of Offian, this hero is further diftinguifhed by his patronymic of *Mac-Drui-Bheil*, or " the fon of the Druid of Bel," probably the Arch-druid of the Caledonian kingdom.

The Druids, for fome generations back, had been at variance with the family of Fingal; and this feems to have been the laft ftruggle which they made for exiftence. They had got fome aid from Scandinavia, and feem to have been no ftrangers to war themfelves. But all their prowefs, affifted with the incantations of their allies, was too weak to cope with a race of warriors. They were forced to fubmit; but their conquerors, having nothing to fear from them, permitted
- them

of oaks. In the bofom of its grove is the circle of ftones. Dim unfiniſhed forms figh, within their gray locks, around it. The fons of the feeble hear the found; and, trembling, ſhun the awful ſhadowy fpot. "The haunt of ghofts," they fay, "is there."

But your voices are no terror to the bard, fpirits of dark night, pale-wandering around your awful ftones. No: I tried the ftrength of your arm when alive; I lifted my fpear in battle againſt your mighty Dargo, againſt the terrible fon of Druivel.

A TALE of the years that have fled, on their own dun wings, over Morven.

THE chafe was over in the heath. The wearied fons of the mountain laid themfelves down to reft; their bed of mofs is in the fhade of groves. The hills robed themfelves in the folds of darknefs, and the heroes feafted in Selma. Song on fong deceived, as was wont, the night*; and the found of harps arofe. The howling of gray dogs is heard, in the calm of the fong. Their place is on the top of their rock, and their look is towards the dark-rolling of ocean. Our fcouts repair to its fhore; Sulinroda of quickeft fight, and Calcoffa, foot of fpeed.

SHOULDST thou not now arife, half-wafted moon, from thy bed of heath; ſhould not thy horn appear above the rock of Morven? Lift it, fair light; look down, through trees, on the fleeping roes, and

them to retire to their ſhades, and die in obfcurity.—This poem begins with the following lines:

Tha fuaim am chluafa fein,
Mar thonn ann cein air muir fhaimhe;
Do ghlaodh, Shruthain-dorcha, 'se t'ann,
Ri tormnn ann gleann nan geugan.
'N ad dhoirre tha ra' nan clach
'S taiblife cianail 'nan glaſeide'.
" 'S tiamhaidh fo!"

*Till of very late the cuftom of fpending the winter-night in the tale and fong prevailed univerfally in the Highlands. This gave the mind a flock of ideas and fentiments which it can never derive from the few red and black fpots which conftitute the great amufement of a politer age and a more poliſhed people.

* *Sulin-*

and let the stream of Cona glitter in thy beam. Point out to our scouts the way; and if the dark path of strangers be on the nightly deep, lead them to the feast of Selma. The gate of Fingal stands always open, and bids the benighted traveller to come in.—Break through your clouds, stars of night; Uloicha, pour thy beam!

—But you slumber on your beds, ye lights of heaven. The darkest clouds are your covering; and thick mists, fold on fold, like Ossian's robe, conceal you. No ray breaks through. The heath is dark; and no beam trembles on the sea, save where breaks the wave upon a rock, and sends abroad its sound. Ghosts hear it, as in their ships of mist they pass, and bid their mariners turn away their sails.—Rise, O moon, on the hill of heath; break through your clouds, ye stars of night: Uloicha, pour thy beam!

Gray morning half-appears. The heads of the mountains see it, and rejoice. A low murmur comes on the breeze; it grows on the ear of our scouts. It is the buzz of the morning flies, on their dusky cloud, said Sulinroda*. The hum of the mountain-bees, said Calcossa, coming forth from their mossy hive. The traveller with his careless foot hath touched it; and their thousands rush forth to war.—Nor flies of the morning, nor bees of the mountain, make the noise, replied Sulinroda; is not that an host on the shore, moving through that column of mist, like the moon of night in her steps of silence?

The scouts, abashed, return. They did not perceive the host till day arose; and how shall they behold the mild face of the king? Blushing, they walk with unequal steps: on earth they often pitch their quivering steel. At the foot of a gray rock, as they

* *Sulin-roda,* " a discerner of roads;" *Calcossa,* " light or swift of foot."

they pafs, they halt. One hand beats their breaft; the other ftrokes their beard. A broken ftream leaps down from cliff to cliff: it falls, a thick fhower in their wandering hair. But the fcouts perceive it not; far diftant, in the caves of thought, is their filent foul.

At length the burfting figh of Sulinroda rofe. The eagle heard it in the cleft of her rock. She fhook her fluttering wings, and the fouls of the chiefs awake. " Let us demand the combat of heroes, and return with our fame to the king."

They, went, like two mountain-ftreams that rufh, white, from the heathy hills, and join in the vale of trees their force. They fweep the earth and ftones before them in their courfe, and tofs on every fide, amidft foam, their rooted trees. The boy, from his diftant rock, beholds with fear their terrible beauty. He grafps in his hand the bending oak, as beholding them he backward leans.— Such ftreams were the fcouts of Morven; but in the fon of Druivel they met a fea.—Calcoffa firft is bound. Sulinroda next maintains the terrible fight; but who could fight with Dargo? The hunter hears their noife, as he fleeps beneath the fhelter of his rock; he thinks the paffing thunder hath torn its crumbling brow, and he trembles in his dream. The roe fees him, as filent-bounding fhe fteals by with her fon, the dun kid with the long feet. She wonders he does not fly for fafety, like her, to the ftream of the diftant wood. She fhakes her head, as fhe flies. The thought of her foul is, " Hunter, thou art not wife."

The echo of arms defcended on my morning dream in Selma. I ftretched my hand, in my fleep, to grafp the fpear. The next breeze drove a louder sound againſt my ear; I ſprung awake, and ſtruck the boſs.

THE king aroſe. The ſhield of Morven ſent abroad its ſound. The heroes ruſhed from their hills, like the path of whirlwinds in withered oaks. In their courſe are a hundred ſons of Innisfail. They ſaw the ſon of Druivel with his gathered hoſt. They ſaw his banners float, with their blended colours, in air. " Give me," he ſays, " the equal combat."

HIS chiefs brightened before Fingal. But the youths of Inniſ-fail were ſtrangers. They ſtood, each bending forward as he graſped the ſpear. Their eyes, under their helmets, were fixed on the king: they ſeemed like ſilent meteors under dark clouds, when trembling groves ſee them from afar, and the bounding of roes is to the rock of the deſart.—In the midſt of their ſouls they ſpoke; but no voice of theirs was heard. Fingal ſaw their eyes were flames of battle; and his own people had already got their fame: the children of diſtant ſtreams ſpoke of the heroes of Morven.

CURACH, ſaid the king, lead thou the battle with thy heroes of Innisfail. But, Oſſian, let thy ſhield be near: it has often been a rock that ſheltered the oak of the mountain, when its head was bending beneath the ſtorm, and the craſhing of groves was heard around.

THE aged chief of Sliruth leaned to the trunk of a pine that had been torn, from its dark rock on high, by angry ghoſts, or eddy-winds. With one hand he, thoughtleſs, pulled off its gray moſs; in the decayed ſtrength of the other, he ſtill held his father's ſpear: its gleam was hid beneath the growing cruſt of years. There, the days of his youth rolled themſelves, a ſilent ſtream, over his ſoul.

All the murmur of their courſe, as they paſſed, was the low hum of a ſong. He wiſhed it might travel with his fame to the years to come.—But when he heard his ſon named for the battle, the thoughts of other years retired. Between his gray-hanging locks aroſe the ſmile, as he turned his eye to ſee his ſon. He turned his eye, but his ſight had failed. The night of age around him is dark: its miſts are thick; no light will diſpel their gloom.

" TAKE, Curach," he ſaid, " this ſpear. Often have the valiant, like dry leaves, ſtrewed its path in war. Wield it like thy fathers. My eye is dim: but let them behold thee from their clouds, that their faces of miſt may rejoice.—

" Let me feel, my ſon, thy ſword, ſince age hath dimmed the eye of Sorglan *. Let me feel thy ſword; is it ſharp and ſtrong for the battle? Let me feel thy ſhield; is it a rock of braſs in danger?—It is; but ſtrengthen its thongs: I wore them not ſo weak in the days of my youth, when I bounded to the battle of ſpears; when the blood, like a mountain-ſtream, leapt in my veins for joy.

" CURACH, thy father, in his youth, was a tempeſt that ruſhed through the ranks of war. Seven heroes attended once my ſteps in Iforlo. We purſued, three days, its deer. The pride of Ul-thorran roſe. Never before, he ſaid, was I diſtanced at the chaſe. —On the ſhore he burnt our boat; and twenty of his people he ordered at night to ſeize us in our cave. Iulorno, that beam of beauty in his halls, had heard his words. She ſaw the face of her father dark, as the cloud of Lano before the ſtorm. She loved my ſteps

* *Sorglan*, " open and generous;" *Curach*, " rage of battle;" *Sliruth*, " ſtreamy hill."

steps on the heath. My image grew a lovely tree within her soul, and she trembled for the growing blast. 'If it lay thy green branches low, no leaf of mine,' she said, ' shall flourish; no voice of the spring shall awake my beauty.'—In the evening we found the beam of light in our cave. Her yellow locks wandered, on her blushing face, in the midst of tears, as she told the tale of death.—' Shun,' she said, ' the cave this night; but tell not the steps of Iulorno were nigh it. The soul of my father is dark, as the gathering of night in the narrow house; why should he know that his daughter loves the chief of Sliruth?'

" SHE sunk in her cloud, and retired; like the moon of heaven when she hath shewn the bewildered traveller his path on the heath. He was wandering thoughtless on the face of a rock; the beam shone around him: quick he turns his steps; and blesses the light that saved him.

" WE fought with the warriors of night, and prevailed. We went for Iulorno, but the steel of her father had pierced her breast. Nigh his gate we found her in her blood. She was fair as the dying swan on the foam of the stream of Lano, when the arrow of the hunter is in her breast, and her down is lifted by the breath of gales.—Her brother asked her why she would not rise; and asked us, wondering, why we wept?—I gave the child a sword of light. I reared the tomb of the fair, on the shore of her native land.—Moon-beams shine on the place when all is dark around; and virgin-ghosts breathe there, on the passing breeze, their song. The soul of Iulorno is with them in mist; the music of her voice is mournful. Through every warm shower, the sun smiles on her green turf, and bathes its rays in the dew of her tomb.—Three days our tears fell on the grave of Iulorno; on the fourth we failed in the fhip of Ulthorran.—Such, Curach, were the early deeds of Sorglan; be thy fame, my fon, like that of thy father."

* * * * * * * * * * †

As the eagle comes, ruftling with joy, from her rock, when fhe fees her prey, the young fawn, fleeping in his dun moffy bed below; fuch was the joy of Curach as he bounded down to battle. The murmur of his people followed his fteps: their found was like the noife of a ftream, when it travels beneath a rock; like the thunder hid in earth, when the woods fhake their heads, but no fiery cloud finges their blafted beard.—Dargo came on, red eye of battle, rolling along his hofts, like the ftream of Balva. Silent and flow, but deep and ftrong, is its courfe *.

On either fide of Moruth's ftream the heroes ftride. A while admiring each other they ftand. With joy they bound on their fpears, and meet in the midft of the dark rolling flood. Over them bend in ftormy clouds their hofts, and mix around them fteel with fteel.

† Some verfes defcribing the manner in which the different companies repaired to their refpeƈtive ftandards are here repeated, but their inaccuracy forbids a tranflation. They are fomewhat curious, as they give the names of the different ftandards. On this account, a few of them are here annexed.

Chuir finn amach a dh' fhulaug dorainn
Bratach Fhear'ais oig mo bhrathar,
'S thog finn amach bratach Chaoilte
'N Lia'luideagach aobhach anrach.
    Thogadh afuas mo bhratach fein,
'S a follus mar ghrein ann duibhre;
'S thog finn amach an Lia'luimneach,
Bratach Dhiarmaid oig o Duibhne, &c.

* Some repeat here a defcription of a general onfet; but, as the following fentence gives reafon to fufpeƈt that it is rather a part of fome other poem on the like fubjeƈt, it is omitted. The verfes, however, on account of their poetical merit, are here fet down in the original.

'N fin chuaidh finn ann dail a cheile,
Sloigh nan Druidhcan 's Suinn na Feine,
'S bu luaithe na greanna-ghaoth earraich
Sinn a' dol ann tus na t eug-hboil.
Na bu luaithe na milte do fhruthaibh
A, ruith ann aon flugan o ardaibh,
Bhiodh a heueaich gu treun meamnach
Le toirm gheamhraidh o gach fafach.
Cha bheucadh treun thonn na tuinne,
Nuair bhuailt e ri creagan arda
Le neart na gaoi' tuath 's ann fhaoilteach,
Cha ftuadhadh ri gaoir an ard-chath.
—Ceart choi'meas cumhrag nam fear
Cho'n fhaca mi riabh ri m' latha.

steel. Here the stream runs red. There it breaks white over shields. Blood rests, curdled, on the ooze of its stones; and heroes swell, in their death, the tide.

But who shall give to the song the rage of battle! The shield of Curach falls from its broken thong. He reaches his hand to grasp it. The sword of Dargo cuts it off. Clung to the shield, it swims along the stream. But still the other hand is left.

Three steps he retires. His sword leaps from its dark sheath: its light gleams in air, on high. " Spread, Ossian, before me thy shield; but lift not thy spear against the foe. The fame of the warrior shall arise, only, when foes have the equal combat."

I will not fight with the wounded foe, said Dargo. My fame, in his death, would not arise. Retire, and think of battles that are past. I will contend with that son of the king beside thee.

Curach goes. In his eye is the flame of battle. Lying on earth, he spied a shield: its owner beside it sleeps, nor hears he the din of war. " Bind it, Conchana, with all its thongs to my breast. I will elsewhere reap the field. They shall not see that Curach's hand hath failed."

My spear was lifted against Dargo, as he rose on the bank of the stream. With the stroke he stumbles back: a withered oak is grasped in his fall. The crashing of arms, of branches, and of bones, is mixed.

He rose, and leaned against the tree in his place, His hand lifted still the sword; but I spared the decay of his strength. A-round him his people fall, like the withered leaves of the oak before the wintery blast. The stream leaps, bubbling, over their heads; and spreads, around stones, their hair. Helmets lift, here and there above the ſtream, their nodding plumes.

Lift, ſaid Dargo, thou ſon of the king, thy ſword; I am not fallen yet.—I lift mine, ſaid Curach, as he came, ruſhing through the ſtorm of the battle, and ſtrewing men and branches, with his lightning, along the ſtream: I lift mine, he ſaid, as it deſcended, a flaſh that blaſts the oak, on Dargo.

The chief fell in the ſtream. Its banks echoed around. His people ſhrunk back in their place.—But Cuthon † ſtill rolled our heroes in their diſtant wing, as the whirlwind rolls the pillar of duſt; as the blaſt ſweeps over a plain of ice the driven ſnow. I turned my ſteps to meet him; but Fergus was before me. His ſoul of battle burned at the ſight of Cuthon: his eye was like a ſtream of fire on a cloud of night. He bends forward with the joy of a young eagle, when it ſees its dun prey from Moruth's top. It ſpreads its wings on the ſtream of winds; but the bounding ſon of the roe hears the ruſtling of his courſe, and retires beneath his trees.

Cuthon, a while, ſtood terrible in his place; like a nightly ghoſt when he reſts on Lena. He ſeizes the meteors of heaven as they paſs; he clothes his dark limbs in their terrors, and meditates again the war of clouds above the trembling nations. So ſtood Cuthon, girding anew his arms: but he ſaw his people vaniſh; and ſidelong, he ſlowly, angrily, retired.—Twice, as he went, he turned in the midſt of his doubts, and ſtood like the ſtream of the vale of Balva*, where it knows not which way to turn its courſe.—He looks at length to the place where his father fought. He ſees his red hair wandering on the breaſt of the ſtream.

In

---

† The ſon of Dargo.   * *Balva*, "a ſtill ſtream."

In one hand he ſtill graſps the ſword; in the other he firmly holds the moſſy oak. Cuthon wildly runs. He lifts a mournful load. He bears his father to his hill: the rattling of his arms, and the voice of his fighs, are mixed.

WE ſlowly returned to the king. A little rill met us on the heath. Curach tries to bound over it on his ſpear: but acroſs it the hero is ſtretched. The gurgling ſtream climbs his boſſy ſhield; and leaps, gray, over his wounded breaſt.

GIVE, Oſſian, he faintly ſaid, give this ſword to my ſon. In the green ruſhy vale of Sliruth he purſues the tufted down, as it flies on the wing of ſporting ghoſts. Near him the water leaps from the height of rocks: between two woody banks it falls; the found, deep-murmuring, rifes on my boy's ear. " I hear," he ſays, " the ſteps of my father."—With the unequal pace of joy he runs to meet me; but he ſees the gray ſtream.—Return, my child, and purſue thy down; my eye will gliſten with joy, as I behold thee from my hovering cloud.—Tell him, Oſſian, how his father died; that the battle may grow in his ſoul, when the years of his ſtrength ſhall rife.—Oi-lamin † prepares for me the robe. Her tears fall as ſhe bends over the loom. A thought comes a-croſs her ſoul, and her white hand ſupports her waving head.—Oi-lamin, thy fears are true; thy hero lies now on Moruth's * heath!—Spare then, my love, thy toil. The gray paſſing miſt ſhall yield a robe to Curach.

WE opened the tomb for the chief; and raiſed, amidſt the voice of the bards, the ſtones of his fame. The found reached the ear of his father; as, bending forward, he liſtened for the return of

his

† *Oi-lamin,* " ſoft-handed virgin."   * *Moruth,* " great ſtream."

his son. He thought he was coming with the song of his fame, and he stretched his hand to search for him. The mournful song of the tomb strikes louder upon his ear.—" And has thy father now no son, O Curach!"

He came, groping through darkness for his way. He stumbled on the heath over a hero, whose soul had been travelling through the path of wounds. " How weak," he said with a sigh, " is now become the chief of Sliruth!"

The wounded half-raised his head over a broken shield, that had been fixed with the head of a lance to his breast. " Was the chief of Sliruth," he said, " ever in Iforno?—If thou wast, take this sword; perhaps thou mayst know it. A beam of light I received it, when young. No more shall Ulan-forno lift it."

The memory of the past rushed, like a torrent, into the stream of Sorglan's grief. We heard the bursting of his crowded sigh over the brother of Iulorno, the early beam of his love.

We bore the two to the grave of Curach. Sorglan felt the place where he was soon to rest. And Ulan-forno faintly bade us raise, with the mighty, his tomb. " Send to my hall," he said, " this ashen spear; it may support, in place of me, an aged mother. But no son, no young spouse of mine, is there to behold it. Ulan-forno dies like the young oak on the solitary mountain, when the spirits of Lano breathe over the desart. Its roots are torn by the blast; and no tender shoot from its trunk shall spring. Raise here my tomb, heroes of Morven: send home my spear."

And thy spear shall be sent, said the king; but is that all thy mother shall receive in place of her son! Now the oak flames bright in her hall. The song of the bard is up. He compares the

the bright blaze to the fame of her fon. Joy trembles in her aged foul, and the tear of gladnefs grows upon her cheek. " The fame of Ulan-forno," fhe fays, " fhall be a fun to my evening fteps. A ftreak of light on the mountain fhall be the decay of my years. The young fhall blefs the mother of Ulan-forno."

SHE ftops to wipe the tear of joy from her dim fight. The fhield emits a fainter found. The colour of its bofs is ftained: the face of the aged is pale with fear.—The gray dog howls without. Does he mourn; or does he fee the coming of Ulan-forno?—The aged bard goes out to fee. He refts at the door upon his fpear: his eye travels through the blue land of night. He fees a ridge of clouds failing, on the blaft, acrofs the fea. He knows the heroes of his land have fallen. He bids their hall of air to open, and their fathers bend to receive them. He fees Ulan-forno move before the reft, a taller form. A ftar dim-twinkles through the dun eagle-wing of his creft. Dark-wandering ftreams mark his broken fhield; like the black ooze of the mountain-rock, which points the courfe of the melted fnow.—The cloud varies its form. The bard returns. His face is dark as the meteor at which he looked. His harp is in his hand; but its voice is mournful.—" Hang it in its place, O bard," the paffing form feems to fay; " for in Morven we have our fame."

YES, rider of eddying winds, thou didft receive thy fame in Morven. The king himfelf was not filent in thy praife, when Sor-glan, with the image of Iulorno in his foul, fhed over thee the tear; and the bards mixed thy name with the fong of Curach.— Often do I ftill remember thy name, when thou comeft on thy northern blaft, to hover above the field of thy fame. The children admire thy tall form. "A ghoſt," they ſay, " bends over Moruth; the dim path of the ſpear is in his ſhield and breaſt; and we faintly ſee, through the mark, the burning ſtars."—I hear them, and know it is Iforno's chief. I teach the children the ſong of his fame. They ſay that Dargo, at times, is with him; that the winds lift the red meteor that forms his hair, and that the gray oak is ſtill beſide him †.—I rejoice in their viſits to our hill, where no ghoſt of the departed moleſts them. No; the feuds of other years, by the mighty dead, are forgotten. The warriors now meet in peace, and ride together on the tempeſt's wing. No clang of the ſhield, no noiſe of the ſpear, is heard in their peaceful dwelling. Side by ſide they ſit, who once mixed in battle their ſteel *.

There,

† The poet ſuppoſes the oak to be as eſſential a neighbour to the Druid in the next world as it was in this.

* Oſſian, on ſeveral occaſions, ſhews a liberality of ſentiment which does honour to his character. Here he not only allows future happineſs to his enemies; but, well judging the little differences of this world of too ſmall importance to be renewed beyond the grave, wiſhes for the moſt cordial reconciliation. Thoſe who were at variance here, as he elſewhere expreſſes it, " ſtretch their arms of miſt to the ſame ſhell in Loda." (Poem of Oi-na-morul.)

Such has been the fate of the Galic poetry, that its moſt beautiful paſſages are generally thoſe which have been moſt objected to. To ſuppreſs any of them, on this account, would be as cowardly, as it would be preſumptuous to treat the prejudices that are againſt them with indifference. Every body has as much right in this caſe to judge for himſelf as the tranſlator has, who does all he can to put this in their power, by laying before them the words of the original.

Cuairt nam flath gur ait leam fein
Gu aonach nan tannas gun bheum,
Far chiurre' gach falachd air cul
Sa bheil na feoid a dh'aon run.

Tha codhail nan Cathan ann ſith
'S iad air fgiathan na doininn gun ſtri',
Gun bheum-fgeithe gun fharum lainne
'N co'nuidh thofdach na caomh-chlainne.
Tha ſliochd Lochlinn is Fhinn, gn h ard,
Ag eiſdeachd caithream nan aona bhard;
An uigh cho'n eil tuille ri ſtri'
'S gun uireas' air fiuthann no fri'.
'Tha'n fuil air na blianai' a threig
(Le fnotha gun ghean mar mi ſein)
'S air raon nan rua'bhoc le io'nadh,
On glas-eideadh air mharcachd ſhine.
—Mar fgeul nam blianai' chaidh feach
Air ite'g aonaich, le'n ciar-dhreach,
Tha aiſling na beatha dhuibh's a I hlaithibh;
Mar tha dhamhfa Dearg nan catbaibh.

There, Lochlin and Morven meet at the mutual feaſt, and liſten together to the ſong of their bards. Why ſhould they any more contend, when the blue fields above are ſo large, when the deer of the clouds are ſo many? Like me, they look back with a ſmile on the years that are paſt, and ſigh at the memory of the days that will no more return. They look down on the earth, as they ride over it, on their gray-white clouds, and wonder why they contended.—Yes, heroes of happier climes! you look back on the dream of life, as Oſſian does on the battle of Dargo.—It is a tale of the years that have fled, on their own dun wings, over Morven.

CUTHON * THE SON OF DARGO:

A POEM.

THE ARGUMENT.

DARGO, whose death is related in the preceding poem, being sent away in the night to his place of burial, Ossian and Suloicha reconnoitre the enemy. Some of their incantations and superstitious rites are mentioned. The attitude of Cuthon the son of Dargo is described. On hearing the shield of Fingal they return, and meet in their way with a wounded hero, from whose story Suloicha becomes much interested in his favours.---An affecting incident occurs in passing by Curach's tomb.---The command, this day, is given to Fergus the son of Fingal. His descent to battle, and that of Cuthon, described; with their engagement.--- Fingal, coming to the assistance of his son, puts an end to the battle. Cuthon, leaving the field, dies of his wounds.---He is reconciled to Fingal. His people are invited to the feast; and a lasting peace is concluded, by means of Lugar, whose story is given.---The poem is addressed to the pine that covered the grave of Curach; and the scene is the same with that of the preceding poem.

THE wind of heaven whistles in the moss of thy gray branch, tall pine of Moruth ! The blast bends thy withered top, and strews thy gray hair, like mine, around. Our strength is fled on the

---

* *Cu-thonn*, or contracted *C'onn*, " the voice of waves." This poem is connected with the foregoing; the title of it in the original is generally expressed by these verses:

Sgeulachd air C'onn mac an Deirg,
Air a liona' le trom fheirg;
Dol a dhiola'bas athar gun fheall,
Air uaisibh 's air maithibh na Feine.

" The tale of Cuthon the son of Dargo, when he rushed in his wrath to revenge the death of his innocent father, on Fingal's heroes."

The address to the pine of Moruth is natural; as also the poet's passion for assimilating every object to the state of his own mind. In the absence of his beloved

the wings of years: years that return not again, from the dark wandering of their flight along the ſtreams of the defart.---But we were not thus weak, when roared on the heath of Moruth the ſtrife of battle; when trembled the wide-ſkirted field beneath the ſteps of the terrible Cuthon.---Doſt thou not remember the ſtrife of Cuthon, gray-haired pine of Moruth? It was in the days of thy youth; and thy memory, like the bard's, may have failed. It may have failed; but the light of the days that are paſt, though dim, is pleaſant.

A TALE of the years that will no more return from the dark wandering of their trackleſs courſe over the heath of the defart.

THE battle of Dargo was over; and the heroes repoſed themſelves on their ſhields. Beneath thy branches, O pine, which then were green, three ſtones, children of the ſtream, reared on high their oozy heads. We bade them tell to future times where we laid the mighty Curach. Beſide him I leaned that night, on my ſhield; when ſleep, like the cloud of Ardven, ſpread over my ſoul its miſt. But the forms of other times beamed on my mind, as the ſun on Cona's winding-ſtream, when the ſhadowy hills are dark, and miſts are on the head of deer. Curach roſe from the midſt of a cloud before me, ſuch as lately he appeared in the field. The fire of battle was ſtill in his eye; and a faint meteor, like a ſword, lighted his path through darkneſs. A blaſt lifted his duſky ſhield; no ſinewy arm was below, to graſp its thong. I knew the ghoſt of

---

loved Malvina, and every other human friend, this perſoniﬁcation became neceſſary; and the contraſt between the preſent and paſt days renders it not diſagreeable.---The ſtory of Lugar, or *Dan Liughair*, towards the end of the poem, is generally recited as a detached piece. But as this ſeemed to be its proper place, it was reſtored to it, and a ſentence or two of the other poem tranſpoſed towards the end of it.

of my friend. A while he ſtalked before me, mournful; and often the blaſt had whirled his limbs together; but ſtill he ſeemed like Curach.

"WHY ſleeps Oſſian?" he ſaid, as bending over me, on the breaſt of his blaſt, he leaned: "Should the warriors of Morven reſt, when danger rolls in darkneſs around them?"—He took the pine of Moruth by the head, and ſhook it as he flew. Amids a ſhower of ruſtling leaves, I awoke from my dream, and kindled the flame in the withered oak. The wanderers from the hoſt of Cuthon beheld it, and retired. I called for the ſcout. He came. His ſteps had been over Moruth; he had been viewing the hoſts of the foe.

DARGO they had ſent to the green iſle, where his fathers reſt [*]. Dark-bending over them ſpreads an aged oak. Its waving branches are worn by the gray moſſy ſtones that lift their head in its ſhade. Bards ſing there to Dargo's praiſe; and the forms of his fathers are ſeen above, dark-muſing, on their miſty clouds. Their red eyes are ſad, for they behold the fall of their ſon.

WITH Suloicha the ſcout, I croſs in ſilence the ſtream of Moruth. We hear the voice of the ſons of Loda, as, three times, they call on the ſpirits of their fear. We hear their ſhrieks going round the ſtone of their power.

" Roll," they ſaid, " ye vapours of Lano, that bring death to the

---

[*] This iſle is ſuppoſed to be that of I-ena, to which the laſt remains of the Druids, according to biſhop Pocock, had retired. Its ancient name was *Innis-Druinach*, or " The iſle of the Druids." They were in poſſeſſion of it till St Co-lumba fixed upon it for the ſeat of his monaſtery, towards the end of the 6th century. Their burial-place is ſtill ſhewn, at a due diſtance from the conſecrated ground allowed for the repoſe of their Catholic brethren.

the people; roll your dark-red columns on the hill of the foe. Defcend, Loda, into their dreams with thy terrors. Rife before them in thy awful form. Spread around the flames of thy lightning, and let the thunder of thy courfe be heard.—Roll, vapours of Luno, round the foe. Loda, defcend to their dreams with thy terrors *."

Nor filent ftood the gray fons of other times †, when the children of Loda fpoke. They called; nor did they call in vain. The friends of Dargo heard them, as they paffed in their ruftling blaft. Enrobed in meteors they came, and fhone, at times, around Dargo's fon. Often had the ftrangers fled with fear from the fign, like the roe from the hill of heath, when it waves its crackling flames before her. Bounding fhe flies to the fecret vale of her wood, nor waits fhe to look behind. So, often fled the mighty from the danger of the race of Dargo. But no danger did the king of Morven dread, though fome of his heroes were half afraid.

We faw, as we viewed the foe, the fon of Dargo by himfelf retired. Now, thoughtful, on his gleaming fpear he bends. Now he
fhakes

---

* The Scandinavians ufed incantations fo much, that, in later times, every fcrap of their learning and of Runic poetry was fuppofed to contain fome powerful magical charm.—This paffage is in a different meafure from the reft of the poem. The numbers have in them a fort of wildnefs and ferocity highly adapted to the fubject and occafion of them.

A cheo na Lanna!
Uamhar alla,
Air di ath na fala,
Taoig o'n chala gun deifinn.
Taom, a Lodda!
Fraoch do chorruigh,

'S lion le oglni'chd
Aisling 's brollach na Feine.
N am fradharc eirich
A'd chruth eitti' ;
Torian fhleibhte
'S lafair fpeur ga d' cho'dach.
A cheo na Lanna
Aom nan cara';
'S Luair an cadal
A chruth Ladda nan leir-chreach.

† The poet here means the Druids. It would appear from the following lines, that they had the art of kindling fome fulphureous matter, in order to ftrike terror into their enemies by that phenomenon. See *Hiftory of the Druids*, p. 73.

shakes his arm, and tosses on earth his heavy spear. Quivering it stands. Its studs tremble in moon-beams that glitter through oaken trees. We saw the thoughts of battle and of grief shake, by turns, his soul. The ghost of his father came. On a dark cloud that obscured the moon, he thoughtful leaned. He appeared like the gray-musing son of a rock, when his thoughts are of other worlds *. His red hair streams on winds; and his sighs are heard, like the voice of the breeze in Lego's reedy banks, when the ghosts of the dead wander there in mournful mists, without their fame.

The shield of Fingal sounds. The hills with all their rocks reply. The roes hear it, and start from their mossy bed. The fowls hear it, and shake, in the desart-tree, their fluttering wing. The wolf, wanderer of night, hath heard it, as he made for the slaughtered field, in hopes of prey. Sadly growling, he returns to his den; his hungry eye is red.—Shun his path, ye children of the deer.

We directed our steps to the king. Suloicha looked if the gray stars had retired in the east. His foot stumbled; it was on one of Dargo's chiefs. At the side of a gray rock he leaned. Half a shield is the pillow on which rests his head; over it wanders in blood his hair.—Why, he said, do thy wandering steps disturb the warrior's repose, when he can no longer lift the spear? Why didst thou banish, like a blast of the desart, my dream; for I had seen the lovely Roscana? My soul might have fled with the beam of my love; why didst thou call it back from its flight?

---

* By this is meant either a contemplative Culdee or Druid.

What was that beam of thy love, Roscana? replied Suloicha[*]. Was she fair as the down of the mountain; were her eyes like stars that sparkle through the thin shower; was her voice like the harp of Ullin; were her steps like the wave of the breeze, when it softly pours on the scarce-bending grass; and her form like the moon sailing in silence from cloud to cloud, in the calm of night? Didst thou find her, like the swan, borne on the breast of the wave; lovely, though lonely, in her grief?—Yes, thou didst; and that Roscana was mine. Stranger, what hast thou done with my love?—

" On the bosom of the wave I found the fair. In her skiff she had been sailing to the cave of her isle. There, she said, a chief of Morven was to meet her. But he did not come. I solicited her love, and invited her to I-una's plain. For three moons she bade me wait. Suloicha, she said, perhaps may come. Faster than the last moon she pined away. Before its light was quite gone, she failed. Like the green pine of I-una, which withered in its youth, she failed: its branches, by the blast, are left bare, and the children of music forsake its boughs.—On the shore of the isle, I raised the tomb of the fair. Two gray stones are there half-sunk in earth. A yew spreads its dark branches nigh: a murmuring fount breaks from the ivy rock above, and bathes the foot of the mournful tree. There sleeps the lovely Roscana. There the mariner, when he moors his vessel in the stormy night, beholds her fair ghost, enrobed in the whitest of the mountain-mist. ' Thy form,' he says, ' is lovely, O Roscana; fairer than my sails is the cloud of thy robe.'—Such have I seen her now in my dream; why was

---

[*] *Suloicha,* " one that sees well at night;" *Roscana,* " fair countenance."

was not my foul allowed to fly with the lovely beam of light? Come back to my dreams, O Rofcana; thou art a beam of light, when all is dark around!"

CHIEF of I-una, thou haft raifed the tomb of my love! If no herb of the mountain can heal thy wounds, thy gray ftone and thy fame fhall rife on Morven.—Rofcana! haft thou pined for me? Young tree of Moi-ura, are all thy green branches withered?— The wars of Fingal called me; I fent the fcout; but neither his fkiff nor he have fince been feen. In the morning, my firft look was on the deep; and in the evening the laft caft of my eye was on the main. Through night, my head leaned over the rock; but I beheld Rofcana only in my dream. Chief of I-una!—but thy voice has failed. Thy face, amidft moon-beams, is pale: thy eyes are flames that are dead. Friend of my Rofcana! thy tomb fhall rife.

LIKE the fall of a lofty oak in the calm gathering of night, when the woods and rocks fhake with the found, the fhield of the king again is heard. It calls his people together. We bend on our fpears with the fteps of fpeed; our way is by the tomb of Cu-rach.—Who mourns in filence on its green turf? he heeds not either the fhield of the king, or the gray dawn of the morning. It is Coffagalla. He miffed his mafter at home. His ears are up, upon his rock: he fnuffs the wind in all its points: he turns to every breeze that fhakes the tufted grafs; but his mafter is not there. No ruftling leaf, no fparrow's wing in the wood, ftirs unobferved by Coffagalla. But Curach is not come. He feeks his fteps in the battle. He finds his hand on the edge of the ftream: the foam a-round it is ftained with blood. Mournful he bears it with him, and his stream of tears descend. He lights, as he walks along, on Curach's grave. On his breast, above it, the white-footed dog is stretched. Under his neck lies the arm.—I see him as I pass: the tear is in my eye: I think of the white-breasted dog and Oscar *.— A moment I lean on the head of my spear: the crowding of grief hath swelled my soul. But I must not forget the battle. I step aside to bring the mourner with me; but he will not come. Three times his howl is heard; his soul in the cry is gone. Ah! thou art cold as the clay of earth; no breath is in Coffagalla. Why this dimness of my sight? My soul of battle fails. But the shield again awakes it. His heroes are gathered around the king.

LIKE the many rays of the sun glittering through the watery cloud, when the hunter fears the storm; so, thick rise before Comhal's son the gleaming spears of Morven and Innisfail. Curach is low. A thousand heroes look in silence on Fingal. Who shall have the battle?—Fergus stands behind: no field of such fame had yet been his. In his hand he holds his spear: without thought he tears away the rough beard of its shaft; the mark of its strife in war. His breast beats with hope. Battles swell in his soul: the blood glows in all his veins. His eyes are two stars in watery mist, when

---

* Alluding to the death of Oscar, and the grief of Bran on that occasion; a scene so affecting, that few passages of Ossian are oftener repeated than that which describes it in these beautifully-tender lines, which I may be pardoned for giving in the original, as the translation is already so well known.

—Chruinnich iad uime na fluaigh,
S gach aon neach ri buirich thrnagh;
Cha chaoineadh Athair a mhac fein,
S cha ghuilcadh a bhrathair e:

Cha chaoineadh piuthar a brathair,
'S cha chacineadh mathair a mac;
—Ach iad uile anns a phlosgail,
A geur-chaoine' mo chaomh Oscair.
 . . . . .
" Donnalaich nan con rem thaobh,
Agus buirich nan fean Laoch,
Gul a phannail fo co snitheach,
Sud is mo a chraidh mo chroidhe.
Cha d' fhidir duine roimhe riabh
Gur croidhe feola bh' ann am chliabh;
Ach croidhe do chuibhne cuir,
Air a chu'dacha le stailinn," &c.

TEMORA, D. I.

when the night is silent, and the winds are retired to the defart. Over heroes that stand between, they view the mild face of Fingal.

WHERE, said the king, is the young eagle that rushed so late, with ruftling wings, through the paths of danger? No light staff in a boy's hand was thy spear, my son; it was no thistle's down with which it strewed the field. I see its beamy shaft marked with the scars of battle.—This day, be thou first in danger and in fame. Near thee, on his rock, shall be the steps of thy father: be like the eagle among the fowls of the heath, strong-winged son of Morven.—Bid the mighty bow before thee, but bind up the wounds of the feeble. The fame of heroes grows, as fall before them the proud in arms. But if the blood of a low-laid foe is on their spear, bards give their name no room in the song, and heroes turn away on their gray clouds when their ghofts appear in the course of winds. Fergus, spare the low; but when the mighty oppose, be thy arm like a grove on fire. My voice on the heath shall be a breeze; it shall raise on high the flame.

LIKE the dark-rolling of a tempeft, when it shakes the deep with all its isles, and heaves the white-headed billows, like mountains of snow, upon the shore of rocks; so Cuthon with his hoft came on. The aged hunter hears the sound, as he rises in the woody vale, from the foot of a rock, on the mossy bed where slept the roe. He turns about his ear. " It may be the deep murmur of thunder, rolling along the distant heath; but I see not the lightning, in its course, appear.—It is," then he saith, " the tempest of ocean: I will ascend the rock and behold its terrors."—He climbs the gray rock; but the face of the blue sea is calm: the sun lifts half his face above

the

the eaſtern hill; his beams glitter, through the warm ſhower, on the gray beard of the hunter, as he leans forward on his ſpear, liſtening to the growing din.—He ſees the hoſt of Cuthon. " Shall I not ruſh," he ſays to his ſoul, " to the aid of Morven?"—Thou needeſt not, fighter of the wars that are paſt: thou mayeſt wait on thy rock till the ſtrife is over; for the warriors of the king are many, going down in their terrible joy.—See! Fergus moves with kindled wrath before them, tall as a ghoſt of the defart, when he comes ſhaking the waving heath with his ſteps. He catches the green groves, as he paſſes, in his hands, and overturns them in his ſport, as the whiſtling boy lops, with his playful ſtaff, the flowers. In his head is the voice of thunder; his eye is the place of the lightning, and meteors form his waving hair. The nations ſee it, and tremble.—So moves Fergus. A troubled cloud behind him move his heroes.

THE battle joins. Moruth ſhakes. The ſound of ſhields, the craſh of ſpears, and the voice of bards, aſcend. Whales tremble on their waves. Roes bound towards the defart. Fowls, on their ruſtling wings, fly over their mountains; or, trembling, fall with fear*. The white-handed daughters of the bow are aſleep on their mountain of groves: they hear their noiſe, as they paſs thro' pines over their booth: their dreams of danger riſe; they draw their veil over their head, and tremble for heroes.—Nor is your trembling without cauſe, white-handed huntreſſes of Moruth;

many

---

* The Galic reader will wiſh to ſee theſe lines in their native terror.

Le ſgreadail an lanna girbha
'S le caoitibh teine o'n cruaidh arma;
Chuir iad iaſg nan cuantaidh fluadhach,

Ann an caoilte caola fuara.
Chuir iad feidh nam beanntaidh arda
Gus na gleanntaidh fuara faſail;
'S eunlaith bhinn-ſhoelach nan euillteach,
Anns na ſpeuran le crith-oillte.

many of your heroes are low, and fhall no more purfue the deer.—
Many rills wander red on Moruth's heath: many a tall tree
ftrews all its branches there. Heroes lie, like groves overturned by
the lightning: their green branches fhake their fickly heads in all
the winds.

Two eagles rufh from oppofite rocks, and fight on the dark pillar of a cloud between. The blaft toffes them from fide to fide, and the ruftling of their wings is heard afar by quaking birds. Thefe eagles are Fergus and Cuthon, in the midft of their ftrife of fteel. Long and terrible is the combat of the chiefs; but neither this nor that prevails. A fon of Loda lifts, at length, his fpear between. " Why fhould not," he fays, " the hawk of heaven feaft on the fon of the king?"—Die thou, but not for the hawk, faid Fergus, as quick he lifts above him his blafting fteel. His head, fixed in the helmet, falls muttering to the earth, and marking, in its way, his own blue fhield. The body ftill had ftood, propped by the pitched fpear.

FINGAL beheld the danger of his fon, and half he drew his fword. But ftill he ftands in his place. " Why fhould I deprive the young hero of his fame; why fhould I make the mother of Fergus fad on her cloud?—No; beam of my early love, let not thy face be dark; our fon fhall yet prevail."

A GHOST of other times is riding by, on his wind. He fees with wonder the terrible ftrife of the warriors. " They refemble," he fays, " the heroes that have been *." He alights from the car of winds. He defcends with all his clouds, and ftands on the heath

to

---

* That predilection in favour of former times, fo common with old men in this life, is here very naturally afcribed by the poet to a being of another ftate.

to gaze on the ſtrife of heroes. The ghoſt, with his miſt, hides his ſon from the king; nor did many of the people ſee their chief.

Fingal trembled for his hero. He ruſhed in all his terrors from his place; like the boar of Gormul, when, wandering on the heath for food, he ſees the ſteps of the hunter towards the place of his young. The rocks hear his voice, and ſhake with all their branchy trees.—So ſhook the voice of Fingal the rocks of Moruth; and his bard poured before him, like the roar of a red mountain-ſtream, the ſong.—Morven kindled, like the decaying fire, on the heath of Lora, when the ſpear of the hunter ſtirs it, and all the winds are awake. It ſpreads its flames from hill to hill: its columns of dark-curling ſmoke, with all their thundering noiſe, aſcend. Ghoſts ſport in its clouds, and paſs through the darkneſs of its flame. The roe hears its ſound at a diſtance. She thinks of her ſon in his moſſy bed. The big tear trickles from her eye. She flies to look for his ſafety.

The people of Cuthon fled, or fell. We purſued them over the ſtream of Moruth. Cuthon himſelf ſtood, wounded, in his place, like a rock which the ſea hath half-conſumed below. The mariner, as he paſſes, fears its fall, though ſtill it ſeems to defy the ſtorm.— He ſaw the coming of the king, and graſped with joy his ſpear. But Fingal ſaw his blood, and would not lift the ſword. Sullen, after his people, he retired. His ſteps are ſlow through Moruth. The furtheſt bank is ſteep. Its face he thrice attempts to climb; but thrice in the attempt he fails. He clings by a withered thiſtle; but it yields.—Backward in the ſtream the mighty falls!—Moruth ſounds along its winding courſe, like the fall of rocks with their

ſhaggy

shaggy woods, when the thunder rolls above them in clouds, and the valleys, with all their herds, are trembling.

We flew on our spears to assist the chief: but his face was pale, and the darkness of death was gathering about him, a night without moon or stars.

And art thou fallen, said Fingal with a sigh, art thou fallen, who hast this day been so mighty?—How fleeting is the life of the warrior!—In the morning he goes forth to strew the plain; but his friends receive him a clay-cold corse at night!—His aged mother and spouse of love prepare the feast, around the blazing oak. At times, they listen for his return. The tread of feet is in their ear; the pale moon points out the crowd. " He comes!" they say, as with joy they rush forth.—They meet his bier!—The life of the warrior is a wintery day; short, dark: its streaks of light on the heath are few.—Fergus, bid the friends of Cuthon take him. Bid them also, this night, partake of the feast of Fingal; the deer of their own hills are distant.

Cuthon heard the king, and reached his hand; while a few words trembled on his lips. " Fergus, take thou that shield; Fingal, king of heroes, be thine the rod *. My soul mounts on the meteor's wing † to the abode of the brave and good. With my

fathers

---

* The Druids, and most other pretenders to supernatural power, are said to have worn a white rod, called *Slatan druì'achd*, i. e. *the Druid's rod*, or *magic wand*. The virtues ascribed to this weapon were so great, that we may suppose it would not be forgot in a day of battle. But whether it is this precious wand, or his spear, that Cuthon is here resigning to Fingal, cannot be determined with certainty, though the first is most probable from the name in the original:

Gabhfa Fhear'ais mo sgia
'S aig Fionn nam fiann biodh an t fat.
See *Hist. of the Druids*, p. 10.

† Tha m'anams' *air rioluin* a triall
Gu ionada fal nam flath.

That souls on their departure from the body take their flight to the other world in such vehicles, is an opinion which still prevails, in some measure, among the

fathers let my body be placed: let our reſt be together in the green iſle."

We move to the feaſt along the heath. We diſcover through the trees, the ſteps of age. It was the feeble hunter on the rock; he who trembled for Morven's heroes. Thrice had he tried to toſs the ſpear on which he leaned, and thrice his ſighs aroſe. He felt the trembling of age on his hand, and ſaw his locks white with the ſnow of years, as with them he wiped away the tear that dimmed his ſight.—But when the danger of Morven grew, his youth returned, and all the thoughts of feeble age were forgot. He ran to aid them from his rock. He ſaw, when he came near, the ſtrife was over; and returned again, low-humming the ſong, to his wood. The robe of other years, we ſaw, had failed. His worn-out ſhield and gray beard, ſupply along the breaſt its want. Behind, it is alſo torn; but the ſkin of a boar conceals the rent. —" Bring," ſaid the king, " to the needy this robe; and bid him come with our people to the feaſt."—" The garment," he replied, " the gift of the king, I take; but cannot wait, this day, for his feaſt."

Fingal knew the voice of Lugar; he knew the gray dog of his friend. He went with his wonted joy to meet him; but bade his people ſtand away, that the aged might not bluſh.—Chief of Moiallin, he ſaid, where ſo long haſt thou been? I rejoice to ſee the friend of my youth. A hundred fair cows, with all their calves, thou gaveſt me then on Drimcola's heath. Twenty horſes alſo

were

the vulgar Highlanders, who generally believe that certain meteors, to which they give the name of *Dr'eug*, portend the death of eminent perſons. This Druidical notion, with ſeveral others, owes its long continuance to the frequent repetition of Oſſian's poems.

* The

were thy gift, the children of the rein; and five ships, safe riders of the sea, with all their sails and nodding masts. The like boon, Lugar, shall now be thine. No generous deed shall ever be forgot by Fingal.

I am not Lugar, the aged replies: I had rather die without a friend to lay me in the narrow house, than take the bounty, due only to him, in his stead*.

—" To thee it is due; and thine shall be the gift. But first thou shalt, for seven days, prolong in Selma the feast. Seven heroes shall then guide thee home. They will remain in Moi-allin to smooth the road before thy aged feet; to ward off every rougher blast that might toss thy gray hairs."

FINGAL led the aged by the hand. We pursued our way with the people of Cuthon, to the feast. A gray stone met us on the heath; and the words of peace were heard from Lugar.

" WHY

* The attachment of Lugar to his friends was great, when it made him forget all the feebleness of age, and rush down, with the ardour of a youthful warrior, to battle. But his modesty under his reverse of fortune, and the spirit with which he bore his poverty, are more striking features in his character. The generosity and delicacy with which he is treated by Fingal are no less remarkable. *Dan Liughair*, or "the song of Lugar," beginning with

La gan deachaidh Fionn do thigh Le'ir
Pu lionar ann ceir agus fion, &c.

is still a favourite of all admirers of ancient Galic poetry; and is so sure to meet with the approbation of the hearers, that a sentence to that purpose, supposed to have been first spoke by some Culdee, or son of the rock, to whom Ossian repeated it, is generally added to it.

" Mile beannachd dhuit gach re,
Oisin fheilidh is binne gloir;
Arson aon fgeoil co maith blagh
Sa dh' airis thu riabh red' bheu."

The modest shyness of Lugar is still highly characteristical of the generality of his countrymen, who wear the best face in the world under the galling load of oppression and the pinching rigours of poverty. With the greatest industry they conceal from all about them how small *a handful of meal is in the barrel*, giving cheerfully away, to the very last, a share of it. And there have been frequent instances of nobody's knowing that the *little oil in the cruise* was spent, till the lamp of life, for want of a supply, was quite extinguished.

* The

"Why," he said, "should they who go together to the feast meet in battle any more? Why should the voice of strife be heard among the race of those who reaped the field together, in the years that are long since past; among the race of those who now ride, hand in hand, upon their clouds; never sad but when they see the war of their sons. Raise this gray stone, the daughter of the rock, on the heath of Moruth. The children of the years to come shall mark it. They will ask the aged warrior what it means. 'Lead me,' he will say, ' to the place.'—With short, equal steps, they walk beside him. The blunt spear supports his hand; and his gray dog, blind with years, attends his steps. The evening is calm. The song of birds is in the woods; the voice of hinds is on the hill; but the aged hears them not. The sun is bright as it goes down. He half-sees the parting beam: its rays are glittering in his few gray hairs. In two white, parted locks, like mine, they hang before him, as he lowly stoops, and wave around the blunted spear.—He hath reached the place; he hath felt, with joy, the stone. ' It is,' he cries, ' the stone of Moruth!—Here,' leaning to it his weary back, he adds, ' here your fathers met in peace: they laid their hands together to rear this gray stone. Forget not, children, the peace of your fathers; remember it when you behold the stone of Moruth *'—Speak, O stone, to the years that

---

* The custom of setting up such pillars to ratify agreements and to commemorate them, seems to have generally prevailed among ancient nations. We find frequent instances of it in Scripture: (see Gen. 31. 51. and Josh. 24. 26.) The Ἑρμαι, Fauni, Termini, all the Mercurial heaps and pillars among the ancient Greeks and Romans, and those pillars which the old Ethiopians and Arabs held in such veneration, had probably the same origin. The excessive regard paid to these objects, and the custom of calling them to witness their most solemn protestations, led men by degrees to think there resided in them some divinity. The little heaps or mounts called *Si-dhuin*, or *hills of peace*, so frequent in the Highlands,

that wander beyond the fun, and fhall not for ages come forward to hear its morning voice: tell them, and the children who fhall behold them, that here we bade the battle ceafe.—Let the mofs of years cover thee, thou fign of peace on Moruth; let the ghofts of the dead defend thee. Let no unfriendly hand; no ftormy blaft, while Moruth's heath fhall laft, or that dark ftream fhall run, come nigh thee!"

THE night was fpent in the feaft. With morning the people of Cuthon retired. The bards raifed the mournful fong to their chief; nor were the harps of Morven filent.

CUTHON! thy arm was mighty, and thy foul of battle great. Often have I feen thee hover, a dark cloud from ocean's mift, above the field of thy fame. But now I fee thee not; though at times I hear thy blaft in the gray hair of Moruth's pine. I hear thee, when I fit beneath it, as now, in the gathering of the evening fhades, and liften to the murmur of the paffing ftream.— Sweet is thy nightly fong, O ftream; fweet is thy hum in the wandering of thy courfe.

BUT it is late, and the bard will retire from the ftorm of night; for the ruftling wing of the heath-cock, lighting on his moffy bed, is heard. Is not that his voice, bidding his mate to hafte her home?—Mate of mine! Evirallin! the time hath been when thus I cried, from my booth, to thee. Now I cry; but there is no friend to anfwer, fave the mimic rock, and the voice of the hollow ftream. Fingal is with his fathers. Ofcar is no more. Evirallin is

lands, are ftill approached with awe, and fuppofed to be inhabited by *genii*.—They were generally fituated on the boundaries between different clans and poffef- fions; and probably contributed much to maintain among them peace and good neighbourhood.

† In

is in her cloud; and the voice of Malvina is silent*. My fathers, when shall Ossian be with you? My friends, when shall the the bard join you? When shall the short days, the long nights of my many-coloured life be over? My friends are gone: their memory, like the stones of their tomb, is half sunk; and the place of their abode is desolate.

But such changes are not the lot of the bard alone. Lugar! thou hast had thy share. I have seen the heroes feast in thy hall. Thy lights of wax were many; and plentiful was thy feast of shells. Though a cold, shapeless ruin now, thy palace was then the abode of a king †.—Such have I seen the dwelling of Lugar. But as the warm season, in the rolling of years, is changed; Lugar wandering, with his spouse, in want again was seen.—I passed through Moi-allin's vale ‡: but the house of Lugar was empty.

---

* In the following poem Malvina is a speaker; so that it seems to have been composed before this.

† The whole contrast of this passage is beautiful; but the two lines of which this sentence is a translation are exceedingly striking, as the opposition is so quick, and a group of interesting images are strongly painted in them, with only a single touch.

    Ged tha e 'n dlugh na aibhist fhuair,
    Bha e uair a b' aros Righ!

‡ Perhaps there was never any language better adapted for poetry than the Galic, as almost all its words are not only energetical, and descriptive of the objects they represent, but are also, for the most part, an echo to the sense. Harsh objects are denoted by harsh sounds, in which the consonants greatly predominate; whilst soft and tender objects and passions are expressed by words which bear some analogy to them in sound, and which consist, for the greatest part, of vowels. Hence, in the hand of a skilful poet, the sound varies perpetually with the subject of discourse, and assumes the tone of whatever passion he is at the time inspired with. Any person acquainted with the Galic, will see the justness of this remark, from the different specimens inserted in the course of these notes. It is generally so obvious, that a stranger to the language may observe it, notwithstanding the number of quiescent consonants which oppress the Galic. In p. 244, for instance, the "hoarse-roaring of a wave

The kid of the roe fed on its green top where inward it fell, in the hall of heroes. The owl, in his window, covered her head with the ivy-branch; and the fwallow fluttered around her. The deer cool their fides in the ftream before his door; and feem as if they were mufing on his lot.—Sons of the mountain, have you feen Lugar? Ah! you are glad, for his fhafts will no more difturb you.—But yourfelves, like him, fhall one day fail. Your companions will look for you in the vale which you ufed to haunt. Your fons will fhake their heads, for they know not where to find you.

VARIOUS, O life, like the feafons of the year, are thy changes! Once, I fmiled in the fummer of youth; and laughed, like thee, tall pine, at the winter's ftorm. My leaf like thine, I faid, fhall always be green, and my branches in age fhall flourifh. But now my withered arms are bared of all their leaves; and my gray hair, like thine own, is the fport of winds, and trembles in every blaft.

TALL

wave on a rock" is defcribed by words which prefent the letter *r* in almoft every fyllable:

———— ftairirich
Meafg charraige cruaidh a garraich.

And a fimilar idea is exprefled much in the fame manner in p. 247:

Gan ruaga le ftoirm toirt nualan
A'r carraig chruaidh meadhon barach.

On the contrary, any perfon who turns his eye to the fpecimens in p. 145 and 202, where the poet is under the influence of fome of the fofter feelings, will find the moft predominant founds to be *ci, ae, aoi, eo, eei*, and the like.----The original of the paffage which gave rife to this note, is added as a further illuftration of the remark. Grief is the predominant paffion in it; and *ai, iu, ua, uai*, &c. are the predominant founds.

A' finbhal gleannan na Moi'alnin
Fhuaras ua fhafach tigh Liughair,
Minnein na h carb' air a dhruim uaine,
'Sa fuaine finte 's an fhardaich aoibhein.
Na uionaig bha inn na h oi'che,
'S eigheann a' cuir duibhr' air agh. idh,
An gaoth-n ga chuartach; 's na ciar-aighean
Beul a thighe 's an t fruth, foi fmuairein.
A fhliochd nan fleit.hre, 'm faca fibh Liughar?
Ach 's cubhaidh gur ait leibh nach beo e.
Ach failnichidh fibhfe mar cifin,
'S biaidh ar daimhich aon latha gar fcoruich.
Crathaidh ar clann an cinn le fmalan;
Cho'n aithne dhoibh gleann ar co'nnidh.'

TALL pine of Moruth, we have once feen better days; but they have fled, on their darkly-filent wing, over the heath to the defart.

THE FALL OF TURA:

A POEM*.

THE ARGUMENT.

FINGAL, on his return from an excursion which he had made to the Roman province, is received by the congratulatory song of the virgins in his palace of Tura. While they are at the feast, a bard arrives to intreat the aid of Fingal in behalf of Ci-
'va-dona, whose story is told. In the morning a part set out on this expedition, while the rest pursue the chase, leaving only the women and children at home, with Gara to attend them hard by, in case of any alarm or danger. Unfortunately the house took fire, while they were asleep; and all that were in it perished. This loss is described, and pathetically lamented, by Ossian; and by Malvina, to whom the poem is addressed in the beginning, and who bears a part in the end of it.

WHO comes, pouring his voice on the night? Art thou a ghost that hast not received thy fame? Is thy wandering still on the vapour of the fenny mist; and dost thou come with thy complaint to Ossian's ear?—Pour thy voice, then, son of night! my ear, within its gray lock, leans forward to thy tale. Pour thy voice, ghost of night! that the bard may know thy name.

R r THE

* This poem is known by the names of *Lofga Taura*, and *Laoidh Ghara's nam ban*, " The burning of Tura," or " The elegy on Gara and the maids of Morven." The unfortunate accident which it records, partly accounts for the sudden decline of the bard's family and friends.---The latter part of the poem is generally repeated as a separate piece, by the title of *Offian a' caoi' nam Fiann*, " The lament of Ossian for his friends."

ᵇ Mal-

THE FALL OF TURA:

THE found comes, growing on the wing of the rolling breeze. It comes, like the figh of the mountain-ftream that falls, between trees, from the height of rocks. It rifes from its dark bed, at times, through the mift of foam, and reaches by halves the ear of the hunter. "Lora!" liftening from his booth he fays, "the voice of thy weary ftream is fweet; I love the murmur of thy fteps through the rocky vale, though it often foretels the ftorm."

YES, hunter of rocs, the evening voice of Lora is fweet; but fweeter far is that in Offian's ear. It is foft as the found of departed bards in the gale of the reed. It is foft and mournful, as the fong of Malvina when fhe fees the ghoft of Ofcar: the evening is calm, and the breeze fcarce waves the down of the lonely thiftle. —It is fhe; it is the love of my Ofcar; Malvina, lonely bird *. She comes, like the moon on her folitary mountains, when her fteps in clouds are flow, and her face through thin mift is pale. She comes, fair light, to mourn for her fifters' fall. Their place is dark: the mark of their footfteps is loft, as the courfe of the ftars that fell from their blue place in heaven; as the moon when fhe has retired within her dun robe in the fky.—Yes, Malvina, their place is dark; and the fteps of thy grief, on the hill of heath, are lonely.

DAUGHTER of Tofcar, bring my harp. Kindle the foul of the bard with thy voice of fongs. Awake it from the flumber of years: the night of age is unlovely and dark. It is dark, Malvina; but thy fong is a beam of light. Its found is pleafant, as the harp of

fpirits

---

* Malvina, of whom Offian fpeaks fo often in his poems, was the love of his fon Ofcar, who died when he was very young. (Temora, B. i.) Offian always treats her with peculiar tendernefs and affection; which fhe requited, to the very laft, with the moft dutiful and attentive regard.

† Ths

spirits on their gale, when they are seen at noon, on their white ridgy mist, creeping along the silent-winding stream. Thy voice is pleasant: join it to the harp: pour it on my ear, through night, Malvina, lonely bird!

THE times that are past roll back, with their dim light, on the soul of the bard.

WE returned in our fame from the field of Arda *. The steeds of the stranger strode beneath us in their pride; and we rejoiced in the greatness of our spoil. The setting sun was yellow on the groves of the mountain; its beams on Tura were like the gold of the stranger. The face of the lake below is calm. The children admire the hills that hang beneath it, with their ivy-rocks in the midst of woods. They wonder to see the blue smoke of Tura, there, descend. The virgins of Morven stand, like rainbows, upon their mountain. They see the steps of our return; and in the joy of beauty they move to meet us. The sound of their hundred harps is up. The songs of music, mixed with these, arise.

"WHO comes," they said, " in the light of his strength; who comes gleaming in his steel? The steed of the stranger is proud beneath him: he paws with scorn the earth, and tosses on high his gray mane. The clouds of smoke, like the blue curling pillars that rise from Tura, fly, snorting, from his nostrils; and from his mouth hangs the foam of the stream. His neck bends on high, like the bow of the battle; and his two eyes are flames.—Who holds the glittering reins of the steed? who but Fingal, king of men?— Thy fame, O Fingal, is brighter around thee than sun-beams; in

its

* The most of this paragraph, with some others that follow, particularly before and after the song of the old bard, have been supplied from the tales, as the versification is broken and defective.

* The

its light thy thousands rejoice. The smile of peace is on their brow: they are calm as the smooth lake. They are as the river of Cona in the evening of spring, when the children of the stream leap in air for the buzzing wing.—But they that are calm in peace, were a tempest in the strife of war. Before them, strangers of the distant land! you have fled: in their presence, kings of the world! you have trembled. Your warriors, without their steeds and bright arms, return. ' Where,' you say, ' have you left your arms?'— Ask the sons of the mountain, they best can tell. Your own men are silent; they are ashamed: no bard gives their name to the song; no virgin comes, with her harp, to meet them. No; they weep in their secret halls, for their lovers have given their fame to Fingal. Yes, virgins of the distant land, you may weep: kings of the world, you may tremble. But Morven's maids will rejoice; with the voice of songs and the harp they will hail their heroes †."

Such was the song of Morven's maids in the day of their joy; when the gladness of their face was like setting sun-beams on the mountain of groves, and their peace like the green leaf of the oak, when it hangs, unshaken, over Lubar. Nor did your harps sleep that

---

† The religion, laws, and customs of the Caledonians, had all a tendency to inculcate their grand maxim of *behaving valiantly in war*. Such especially was the tendency of these congratulatory songs of their fair ones when they returned in triumph. With the same view of animating them to a gallant behaviour, the ladies often followed them to the field of action, where they were sometimes more than mere spectators. In the passage cited in the *Note*, p. 300, concerning the death of Oscar, there are, in almost all the editions I have met with of that piece, two lines (there marked in Italics) which intimate that their women were then present. The practice of other ancient and neighbouring nations gives a further probability to this custom, so different from the manners of modern times. See Lord Kaims's Sketches, B. i. Sk. 7.

* Hos-

that night, O bards, on the walls of echoing Tura. Their joyful, trembling voice is up. Their found at a diſtance is heard. The red oak is in a blaze; the ſpire of its flame is high. The traveller ſees its light on the duſky heath, as night ſpreads around him her raven wings. He ſees it, and is glad; for he knows the hall of the king. 'There,' he ſays to his companion, 'we paſs the night. The door of Fingal is always open. The name of his hall is, The ſtranger's home *."

THE feaſt is ſpread. The king wonders that no ſtranger from the darkly heath is come. " I will liſten," he ſays, " if I may hear their wandering ſteps." He goes. An aged bard meets him at the door. On leſs than half a ſpear he leans his bending weight. No ſteel glitters on his blunt ſpear: for the days of his ſtrife are paſt; his battles are all fought, and their noiſe is over.

THE king, with joy, led the ſtranger in. We ſaw his grief-red eye bedimmed with tears: we ſaw their path on his furrowed cheek. His few gray hairs hang, a thin, twiſted lock on either ſide, and mingle with the white beard on his breaſt. A youth ſtands behind him: his down-caſt face is the bed of grief: he bears the harp of the bard.

WE riſe to give the ſtrangers place. We bid them partake of our feaſt that ſmokes around. We bid the light of our joy

diſ-

---

* Hoſpitality is one of thoſe virtues which loſe ground in proportion as civilization advances. It ſtill ſubſiſts to a high degree in the Highlands; though vaniſhing ſo faſt, that, in ſome years hence, its exiſtence in ſome parts may be as much doubted as that of ſome other virtues aſcribed by Oſſian to his heroes. It is not many years ſince it was the general practice to look out every evening, whether any ſtranger appeared, before the doors were ſhut. When any had caſt up, the hoſt had manifeſtly more pleaſure in giving, than the gueſt in receiving, the entertainment. Sed tempora mutantur, et nos mutamur in illis.

* Si-

dispel their cloud of grief, and shine through the mist on their soul. But they were like the gray cloud of the morning, which climbs not half the mountain, though the sun in his brightness shines around.

THE aged, at length, took his harp, and poured in our listening ear his song.

" SITHAMA was a chief of other lands. His halls lifted their heads on Gormluba's banks, and saw their gray towers in its blue winding stream. Mountains spread their arms around the place, and aged woods defend it from the storm. Here, fifty times, the oak dropt its withered leaf on Sithama's head; and as oft bade he the people mark how fast their days decline. ' We wither,' he would say, ' as the grass of the mountain; we fade as the leaf of the oak. Four are the seasons of life, and restless they roll as those of the year. Some fall in youth, as the bud that is killed by the blast: others are like the leaf over which the mildew hath passed in the sultry day. Many fall, like my departed love, in the sickly autumn; and a few remain, like myself, till the winter of age. Since our season then is so uncertain, let us be renowned, he would say, while we may *.'

" The deer of his own hills sufficed Sithama: he fought not to drink, save of his own blue stream. When the feeble fought his help,

---

* Sithama seems to have been of the sect of the Druids. His parabolical manner of conveying instruction is agreeable to the most ancient times, and to those ænigmatical apophthegms which Laërtius ascribes particularly to the Druids. If the whole of this order were obnoxious to Fingal, their confidence of his readiness to redress the wrongs done even to one of them, and the alacrity with which he undertook it, reflect the greatest honour on his character. The highest heroism is to be above revenge, and to subdue one's enemies by kindness.

help, his blade leapt out of its dark sheath, and shone in their aid. The helpless staid behind his shield, and said, Here we are safe.

"The strife of friends arose. Duarma seeks the fall of his brother. The injured obtains Sithama's aid. But the gloomy Duarma prevails. Talmo falls in blood; and Sithama, the friend of the feeble, fails!—Duarma comes to Gormluba's streams. The son of Sithama is young. He admires the boss of the broad shield on the wall, and asks how the spear of battle is lifted. Over the heath he sees the strangers come, as night descends upon the grove. Short, but fast, are his steps to meet them: for Crigal had the soul of his father; he rejoiced in the presence of the stranger, as the green branch in the shower of the spring. He sees the face of Duarma dark; but he reaches his little hand. 'The feast,' he says, ' is spread; why should thy face be mournful?' Duarma makes no reply; but his spear on high is lifted. The youth attempts to fly; but alas! he flies in vain. Across the threshold of his father he is stretched. His soul comes, red, through the path of the spear.— His sister, from her window, sees Duarma's wrath. What shall the helpless Civa-dona do?—' Aged bard, canst thou not help me?' —The withered arm of the bard is propped by half a spear.—She wildly turns her to the other side. The window is there, from which virgins oft beheld their face of beauty in the flood. From its height she throws herself into Gormluba's stream. The bard with his harp goes, trembling, to the door. His steps are like the warrior of many years, when he bears, mournful, to the tomb the son of his son. The threshold is slippery with Crigal's wandering blood; across it the aged falls. The spear of Duarma over him is lifted;

lifted; but the dying Crigal tells, ' It is the bard *.'—A gray dog comes howling by, and in his fide receives the fpear.—The hall is on fire. Its flames are moon-beams in the vale. The bard feeks Civa-dona with their light, and finds her clung to a branch that wandered acrofs the ftream. Crigal is laid in his filent bed, and Civa-dona is clad in his robes. She goes with the bard to feek for aid.—King of Morven, the unhappy two are before thee; give the young and the old thine aid."

THE bard ceafed. The burft of his grief arofe. With the virgin-fifters of Morven Civa-dona retired. She retired, like a ftar behind its cloud, after its watery face hath fparkled a little through the ftorm. In her brother's robe, where it veiled her head, we faw the marks of Duarma's fpear.

THE tear ftarts into the eye of the king. With his gray lock he wipes it off. His heroes forget the feaft. " Reach me," faid Frefdal, " my fpear."

" THE day lifts above the hill his gray head †. Our courfe fhall be to Ardven's chafe. Ten heroes fhall vifit thence Duarma's hall: and the youth who wins her love, fhall remain with Civa-dona."

WE flew, light as ghofts when they retire from day. Gara alone remains at Tura; that no wandering foe may alarm our maids.—Daughter of Tofcar, why that burft of grief? Their hall is the houfe of joy yet. Dry, then, Malvina, thy tears, and give the reft of the tale to the fong.—The fong of grief is a ftream, O Malvina! It melts the foul of the mighty, and carries it along in its darkly courfe. Its murmur, though fad, is pleafant.

DOST

* The character and perfon of the bard were always held facred even by the moft unfparing cruelty.   † Fingal fpeaks.

A POEM.

Dost thou not remember, Malvina, the beauty of the ftranger, when the brightnefs of the day arofe, and the fun fhone on the heathy hill? Yes; for thou didft attend her, on thy fteed to Ardven, and then purfue the chafe with the king. It was then we beheld the beauty of Civa-dona, when thou didft retire, like the moon, behind thy mountains. She fhone, like a bright ftar over the broken edge of a cloud; but who could admire that ftar, when the full unclouded moon was feen?—Yet the ftar of Gormluba was fair.—White were the rows within her lips*; and like the

S f   down

---

* The poet carries the defcription of this lady to an unufual length, either to divert, for a little, Malvina's grief; or to pay the greateft compliment he could to her beauty, by giving fuch a portrait of one whom he allows her to have fo far excelled. The original is beautiful; but has had the misfortune to be confidered as only ideal; infomuch that it has got the name of *Aifling air dhreach mnai*, or "The vifion of the beautiful woman." Such as think it a trefpafs, will, it is hoped, forgive the inferting it here, for the fake of its admirers.

Innfeam pairt do dhreach na reul:
Bu gheal a deud, gu hur dlu.
'S mar chanach an t fleibhe,
Bha a cneas fa h eide' ur.
Bha a braighe cearclach ban.
Mar fheachda tla 's an fhireach,
Bha da chich air a h uchd cial'ach:
Be'n dreach fud miann gach fir.
Bu fhoithe' binn a gloir,
Shu deirge nan ros a beul.
Mar chobhar fios ra taobh
Sinnte gu caol bha 'lamh.
Bha 'da chaol-mhala mhine,
Du'-dhonn air liobh an loin.
A da ghruaidh air dhreach nan caoran,
'Si gu hiomlan faor o chron.

Bha a gnuis mar bhara-gheuga
Anns a cheud-fhas ur.
A folt buidhe mar orra-fhleibhte;
Smar dhearfa greine a fuil.

A later poet has been fo ftruck with this defcription, that, on hearing it, he naturally expreffed his defire of being made happy by fuch a beauty; " for whofe love he would render more than love; for whofe regard he would render more than regard; and always maintain an affection, which in the longeft revolution of days and nights, he promifed, fhould neither decay nor abate."—As thefe lines are in the fame meafure with the defcription of the lady, they are generally repeated along with it, as if they had been originally joined to it.

'S truagh nach mife am fear,
Annir nan rofg mall,
D'an tiubhra tufa gradh
Is bheirinn a dha da chionn,
Bheirinn gaol thar ghaol,
Bheirinn gradh thar ghradh;
Bheirinn run thar run,
Is mein thar mein a ghna;
'S nam biodh do chroidhe neo'fhuar,
Gun ghluafad as a chaoidh',
Bheirinnfe dhuit gradh
Nach crionadh a la na dh'oidhct.

down of the mountain, under her new robe was her skin. Circle on circle formed her fairest neck. Like hills, beneath their soft snowy fleeces, rose her two breasts of love. The melody of music was in her voice. The rose, beside her lip, was not red; nor white, beside her hand, the foam of streams.—Maid of Gormluba, who can describe thy beauty! Thy eye-brows, mild and narrow, were of a darkish hue; thy cheeks were like the red berry of the mountain ash. Around them were scattered the blossoming flowers on the bough of the spring.—The yellow hair of Civa-dona was like the gilded top of a mountain, when golden clouds look down upon its green head, after the sun has retired. Her eyes were bright as sun-beams; and altogether perfect was the form of the fair.---Heroes beheld, and blessed her.

We reached the hall of Duarma; but he was fled: he had heard of the fame of Morven. The elbow of his father leaned on a gray stone, as he lay along it on earth. His head hangs down on his hand; and his gray beard is strewed in dust. His sighs are deep on the wind; and his dim, tearful eye is red. He hears the rustling of our feet near Talmo's tomb.---" My son, my son," he cries, " it is pleasant to be so nigh the tread of thy ghost!"---We felt for the aged; we left him a part of the spoil.

We reached the place where Sithama dwelt: but it was dark and desolate. The fox started from its ruins; and the owl rested in the cleft of its broken wall. We looked for the window from which the fair had escaped; but it was fallen. The white stream leapt, roaring, over its heap of stones. We saw where the threshold had been marked with Crigal's blood. It had rested in the hollow that was worn in the stone by the frequent foot of guests.---Civa-dona

was

was sad; but we left Frestal to cheer her: it was he who had won her love.

FINGAL still waits us on Ardven. There we partake of his feast of deer.---Night comes: sleep descends: ghosts rise with all their mournful forms in our dreams. The harps of their bards are like the song of the tomb; their sound comes to our ear like the mountain-sigh, when it is heard from afar before the storm. Over us, in dark shapeless mist, they hang. The blast in frequent eddies comes: it rolls before it all their limbs. But still the forms return. They bend over us, leaning from the breast of their cloud; and often they heave the sigh.

THE sleep of the king was fled. Thrice had the faint howlings of ghosts awaked him. He ascends the hill to hear their words. He looks about him from the height. He sees the curling pillars of smoke ascend to the stars: he sees the spiry flames lift their dark-red head on high, above his hall. His shield is struck: his voice is up. " Tura flames through heaven!"

WITH the thunder we start, at once, awake. We fly like lightning over the heath of Colra. Its dark stream meets us in the vale. Each bounds over it, on his spear, with speed. The son of Ratho tumbles from the height of his. " Heed me not," he cried; " but fly: fly fast, and save my love."—In the current, twice he lifts his white eye above the stream: but, the third time, he sinks and dies.

WE came to Tura; but it was too late. The flames were hiding, in dark-red ashes, their head: the ruin falls, in heaps, above the dying coals. The door, half-burnt, is still shut; as the daughters of Morven left it, when they had retired to rest, in the midst of their joy. O why did they not find the way to it, when the flame of the kindled heath awoke them!—No morning, with its calm voice, shall ever dispel your slumbers, daughters of the mountains! The voice of the lover, no more, shall say "Awake."

WE turn to the ruin our back. We bend, in sadness, over our spears; and loudly bewail our loss.—Our hundred helmets, and our hundred bossy shields; our coats of mail, and swords of light; our hundred hounds, the young children of the chase; our studed reins, the rulers of proud steeds; and all our banners, redgreen meteors that streamed in air;—all these, were, that day, forgot; no hero remembered they were in the hall.—The burst of our grief was for our hundred fair, and for their little sons; that young grove of trees, growing in their robes of green, in the showery sun-beams of the spring.---They were young trees; but the flame catched their green heads, and laid their beauty, amidst ashes, low.---Malvina, fair light! it is not without cause thou art sad; for all the bright beams that attended thy course are extinguished. One mournful grave contains the remains of thy sisters.

WE stood all day, like the dark stream which the ice hath bound in its course on the mountain of cold.---The darkness of night would return unperceived, if a voice had not awaked us from our grief.---It is the burst of the voice of Gara. We look for him in the tower where he had rested; but he is not there. His voice ascends from a cave. The sad mourner there is stretched in grief. ---In the troubled dreams of his rest, the crackling flames had assailed his ear; he thought the foot of the foe approached. With a louder crash the roof falls in. The shield of the king, he
thinks,

thinks, is ſtruck. At once he ſtarts awake. His hair had been caught in the opening end of the beam on which he ſlept: he leaves it there, with all its ſkin. He ſees Tura low: he knows not that his blood, a red ſtream, deſcends. His pain, amidſt his grief, is forgot. " Virgins of my love, I will not ſurvive you," he ſaid as, expiring, he fell on the heath *.

NOR didſt thou die alone, O Gara: the days of many other heroes, in their darkly-ſilent heath, were few and mournful. They pined away like green leaves over which the mildew hath paſſed: they ſink in ſilence amidſt the moſſy heath of the hill. Like ghoſts that have not received their fame, they ſhunned the voice of joy †. They retired to their caves when roſe the ſound of gladneſs.

MAL-

* The *ur-ſgeuls* give a different account of the death of Gara, and relate ſeveral ſtrange ſtories concerning him, ſuch as his having been beheaded on the thigh of Fingal, &c. but theſe tales are maniſeſtly late and ſpurious, and therefore rejected.

† The melancholy ſtate allotted, after death, for ſuch as had not " received their fame," muſt have ſtrongly excited thoſe who believed it, to diſtinguiſh themſelves by ſuch brave and virtuous actions as might merit the praiſe of the bard. We juſtly laugh at many of the ſuperſtitions of our forefathers: but as, in the progreſs of all ſtates, ſuch a period muſt be, we have alſo reaſon to admire the wiſdom with which the Druids managed this engine, ſo as to make it generally ſubſervient to the intereſts of ſociety.---The ſuperſtructures of ſuperſtition, like very old towers, appear now odd and fantaſtic, as well as extremely incommodious; but they were uſeful in their own day, and moſt of them well adapted to the neceſſity of the times.

The firſt Chriſtian miſſionaries, in theſe countries, were ſo ſenſible of the advantage to be derived from ſome of theſe ſuperſtitions, among men who were not yet ripe for bearing the clear light of truth, that they did not ſo much attempt to ſtop their ſource, as to turn them into a new channel. With them, for inſtance, whoever was not initiated into the Chriſtian religion by baptiſm, was forced to wander after death, a mournful ſolitary ſhade, in the ſame ſtate as formerly thoſe who had not " received their fame." It was a notion in the Highlands till of very late, that the faint voices of children who had died unbaptized were heard in the woods, and other lonely places, bemoaning their hard fate.---All countries, as well as this, had once their ſuperſtitious æras; only they are the happieſt, which have got the ſooneſt through them.

MALVINA †! my cause of grief is great. Thou haſt loſt thy ſiſters, fair lights upon the mountains; but I ſurvive the race of heroes. I ſearch for them with my hands among the ſilent ſtreams which they uſed to haunt; but their tomb is all I find. Alas! the children of the years to come ſhall not perceive even this; they will ſeek it on the mountains, but ſhall not find it.—The chief of the days that ſhall be, will ſtand on the green hill where Tura was. Cona rolls below him in its pebbly bed. Its ſtream wanders, loſing its way, through woods; herds, along its banks, are ſeen to ſtray. Blue Ocean trembles at a diſtance. Iſles lift their green, frequent heads, above its wave; and the bounding mariner is ſailing towards the coaſt.—" This ſpot," the chief will ſay, " is lovely: here raiſe for me, in view of whales and roes, the lofty houſe."— They dig the green mound; the mound where Tura roſe. Spears, half-burnt, lift before them their heads; broken ſhields, amidſt aſhes, begin to appear. " It is the tomb of heroes," he will ſay; " ſhut again the narrow houſe." He calls the gray-haired bard, and aſks whoſe memory is contained in the tomb. The bard looks around for the light of the ſong: but his ſoul of age is dark; his memory has failed. He looks for his companions; but he ſees their tomb. He ſtands, perhaps, a ſolitary tree like Oſſian.—A ſolitary tree am I,

---

† What follows of this poem is generally repeated by itſelf under the title of *Oſſian a' caoidh nam Fiann;* but as it ſeems to have been originally a part of *Loſga Taura,* it is here reſtored to it. The great number of names, towards the end of it, occaſions ſuch a difference in the recitation of that part, as made it impoſſible to determine the true liſt with any degree of certainty. The catalogue of names, when repeated by itſelf, begins generally with theſe lines:

So far am faca' mi n Fhionn,
Chunacas ann Cian agus Conn,
Fionn fein is Oſcar mo mhac,
Raoini' Art is Diarmad donn.

I, O bard, on the lone mountains; its companions, one by one, have forsook it: drooping, it mourns their departure.

MALVINA.

AND are not the sisters of Malvina, likewise, green trees that have failed? Yes; and no young plant, in their room, is growing. The virgins are no more, and my cause of wo is great. In the day I look for them; but no trace of their steps is to be found, save the green tomb with all it stones of moss. In the season of night I mourn for them; but they are lights that have retired from their blue place in the heavens. I am like the gray star of the morning, when, sickly and pale, it mourns behind its companions. It mourns for a little, but its own light will soon grow dim. The huntress, rising on the heath, shall look up, but shall not see it. "We too," she says to her companion, "one day shall fail."

OSSIAN.

THE heart of Ossian is sunk in the night of his grief. It is like the sun in his dark-crusted cloud: no ray of light bursts through the gloom: no smile alights on the mountain-top; the silent valley, around its dark stream, is mournful.—The heroes have withdrawn their light, which shone, like the brightness of my arms, around me.

MALVINA.

THE lights around Malvina have also failed. My heart is like the moon when her darkness grows. I draw, like her, my veil over my face, and lament my sisters in secret. Yes; fair lights, I will not forget you, though you have hid yourselves in darkness: your memory is mournfully-pleasant.

Os-

Nor can I forget you, rulers of the storm of battle, though you now rest in your peaceful slumbers. Your image still dwells in my soul, though I shall see you no more, as once I have done, on the brown heath.—Here have I seen Fingal, king of men; Oscar and Ryno, beams of light; Artho of beauty, and the dark-brown hair of Dermid. Here have I seen the son of Lutha, the meek; and that soul without guile, Conchana; with the son of Garo the bold, the three Finans, and Fed. Here burnished the helmet of Eth; here whistled in winds the dark locks of Dairo; and here streamed, like banners, the red hair of Dargo. Here Trenar grew like an oak; Torman roared like a stream; Ardan stalked in his pride, like a tree lifting its green head above the valley of mist; Murno and Sivellan, beside him, smiled over blue shields. Clessamor of mighty deeds was here; and here the polished steel of Fercuth. Here arose the voice of Carril; and here thousands listened to the harp of Ullin. Here have I seen Moran and Fithil of songs; Connal of soft words and generous deeds; Lamdarga with his spear of blood; and Curach, whose arm was an host in the hour of danger.—And where art thou, Lugar, whose door was never shut; where is now thy voice, Fadetha of the loudest cry? where, Ronuro, are thy golden locks? where, Colda, are thy feet of deer? and where, Lumna, thy spear of battle? Where is mildly-looking Ledan; with Branno of arms, and Toscar of youth? Where are the hunters of the boar on Gormal, Machrutha, Colmar, and Comalo; Fillan, my brother of love, and ruddy Fergus of the mildest speech? Where is Crugal, blazing in his steel; and Dogrena, the light of heroes on the plain? Where, Aldo, is now thy beauty? and where,

Ma-

Maronnan, the strength of thy blue shells? Who will shew me the steps of Duchomar, the black but comely; or the face of Crigal, beam of love? Suino, Sorglan, and Conloch, have also failed; the three mountain-streams in our battles. Connal, the meteor of death, is no more; nor Gaul, the whirlwind by which our foes were scattered.—Heroes of my love, you have failed; none of you remains to shed the tear on the tomb of Ossian. No friend shall raise my gray stone, or prepare, on the lonely heath, my narrow bed. No; the heroes of Morven have all failed. But their memory shall dwell in the soul of the bard.

MALVINA.

SISTERS of my love, you have also failed: but in the soul of Malvina you still remain. My departing breath shall be a song in your praise.—Yes, Evirchoma, Darthula, Sulmina, I feel your warm beams pass often over my soul. They are like sun-beams of autumn, when they fly over the dark-brown heath of Lena; and the watery bow, with all its tears, is nigh.—Gellama, Moina, Minona! you once shone on these hills, though dim is now your beauty. Melilcoma, Colmal, and Annir, did your form of comeliness continue! or are you, in your thin clouds, still admired by heroes? Crimora, has thy beauty lasted! Gelchossa, where are the steps of thy loveliness?—Dersagrena, what is now become of all thy brightness? and where, Oi-thona, dost thou pour thy voice of love? Like the harp of the bard, when the chief of the people is dead, it was sweetly-mournful.—And, why should you be forgot, Evirallin and Clatho, fairest of all the lights that have shone on Morven! Joy is a stranger in Selma, since you have set in darkness: the songs of virgins ever since have ceased; and the harps of the bards

T t   are

are silent.—But the tears and the voice of Malvina would fail.—Fair beams! you have left your sister mournful.—Dimly she shines upon the solitary mountains, and her steps are lonely. Pale and sickly is her countenance, as the face of the moon when it appears in heaven, a gray cloud, in the season of the sun, after all the stars of its course have retired.—-Sisters of my love! you are stars that have failed; but your memory is still with Malvina.

OSSIAN.

* CEASE, Malvina, from thy tears. Thou makest the aged sad. As the night on her wings is almost past, so the night of our grief will soon be over. It is like the dream of the huntress of the roe, in the cleft of her rock. In thought she falls from the height of hills: she alights in the stream below: her soul, like the white-breasted bird of the stream, is now above, and now beneath the flood. She cries to her love, but he cannot come nigh her: her soul flies on clouds: she sees him behind her, mournful at the tomb of her rest. She longs for his coming, for she is sad.—Her own sigh awakes her: she lifts her head beneath her rock; and the dream of her terror is over.—Such a dream is our life, huntress

---

* In this place there is sometimes repeated a passage which seems rather to have been the opening of some other poem than any part of this. As it is tender and beautiful, I shall here give the translation of it.

Oss. Why flow thy tears like the stream of the fountain; why sighs thy voice like the gale of Lego?

MALV. Dost thou ask the cause of my grief, when the thistle grows in Selma, and the bats dwell in the house of Fingal? I listened to a noise in the blast; but it was not Cuthullin's car: I saw a beam of light on Lena; but it was not the spear of Oscar.—-Oscar! thy spear is a dweller of the tomb, and thy shield is become dim in Selma? I saw its boss; but it was covered with mist, and its many thongs had failed.

Oss. Love of my Oscar! we too shall fail, and Selma itself in its green tomb shall moulder.—-But the slumbers of the tomb are sweet, O Malvina! let not thy soul grieve for those who dwelt in Morven. They have been beams that shone in heaven for a season, and their path was marked with day.—--

A POEM.

refs of woody Cona. Our friends, before us, shall soon awake us. In the voice of the reedy gale, dost thou not already hear them say, " Malvina and Ossian are soon to join us."—Malvina! their sound to me is pleasant. It is like the murmur of Lora to the traveller of night, when he comes, wandering, over the desart. His face is towards Selma; but it is hid in darkness. No light but the stormy meteor is seen on the heath. The narrow-winding path on the brow of the mountain is lost; and the shriek of ghosts is heard around. At length he hears the voice of Lora, leaping from its broken rocks. His joy returns. " Selma," he says, " is nigh!"—Such * is the joy of Ossian wandering in darkness,

* This passage and one or two more of the same kind, seem to rise somewhat higher in sentiment than the general strain of these poems. As this, in the opinion of many, may render their antiquity more doubtful, I have here inserted the original, in order to give such as understand it a fair opportunity of judging for themselves. Some of the lines, it is possible, may have been altered or interpolated; but as the most of them, from their antiquated air and obsolete expression, are manifestly old, I was loth to reject any of them upon a mere suspicion. Passages of this nature assume a very different look in a translation from what they have in the original, as they must be stript of their ancient garb, and dressed out in those expressions that are appropriated by modern composition. Besides, as all metaphors do not run equally well in all languages, nor the same images tally in one tongue so well as in another, several alterations must be made in order to give the style an uniform look. Some small variations, on this account, have been made in the passage before us; particularly, the words rendered " the light of our joy shall not be darkened," are in the orginal " the light of our joy shall gleam as the blade of Luno." The genius of the English language requires frequently a little softening of those images which appear natural and unaffected in the Galic.

'Sco ait is fin Ossian anrach
Ri claisdin cagar nan laiuhse
Ga chuirre' gu talla a thiunsir,
Aite-cu'ail nan caomh air iontrain.
 Ann talla nam flath am bi bron,
Ne saoi le deoir air a ghruaidh,
An t athair an caoi' an t Oscar,
Sam mair ofnai' Mala-mine?
 An fpionar Aoibhir-aluin o Gradh,
No'n loisgear aros nam Fiann;
An fgarar na cairdean o cheile,
No'n dealnigh an t eug gach diais?
A reul na maise! ni h amhluidh,
Ach dealruidh mar lann an Luin ar follus;
Arn aoihhneas mar an fluirge cha traigh
Scho'n shailnich mar aghaidh na Gcliaich.
 Ar canimh mar shulluis a chaochail
'Sna speura faoin os ar cionn
Cha bhi nis mo; ach taomaidh
Le ceol aobhach an aiteal tharuinn.
—Inghean Thofcair, uifeag at aonar
Leig air faondra mata do thuirfe.

nefs, when a voice tells him, that, foon, he will reach his fathers. —Malvina, fhall we not then meet the friends for whom we mourn; and, in their converfe, again rejoice?—Shall there be any grief dwelling in the clouds; fhall there be any mourner there? ---Shall the father, in that place, lofe his Ofcar; or Malvina mourn over the tomb of her love?---Shall Evirallin, there, be torn from her Offian; the hall, like Tura, be burnt; or the friends by death be divided?---No; fair beam! the light of our gladnefs fhall not be darkened: our joy no more fhall wafte as the moon, nor fhrink as the fea, and retire. Our friends, no more, fhall be ftars that forfake their blue place, and leave their companions mournful. No: they will always attend us in the joy of our courfe; they will pour their light and their glad fong around us. ---Give, then, thy tears to the wind, daughter of Tofcar! ceafe from thy grief, Malvina, lonely bird!

CATHLAVA:

CATHLAVA*:

A POEM.

The ARGUMENT.

Ronnan having sent his scout to assist Sulmina in her escape from her father's house, looks for her in vain all night. In the morning he consults an old Druid, from whom he learns that she had been intercepted and carried off by Lava, to whom her father had formerly promised her in marriage. Ronnan, with his followers, pursues Lava, and lands in the night upon his coast, where he meets with an old man, to whom he had early owed his life, and to whom he makes himself known after he had heard his story. Next morning, the two parties having engaged, Lava is slain; and Sulmina, who out of concern for Ronnan had come to the field in disguise, is found there, after the battle, mortally wounded. Ronnan, having established his old friend Runma in Lava's possessions, returns home; carrying with him the body of Sulmina. The poem is addressed to the son of Arar, who appears to have been a young bard.

THOU sittest by thine own blue stream, son of Arar; thy harp lies silent by thy side: why dost thou not praise the departed? Around thee, they hover on clouds, dark-bending over the place of their rest. But no voice is heard, save that of the rustling breeze, and murmuring brook. Why so silent, son of Arar? Dost thou not know the sons of fame are around thee?

" Thou knowest the fame of the departed, Orrant† ! the deeds

of

---

* *Cathlava*, " the battle of Lava." This poem is sometimes called *Dan an sbir leidh*, " the song of the gray man," from the appearance made in it by an aged Druid.

† Since the order of the bards has ceased, almost all the ancient Galic poems are ascribed to Ossian. To the most, and best of them, he is justly entitled; but as this seems to be only an imitation of his

manner

of other times are funbeams around thy foul. Take then the harp, and let the bard of youth hear the fong, that he may pour its light on future times. So fhall their names be not forgot on their hills when thy harp is hung in thy filent hall; when thy voice of mufic is ceafed, like the gale when it fleeps in the trees, in the calm evening of autumn."

MY voice indeed fhall ceafe, and my harp ere long be filent; but their fame fhall not be forgotten. Thou mayeft liften to their praife, fon of Arar, and leave it to the bards of the years to come.

ON thefe hills lived Dumor of fpears; his daughter of beauty moved graceful on his hills. Her harp was the joy of his hall. Lava faw the maid, and loved her. His arm was ftrong in the wars of Dumor, who promifed him the fair Sulmina. But the maid refufed her love, and gave her foul to Ronnan;—Ronnan of the fair hair and mildeft look, whofe dwelling ftood by the ftream of Struthorman. He heard of Sulmina's grief, and fent his fcout to bring her to his hills.

SHE went with the fon of night: but Lava met her on the heath. An oak and a thoufand thongs confine the fcout: a dark-wombed fhip receives the maid. Loud were her cries, as they bounded over the ridgy deep: "Ronnan, relieve me; O Ronnan, relieve thy love!"

BUT he hears thee not, haplefs maid! By the fide of a ftream he fits, thinking thou doft come.

" What detains thee, Sulmina, fo long? What keeps my love from the ftream of her promife? I liften, but hear not the foft tread

---

manner, the name of Orran is here retained, though that of Offian is no lefs frequently ufed by thofe who repeat it.

Co b' fhearr fios na thu fein,
Offian, air beus na dh'fhalbh? &c.

tread of thy foot; it is but the breeze, ruftling in the aged tree of Senar. Come, my love, like the roe to meet her companion: why are thy fteps fo flow on the heath of Gormul?

The night is long without my love. Why ftand ye ftill, ye travellers of the blue fky? Have you forgot to run your courfe; or are you, like me, waiting for your loves?—Sun of the morning, why doft thou forget to rife; why doft thou fleep fo long in thy eaftern chambers?—I know it; thou haft met with thy Sulmina; for I fee not her fteps in the heavens. Yes, you are together, fair lights! with your children, the leffer beams, in their green, trembling beauty, around you In your chambers of clouds, you are together, and there the night is fhort. But, here, it is long; for the blue eye of Sulmina is abfent.—Lift thy yellow head from thy eaftern cloud, fon of the morning! Shine on the path of Sulmina, O fun! and bring her to the hill of her promife.

The gray-dark morning comes. The fun fhines; but it brings not his beloved. He fees a cloud rife before him. It affumes the form of Sulmina. His arms are fpread; he flies to grafp the fhape. But a blaft, dark-rufhing from the mountain, comes. Its path is through the form of Sulmina.

Ronnan feared the fign. He went to the aged Senar*. Under

---

* *Sean'ar*, "the man of age." He appears to have been a Druid, living in his grove of oaks. His appearance is in the original fo awful and ftriking, that the poem, as already obferved, takes frequently its name from it.

Au crith-thaice ri luirg fein,
Fui' gheig dhoillein dharaich,
Lan ogluidheachd:— a' crom-aomadh,
'S fheafag aofda fios mu bhrollach.

—Air lar tha fhuil a' dearcadh
Ach anam ann co 'radh thaibhfe.

The reply of this oracle is clear and laconic,

Macan ann fis cruaidh,
Barca; thar cuan, na deann;
Shuilmhine! 'scruaidh leam do ghlaodh,
A 'taomadh air tuinn gun fhurtachd!

It was from this pretenfion of the Druids to fupernatural knowledge, and from the many

der the awful shade of his oak he finds him, leaning on his own trembling staff. His head of age stoops to the ground; his gray beard hangs down on his breast, and his dim eyes are fixed on earth. But his soul is mixed with the spirits of air, and his converse is with ghosts.

WHAT seest thou of my love, said Ronnan; what seest thou of Sulmina?

I SEE, said the aged, a youth tied to an oak: a vessel rides the wave. Sulmina pours her voice on the sea; loud are the shrieks of the helpless.

SAD is thy tale to me, said Ronnan.—Thou hast not heard its sadness all, said Senar.

MOURNFUL the chief retires. With his spear he strikes the gathering boss. A hundred youths hear the sound, and start, amidst roes, from their beds of heath. We poured from all our hills to the stream of the chief. We passed the night in silence, for great was the grief of Ronnan. The voice of no harp was heard; the sound of no shell went round; no feast was spread; no oak gave its glimmering light, on that night, on the heath of Struthorman. Cold, drooping, and dark we sat, till day arose in the east. With morning we rush to the deep; and virgins, with grief, beheld from behind their rocks our flying sails.

BUT what are thy thoughts in the morning, Dumor; when no daughter of beauty looks, blue-eyed between her yellow locks, within thy darkened hall?—The daughters of the bow conveened on the dew of the dawn. They moved forth to the chase, like fun-

many passages of this kind in the ancient Galic poetry, that the notion of the *se-* *cond-fight*, which so long prevailed in the Highlands, took its origin.

sun-beams on the hill of the cast. They came to the secret hall of Sulmina, but it was silent. " Daughter of Dumor, art thou not yet awake ? Thou didst not use to be the last on the hill of roes. Awake; arise: the sun is coming forth; and the stag, rising in his bed of moss, is stretching all his limbs. Daughter of Dumor, lift thy locks; this day we move forth to the chase of roes.——But ah! she is not here!"---Their sighs, like the shrill voice of the breeze, travel to the ear of Dumor.---Thy grief, Dumor, on that morning was great; but greater far was thine, O Ronnan!

NIGHT is gathering on the deep. The shore of Lava appears like mist. In the silence of night we reach its bay.

DARK and cold was that night, son of Arar; and unsheltered was the place of our rest, in the land of strangers. The obscured stars were seen, at times, through their torn robes of clouds. Some observed their colour of blood, and feared the sign. Frequent was the howling of gray dogs; nor unheard were the ghosts of our fathers. They looked out, at times, from their dark-skirted cloud; but their countenance seemed to be mournful.

RONNAN sat by a mossy stone. The shield of Struthorman hung above him, on a gray branch. The winds whistle through its thongs.---I sung, beside him, the tales of old, and the deeds of his father, when he fought, on the coast of Ullin *, with Commar of many hills.

—CEASE, said the chief, thy song, till the day shall light me to Lava;

---

* *Ullin*, Ireland, or, more strictly, Ulster.

..ava; for my wrath is kindled againſt his race, at the mention of
he wars of Ullin. It was returning thence his father purſued the
eer of our hills, and fought my early death. I was young; I
ould lift no ſpear, nor draw from its ſheath the ſword. One of
is men had pity on my youth; he ſaved me from Lava's ſpear.
)ur arms are ſtill in his halls; my father did not live to demand
hem.

—But what low and broken voice is that from the heath? Doſt
hou not perceive that aged warrior drawing near? His one hand
eems guided by a child; on a ſpear, that ſeems a burden, leans the
ther. Every little rill ſtops his pace, and on the withered furze
he aged ſtumbles.---Who art thou, aged wanderer of the night?
Vhy ſo late on the lonely heath? Haſt thou loſt the delight of thy
oul; or haſt thou cauſe of wo, like me?

" I THOUGHT I heard a voice. Thou knoweſt, my child, the voice
f thy father. Was it not he, bidding me to follow him to the
lace of his repoſe?"

" No; for I loved my father's voice, and I love not that which
hear. Their arms are like my father's arms; but their voice is
ike the voice of ſtrangers."

" And doſt thou ſee their arms? Then fly, my child; for they
re ſent by Lava. Fly thou; and, if they will, let them ſlay me:
or the place is good; I feel the tomb of thy father."

The child with terror flew. The aged, trembling, ſtood. He
tood, like the dun red-creſted fowl of the heath, when the hunt-
:r, unperceived, comes nigh her brown fons. Quick, ſhe bids

her

her little children fly, to hide their heads in mofs; and calls the danger to herfelf, till they are fafe.

Peace be to the aged, faid Ronnan, as he took him by the hand. Peace be to the child, faid I, as in my arms I took him back. We are not come from Lava; neither do our fwords bring death to the feeble. No, their fafety is behind our fhields: therefore reft thou here, and tell the caufe of thy tears.

" Here I will reft: here is the clay-cold dwelling of my fon. To mourn over it am I come with his child. How filent under this peaceful ftone art thou now, my fon; thou whirlwind in the ftorm of battle! Silent is thy tongue, and weak thy arm: thy beauty is decayed, like the faded flower; and thy ftrength, like the withered oak, hath failed. Lamor! where is the boaft of man, when the clod is become thy fellow? Only one fun hath run his courfe fince thou didft, like him, rejoice in thy ftrength, and gladden the dim eyes of thy father. Like him too, darknefs, thick darknefs, forms now thy covering. Yet his light fhall return, and he will again lift his dewy locks in the eaft, and rejoice. But when fhall thy long, long night, my fon, be over; when fhall the flumberer of the tomb arife from his filent dwelling? But thou lifteft thy head, my fon, in other lands; and wandereft over brighter fields with heroes.—Weep on, O ftrangers! for he that is low was brave; and his foul, like your own, was a ftream that flowed when the tale was mournful."

Weep for him we do, faid Ronnan: but how is he fallen fo foon; was it by the hand of Lava?

" It was; and for no other caufe, but that he loved the friendlefs. But in this my fon was like his fathers. It was the mark of our

race, that we always stood up, though alone, to defend the weak. Our shield was a rock of brass before the unhappy; our spear was a tree that sheltered the stranger.---When I was strong in my arms of youth, as the tenant of this tomb was yesterday, I attended the father of Lava, when he took the spoils from the halls of Struthorman. My words were loud against him; for the heroes were absent, and there was none to oppose him. One child indeed there was, who scarce could wield, in place of a spear, a little arrow. That same he heaved, with all his infant-might, against the foe. On the foot of Commar the blunt end of it, harmless, fell. The gloomy chief turned his eye upon the child, and said, ' Hereafter this child may lift a more dangerous spear against us. Let us leave him on that desart isle, where we wait the morning's light.'——
We came to the isle; and often was the spear of Commar halflifted over the son of Struthorman. My soul was grieved for the child of youth. He heard my sigh, and came near me. He admired the brightness of my arms; he clasped his little hand about my knee. He smiled in my face: the tear glittered in his blue eye. ' My father!' he said, ' I love thee.' My heart melted above him: my soul within me was like the rushing of a stream; like the straitened whirlwind in Atha's cleft, when trees in the storm are bending. My secret tears fell in his yellow locks, as he hid his head in the skirt of my robe. As the roe, when she fears the hunter hath observed her haunt, the mossy bed where she hath hid her son,—or as the eagle of heaven, when she thinks that he hath seen her rock,—carries off, in the night, her young; so I took the child in my arms, when failed the light. I bore him through the waves to his mother, who wept like the cloud of the
shower,

shower, upon the lonely shore. She gave me this spear, and called the name of her child Ronnan *. But of Ronnan have I heard no more, till Lava came from the wars of Dumor, and told the mournful maid of his love, that he had left him wounded by the stream of his land.---My son knew my love for Ronnan. ' I wish,' he said, ' I had been near to lift the spear of Struthorman. It would rejoice to defend its owner.'---His words came to Lava's ear. His people gathered around my son at the feast.---This grave may tell the rest. Mark it, strangers; and when you pass, shed over it a tear, and say, ' This is the tomb of Lamor.'---Yes, and it will soon be the tomb of Runma. But if ye know the friends of Ronnan, bring them that child, that they may defend him; and give them this spear, for they will know it."

The sigh bursts from the breast of Struthorman's chief. He falls on the neck of the aged. " In me thou hast thy Ronnan!"

Their tears fall, mingled, on the grave of Lamor. Heroes drop their spears, and weep, with joy, around them.

---But what noise is that, like the sullen murmur of a stream, when the storm is about to burst? It is the foe with their numerous host. They have perceived our coming, and their steel faintly glimmers to the dawn of the morning. Their light is like the thin stream of a rock, when sun-beams, bursting from between two clouds, are travelling through it.

Ronnan hears the song of battle, and the joy of his countenance

* *Ro'-thonnan*, " through waves;" alluding to the manner of his escape. He may have, probably, been the father of that Ma'ronnan (or *son of Ronnan*) mentioned in Ossian's battle of Lora:

Freitcach bliadhna ri mur Fhinn
Thug an diais bu chaoin dearg dreach,
Deagh Mhac-Ronnain nan sleagh geur,
Is Aildhe nach d'eur neach.

nance returns. He ſtrikes his ſhield. His heroes are around him, a thick cloud, the gathering of the tempeſt on Dura.

As the ſpirit of night moves, with the collected blaſt of heaven in his courſe, when he prepares to pour his force on the groves of Ardven; when oaks hear its ſound at a diſtance, and, trembling for its approach, already ſhake their leaves: So ruſhed Ronnan to the battle on the head of heroes.---Nor leſs terrible is the courſe of Lava. The ſound of his people is like thunder in clouds, when Lara's fields are diſmal. A thouſand helmets nod on high; like a grove in flames is the blaze of ſpears.

But who ſhall tell the rage of battle? Thou haſt ſeen, ſon of Arar, two black rocks rolling from oppoſite hills to meet in the valley below; a cloud of ſmoke riſes behind, and follows the tract of each: ſuch was the terrible onſet of the people. Swords claſh, and ſhields reſound: heads and helmets fall: the dead are mixed with the dying: blood runs in a thouſand ſtreams, and the ſpirits of fallen heroes aſcend on its thin airy ſmoke. See! to the edge of every cloud they cling, as clings the bur to the eagle's wing when ſhe leaves the valley of dun roes, and flies to Moma's cloudy top.

But what eagles are theſe two, that ſtill contend with ruſtling wings on the heath? No gray kid, no red-creſted cock is the prey for which they ſtrive, as from ſide to ſide they bound, and pour death in ſtreams from their ſteel.—See! one ſtoops on his knee. His ſhield ſupports the half-fallen chief, as the rock ſupports the pine, which the ſtorm has half-overturned on Dunora.—Yield thy ſpear, ſaid Ronnan; reſtore my beloved Sulmina. I ſeek not the death of my foes, when they lie before me on earth.

YIELD

YIELD I muſt, Lava replied, for my blood is ſhed; the ſtream of my life hath failed.—Sulmina muſt be thine. Behind that rock, in her cave ſhe reſts. She looks down from its door on a blue ſtream, where waves an aſpen tree.—Sulmina muſt be thine: but let her raiſe my tomb; for ſhe was the love of Lava the unhappy.

He ceaſed. He ſunk on his ſhield; and his people fled. Ronnan bade us ſpare them in their flight, as, ſwift, he aſcended the rock to find the place of his love.—The blue ſtream he finds; and the cave on its woody bank. But no Sulmina is there. The lone wind ſounds in the empty womb of the rock. The withered leaf wanders there, on its ruſtling wing; and no tract is found, but that of the lonely fox.

" WHERE art thou, O Sulmina, my love! Doſt thou hide thyſelf from Ronnan?—Come, Sulmina, from thy ſecret place; come, my love, it is thy Ronnan calls thee!"

BUT thou calleſt in vain, ſon of grief; no one replies to thy voice, ſave the rock and echoing ſtream.

AT length the howling of his dog is heard, in the field of fallen heroes. Thither he turns. There he finds Sulmina. She had ruſhed to the battle to aid her Ronnan. But death, on the point of a wandering arrow, came: its barbed head is in her breaſt of ſnow. The ſparkling light of her eye is become dim; the roſe of her cheek is faded.

RONNAN, pale like her own half-breathleſs corſe, falls on her neck, as drops the ivy when its oak hath failed. Sulmina half-opens her heavy eyes. The peaceful ſhade of death cloſes them again, well pleaſed to have ſeen her Ronnan.

LONG

Long we bended our heads in silent grief, and shed our tears around Sulmina. At length the slow steps of Runma came. He spoke the words of the aged.

"Will sorrow recal the dead; will the cries of the living dispel their heavy slumbers? No; they still sleep on, carelefs of the cry of the mourner. But they are only gone a little before us to the land of their rest. A few more fleeting days, on their silent, swift-gliding stream shall pass, and our steps shall be in air with our friends. Do you not already see the cloud-skirted robe prepared for Runma. Nor shall Ronnan be long behind. The stream of grief wastes the bank on which his beauty grows. The young tree, that lifts there its green head, already half-bends over it in its fall. Let, then, our deeds of fame be many, while we can; and let not our winged days be wasted in mourning——Grief is a calm stream, O Ronnan! the steps of its course are silent. But it undermines in secret the beauteous flower that grows on its green bank: drooping it hangs its withered head; it falls while its leaf is but tender *."

Ronnan arose; but still he was sad. He gave the halls of Lava to

---

* The following lines have in the original all the beauty of the objects which they describe, and all the smoothness of the stream which they speak of. Such soft and mournful sounds as *oi, ai, ui, iui, uai*, &c. occur so often in them, that the eye or ear, of even a stranger to the language, will at once perceive that they are expressive of some of the mournful and tender feelings. In this respect they are an illustration of the remark made in a former note, p. 310, 311.

Tha Bron mar an fruthan diamhair
Aig iarruidh fui' iochdar na bruaiche;
Tha 'n gallan cheanadh ag aomadh,
A thog ri thaebh a ghengan aillidh,
Tuiteadh ar bron, mata, 's circadh ar cliu,
'S ar n uin' a' ruith air barraibh sgiathan.

S' ciuin, a Ronnain, ceime a bhroin,
'S e caithe gu foil a bhlidh uaine;
Tha 'n t ur-ros air a chaithe fui' bhonn
'S gu trom, trom, tha cheann a' fearga.

to Runma and the fon of Lamor: Fermor and the fcout of night he left to defend them.

WE brought Sulmina over the waves in Ronnan's fhip; and here we raifed, amid fighs, her gray ftone. Here too refts the youthful Ronnan, whofe arm was once fo ftrong, whofe form was once fo fair. His days were fad and few, on the hill; he did not long furvive his beloved. Under that mofs-clad ftone he was laid, where grows the ruftling grafs. He refts befide his Sulmina. One lone thiftle bends between their two gray ftones its head, and fheds on either fide its aged beard. Often when I fit here to the glimmering light of the moon, I fee the faint forms of the two on its watery beams. I take my harp, and fing their praife. Glad, they depart on the wing of winds.

WHY art thou fo filent, fon of Arar, when the children of fame are around thee?

THE DEATH OF ARTHO[*]:

A POEM.

THE ARGUMENT.

ARDAR, lamenting the lofs of his fon Calmar, is informed of the death of his other fon Artho, as he looked for his return from battle. The fon of Arman comforts him by relating to him the gallant behaviour of his fon. He informs him alfo of his own paffion for Colval, who had been in love with Artho.—Her death is related; with the defpair of Artho: and the poem concludes with fome reflections of Ardar upon their fate, and upon his own fituation.

SAD are my thoughts while alone! Thy memory comes, with all its grief, on my foul; Calmar, chief of heroes. Thou wert a fun-beam to thy friends in peace; a flafh of lightning to thy foes in war. My fon rufhed, like a whirlwind, to the battle: many a young oak has been ftrewed in his troubled path. The return of his renown was like the fun when it fets. The heart of the aged, over him, was glad; I bleffed the mighty in battle.

BUT,

[*] This poem, which goes under the name of *Bas Airt 'ic Ardair*, or *Tuire' an Aofda*, appears to be the work of fome ancient, but unknown, bard. Poffibly it might have been compofed by Ardar himfelf. At leaft no other poet appears throughout the piece; in which circumftance it differs from all the preceding poems. It begins with the following lines.

'S cianail m' aigne 's mi 'm aonar,
Calmar ag eiridh am fmuainte;
'S a' liona mo chroidhe le mulad,
O nach faic mi tuille mo dhea' mhac.
Bu chofail e'n fioth ri gatha greine,
'S am boile-chatha ri teine fpeuran;
Bu lionar gallan anns na roidibh,
'S e ruith mar ionia-ghaoth fios gu co'rag.
Bhiodh a phille' mar ghrian ri faire,
'S an t aofda le gean cuir falt air.

But, Calmar! thou art now no more; and the fun that fhone in the houfe of thy father is fet. Fuardo was a ftorm that feized my early fun; in one morning he extinguifhed all his beams. Darknefs, fince that day, dwells in Ardlia; for Artho is but a faint ftar, befide the light of his brother. Yet thou, my fon, art alfo brave. But ah! thy arm may fail in the firft of thy battles; for thy father cannot defend thee. I attempt to lift the fpear, but I fall to earth when it does not fupport me. I attempt to lift the fhield, but my knees tremble under its burden. O that I faw my only fon return, in the midft of his renown, from battle!

But who comes in the beauty of youth, and ftately as an oak of the mountain? His fair locks, like leaves, are waving around him. He is of the race of Arman, from the battle of the fpears he comes.—Hail, thou beam of youth! whence are thy wandering fteps? Art thou from the battle of heroes? Say, does Artho live; does he return to his gray-haired father? But why fhould I afk? thy mournful looks tell that he is now no more. Soon haft thou left me, my fon, in darknefs; Artho, fhall I no more behold thee? —Calmar is gone; Artho is low: O that I too had been with my children! In the evening of life I am left without a fon; like a blafted oak that is left alone on Malmor. The breeze fhall defcend from the mountain, and the blaft fhall blow from the defart; but no green leaf of mine fhall either meet. The fhowers of the fpring fhall come, but no bough of mine fhall flourifh; the fun fhall fmile through the drops of dew, but no green branch of mine fhall behold it. The wind whiftles in my gray moffy head; its voice is, " Thou fhalt foon be low."—One comfort is all I expect before then; tell me, fon of youth, how fell my fon?

" With-

" Without his fame thy fon did not fall in battle; the mighty marked, with wonder, his courfe, as he ftrode in the midft of foes. Like the thunder that breaks the groves; like the lightning that lays low their gr en heads, when fudden burfting it fpreads terror, and again returns; fo fought, fo fell thy hero. The foes were troubled at the fight of Artho; they fled, they fell. Death from the hand of Artho roared behind them, like the rolling of a rock from Malmor, when it crufhes the trees in its courfe, till it finks in the lake below them. Such were thy deeds, fon of fame! But the arrow of death came in the blaft; and the people are fad, for mighty was he that is low."

Pleasant to me is thy tale, fon of Arman; it is like the beam that difpels the clouds of night. Thou haft fought like thy fathers in their battles of youth, O Artho! and thy name, like theirs, fhall be found in the fong. When the valiant fall, a ftreak of light behind them is their fame; their friends behold the beam, and are glad. But the feeble die, and are remembered no more; their friends are beheld with fcorn by mighty men. They walk in the filent valley alone, and fhun the eye of heroes.

But, fon of Arman, why that figh; why thefe wandering looks? Haft thou loft a brother of love; or is thy foul troubled for the fpoufe of thy youth!

Nor have I loft a brother of love; nor have I a fpoufe that longs for my return from the battle. My fighs are for the fair of Carnmor; for her my wandering looks. My thoughts are of her in the day; of her are my dreams in the night.—But her foul is full of Artho. She faw the youth move to battle, and fad was her troubled foul. She came to that hill, and followed him far

with

with her looks. Her mournful eye was wet, and her sighs were heard by secret streams. " On this cold rock," she said, " I will sit, till Artho of love return."---I am come to meet the sun-beam of my soul. But the rock is dark; no beam of light is nigh it. The rock without Colval is dark; but darker still is my soul with all its grief, for I see not the steps of my love. I see not her that was fairer than the down of the mountain, or the new-fallen snow on the waving tree *.—But who comes from Malmor with disordered looks?---It is she—it is my love: but ah! how changed! Pale is her cheek, and wild her look; she has heard that her beloved is low. But hark! she speaks.

COLVAL.

WHAT detains thee, O Artho! ere now thou didst promise to return. Ill-boding thoughts distract my soul. Shouldst thou fall, my love, can I survive thee, and wander on dark mountains lonely?—No: tear the ivy from the oak, tear the eagle from her dun-robed prey, and tear the offspring from its parent of love; but tear not my soul from Artho.—But who is it I see? Is it my love returning from the battle? Ah! no; it is the son of Arman.---Trouble me not, O Farno; I cannot love thee. What hast thou done with Artho? Will my love return no more; is he low in the strife of steel? Yes, he is low; I see his robe in the passing mist.---Leave me not, O Artho; leave not thy love; for she too comes on her cloud. Not hills with all their deer, not mossy streams with all their roes, can give joy to Colval when thou art gone. Artho, I come; O leave me not, my love!

FARNO.

---

* Two lines in the original of this passage are so beautiful, that they frequently enter into descriptions of female beauty:

Bn ghile bian na canach fleibhe,
No ar-fhuicadal air bharra gheuga.

FARNO.

Ah! she falls; she faints; she dies away.—And art thou gone, faireſt of maids? In thee alone did my ſoul delight, though thy heart was fixed on Artho. Thou art gone, and what charms has life to me? No, farewel to all the delights of youth; farewel to all the joys of life. Farewel, ye hills of Carnmor*! and farewel, ye moſſy towers of Ardlia: Colval is gone, and pleaſure is no more

to

---

* So great was the attachment of the ancient Caledonians to their hills, which ſupplied them with the means of ſubſiſtence at ſo eaſy a rate, that we often find them not only taking a ſolemn farewel of them at death, but alſo imagining that a part of their future happineſs conſiſted in ſeeing and travelling over thoſe ſcenes which in life afforded them ſo much pleaſure. Of this, the following extract from a ſmall poem, called *Miann a Bhaird*, affords a beautiful inſtance.

—" But hark! I hear the ſteps of the hunter. O may the cry of thy hounds, and the ſound of thy darts, thou bender of the yew, be often heard around my ſilent dwelling! My wonted joy, when the chaſe aroſe, ſhall then return, and the bloom of youth ſhall glow in my cheek that was faded.---The marrow in my bones ſhall revive, when I ſhall hear the ſound of ſpears, the bound of dogs, and the twang of ſtrings.—With joy I ſhall ſpring up alive, when they cry ' The ſtag is fallen!'

" I ſhall then meet the companion of my chaſe; the hound that followed me late and early. I ſhall ſee the hills that I loved to frequent, and the rocks that were wont to anſwer to my cries. I ſhall ſee the cave that often received my ſteps from night; the cave where we often rejoiced around the flame of the oak. There our feaſt of deer was ſpread; there Treig was our drink, and the murmur of its ſtreams our ſong. Ghoſts ſhrieked on their clouds, and the ſpirits of the mountain roared along their hollow ſtreams: but no fear was ours; in the cave of our rock ſecure we lay.—I ſhall ſee Scur-elda tower above the vale, where the welcome voice of the cuckow is early heard.---I ſhall ſee Gormal, with its thouſand pines; I ſhall ſee it in all its green beauty, with its many roes and flights of fowl.---I ſhall ſee the iſle of trees in the lake, with the red fruit nodding over the waves.---I ſhall ſee Ardven, chief of a thouſand hills: its ſides are the abode of deer; its top the habitation of clouds. ---I ſee---but whither, gay viſion, art thou fled?---Thou haſt left me, to return no more.

" Farewel then, my beloved hills; farewel, children of youth. With you it is ſummer ſtill: but my winter is come; no ſpring, alas, is to ſucceed!

---" O place me by the green ſide of my ſtream;

to me. I ruſh back to the field of death, and open my breaſt to ſome feeble ſteel. Then Colval I ſhall ſee again.

ARDAR.

BLESSED may you be, children of youth! lovely were your ſouls; but why ſo ſoon departed? Happy the young who die in the days of their joy. They feel not the burden of years; they ſee not the days of trouble: Days in which the ſun on the mountains is dim; and dark years creep ſlowly on the heath of mourning. Slow rolls the tide of years to me, O my fathers! Why do I wander on Ardlia when my race hath failed? Come, ye fathers of Ardar! convey me to the place where the ſons of my love repoſe. ---Is that your voice I hear in the breeze?---Yes, and I go in the ruſtling of your courſe: in the fold of your wandering blaſt I go. There Artho and Calmar I ſhall ſee again; and ſad and alone I ſhall be no more.

ſtream; place the ſhell, and my father's ſhield, beſide me in my narrow houſe.--- Open, open, ye ghoſts of my fathers! the hall where Oſſian and Daöl reſt. The evening of my life is come, and the bard ſhall no more be found in his place!"

F I N I S.

Printed by MACFARQUHAR *and* ELLIOT, *Edinburgh.*

www.ingramcontent.com/pod-product-compliance
Lightning Source LLC
Chambersburg PA
CBHW031813230426
43669CB00009B/1123